Fantasy Film

Berg **Film Genres** series

Edited by Mark Jancovich and Charles Acland

ISSN: 1757-6431

The *Film Genres* series presents accessible books on popular genres for students, scholars and fans alike. Each volume addresses key films, movements and periods by synthesizing existing literature and proposing new assessments.

Forthcoming:

Fantasy Film

A Critical Introduction

James Walters

Oxford • New York

For my parents.

English edition
First published in 2011 by
Berg
Editorial offices:
First Floor, Angel Court, 81 St Clements Street, Oxford OX4 1AW, UK
175 Fifth Avenue, New York, NY 10010, USA

Berg is the imprint of Bloomsbury Publishing Plc.

Library of Congress Cataloging-in-Publication Data

Walters, James (James R.).
    Fantasy film : a critical introduction / James Walters. — English ed.
      p. cm.
    Includes bibliographical references and index.
    ISBN 978-1-84788-308-7 (pbk.) — ISBN 978-1-84788-309-4 (cloth)
 1. Fantasy films—History and criticism. I. Title.
    PN1995.9.F36W35 2011
    791.43'615—dc22

                                                            2011003156

British Library Cataloguing-in-Publication Data

A catalogue record for this book is available from the British Library.

ISBN   978 1 84788 309 4 (Cloth)
        978 1 84788 308 7 (Paper)
e-ISBN 978 1 84788 843 3 (Institutional)
        978 1 84788 842 6 (Individual)

Typeset by JS Typesetting Ltd, Porthcawl, Mid Glamorgan.
Printed in the UK by the MPG Books Group

www.bergpublishers.com

Contents

Acknowledgements

I would like to thank my series editors, Charles Acland and Mark Jancovich, for their dedication in seeing this book through to completion. I am especially grateful to Mark, whose generosity, support and enthusiasm continues to be a revelation to me; I hope I have repaid at least some of his faith. Tristan Palmer at Berg has handled the publication process with care and commitment, and I thank him sincerely for his efforts.

At an early stage, the University of Birmingham granted me a period of leave to work on the book, for which I am very grateful. More than that, however, Birmingham provides a rich culture of research and critical inquiry that has spurred me on to develop the ideas contained within these pages. My colleagues have supported the direction of this research in a variety of ways, and I am particularly thankful to Dick Ellis and Helen Laville. I have also benefited profoundly from discussions held with students in my film classes at Birmingham. The range of ideas and critical opinions offered in seminars and tutorials has inspired me in ways I cannot begin to articulate. I am very lucky to spend my time with such a high calibre of student, willing to learn and willing to teach me.

I watched any number of fantasy films with my brother, Jonathan, during our childhood and his keen knowledge of cinema continues to be an inspiration to me. Finally, I would like to thank my wife, Amy, and our sons, Isaac, Ruben and Fergus for being such wonderful distractions during the writing of this book. I hope I kept my absences from their lives to a minimum.

James Walters

Introduction

What is fantasy film? The search for any kind of definitive answer can often seem only to present more questions. Indeed, the very term 'fantasy' can become troublesome in discussions of cinema – something that Deborah Thomas usefully addresses when laying out the parameters for her study of the romantic, melodramatic and comedic in American film. Thomas explains that:

> I have argued against using fantasy as part of an alternative schema, both because, in my opinion, the term can be applied to all mainstream American films, and because, in other people's use of it to designate films about the supernatural, it seems to me to be narrowly generic, rather than an example of the broad – but not all-inclusive – sort of category across genres which I'm after.[1]

Leaving aside the particular concerns that Thomas' book will go on to raise and explore, it is clear in her account that definitions of fantasy face a dual dilemma of, on the one hand, being so broad as to include any fiction film that we can conceive of and, on the other, of becoming so narrow that they exclude a host of works that might legitimately belong to such a category. Avoiding fantasy as a definitive term is one strategy for coping with this problem but another approach might be to address directly fantasy's intrinsic tendency to avoid absolute classification – its propensity for crossing the boundaries of genre to surface in works of horror, science fiction, comedy, melodrama, animation and so on. Fantasy is a fragile, ephemeral and volatile element in cinema, prone to emerge in unexpected places as well as shaping itself into the dominant facet of certain fictional worlds. We are left with the choice of whether to suspend such issues by doing away with the term 'fantasy' entirely, or embrace these characteristics in our critical accounts.

Although we might justifiably be tempted to say that any fictional film can be read as fantasy, it also seems to be the case that we intrinsically recognize certain works, or even certain moments, as fantasy. More specifically, we recognize that a conscious effort is being made to depart from the confines of ordinary, everyday existence: from the natural to the supernatural, as it were. We *feel* we are experiencing fantasy as it unfolds. As I watch fiction films, I am aware of being presented with a set of circumstances that could occur within my reality but am equally assured that characters and locations existing in the film could never be found there. When faced with fantasy in films, however, I am conscious of being shown a series of events that, according to the rules of reasonable logic, could *never* occur within my reality. Fiction and fantasy are thus made distinct. The potential risk involved in making these kinds of distinctions is that we might then use such criteria to suggest that fantasy applies to a particular *type* of film, so narrowing our understanding of fantasy and casting aside its essential breadth and diversity. Contrary to this position, my contention in the following pages is that fantasy is just as likely to emerge in a crime thriller about an escaped convict as it is in a story about a mythical kingdom in which the destinies of all creatures are decided by the fate of a magical ring.

Discussion of fantasy in terms of genre is made difficult precisely because, despite our recognition of fantasy at work in certain films, it has the innate capacity to seep into different styles, tones and even genres of film making. But that difficulty is perhaps only made acute when we insist on the absolute rigidity of generic classification. That strategy might involve drawing up a set of rules that determine whether a film can be called 'fantasy' or not, and each potential case could be measured against this set of disciplinary guidelines. Under that system, works falling outside of such criteria could also be discounted with relative ease. Perhaps that kind of concrete discrimination is what the study of fantasy requires, but we could equally maintain that one of the key excitements of fantasy is precisely its ability to emerge in strange and unexpected places, at times making the familiar unfamiliar, enticing through that strangeness. Furthermore, we may resist the straightforward suggestion that placing a film in one genre necessarily excludes it from any other genre of cinema. (This is a thought that we will return to in later chapters.) Historically, definitions of genre frequently shift and realign across periods, a fact emphasized by Lincoln Geraghty and Mark Jancovich in an edited collection centred upon that very theme.[2] They explain that:

> Generic terms are often imposed retrospectively onto books, films and other cultural forms that predate the invention of these terms. At one level, this might seem a fairly innocent activity, but it can do violence to our sense of history. It can, for example, abstract texts from the contexts within which they were originally understood and impose alternative understandings upon them, or it can simply emphasize some details and ignore others.[3]

If we are to conduct any historical analysis of genres, therefore, we must remain acutely aware of the fact that such borders and boundaries are not fixed and that terminology can retrospectively be placed upon certain works of art in order to group them. Across a range of approaches, however, the issues that Geraghty and Jancovich raise should alert us to the mutability and instability of generic terms, at least making us wary of defining genres in ways that are rigid, discrete or absolute. Following their reasoning, such an enterprise could only leave arguments open to contradiction and legitimate challenge.

An uncompromising approach is therefore made precarious. On this theme of genre distinction, Brian Attebery in fact finds the notion of 'fuzzy sets' useful in considering the shifting definitions of fantasy. Taking his lead from the work of Lakoff and Johnson on metonymy and metaphor,[4] he explains that:

> Genres may be approached as 'fuzzy sets,' meaning that they are defined not by boundaries but by a center. As described by George Lakoff and Mark Johnson, fuzzy set theory proposes that a category such as 'bird' consists of central, prototypical examples like 'robin,' surrounded at greater or lesser distance by more problematic instances such as 'ostrich,' 'chicken,' 'penguin,' and even 'bat' … These latter members of the set are described in ordinary language by various hedging terms: they are 'technically birds,' 'birds, loosely speaking,' or even 'birdlike'. A chicken can be a bird to some degree, in some contexts, for some purposes, and be something entirely different, like 'farmyard animal,' for other purposes. Conversely, an insect may be birdlike enough to warrant a name like 'hummingbird moth' or 'ladybird'; the name expresses a perceived grouping.[5]

Attebery's novel and practical way of dealing with this concept in terms of fantasy literature is to conduct a small, non-scientific survey among a group of scholarly acquaintances in an effort to identify the centre of fantasy's 'fuzzy set'. Perhaps inevitably, *The Lord of the Rings* trilogy emerges as the consistent nomination among respondents for the title of quintessential fantasy, something Attebery rightly suggests is 'not just because of the imaginative scope and commitment with which [J.R.R Tolkien] invested his tale but also, and chiefly, because of the immense popularity that resulted.'[6] Tolkien's work has a place in popular culture as arguably *the* central text in fantasy literature and, with the release of Peter Jackson's film adaptations of the books released between 2001 and 2003, that distinction has undoubtedly extended to fantasy cinema. But, while Attebery's brief 'unscientific experiment' reveals the centrality of the trilogy to perceptions of fantasy, around it the picture is especially indefinite or, indeed, 'fuzzy'. As he explains: 'there are, as I expected, no clear boundaries between categories. Fantasy edges into science fiction; science fiction impinges on mainstream fiction; mainstream fiction overlaps with fantasy.'[7] So, while *The Lord of the Rings* occupies a position of stable and defined centrality in Attebery's research, once we move beyond this trilogy of books the landscape of fantasy becomes far less easy to characterize and any number of complications, amalgamations and overlaps can occur.

These overlaps emphasize the fact that fantasy is an especially broad genre, certainly not a niche, and consequently it is the intention of this book to explore that breadth by presenting a series of different configurations of fantasy across cinema. Anxieties over fantasy's status as a genre perhaps derive from its inherent lack of containment and neatness. The unpredictability (or perhaps messiness) of the genre is not something I regard as necessarily troubling – rather, I would consider it a chief attraction – but that characteristic sits uneasily with an understanding of genre as something that can be clearly defined and measured. It is perhaps for this reason that genre and fantasy have endured an uneasy relationship in critical literature. Tzvetan

Todorov's description of a genre of the fantastic (discussed more fully in Chapter 1 of this book) refers to a very particular type of story that 'hesitates' between natural and supernatural explanation, and as a consequence leaves out whole swathes of other fantasy works.[8] As a result, when Rosemary Jackson approaches the subject, she contends that it is possible to 'modify Todorov's scheme slightly and to suggest a definition of fantasy as a *mode*, which then assumes different generic forms',[9] thus expanding the scope for inclusion further. And, in a recent book focussed specifically on fantasy cinema, David Butler suggests that fantasy is 'an impulse rather than a single coherent genre … there are, of course, a number of genres and subgenres in which the fantasy impulse is pushed to the fore.'[10] This resonates with a claim made by Eric Rabkin, quoted in Jackson, that 'The wide range of works which we call … fantastic is large, much too large to constitute a single genre. [It includes] whole conventional genres, such as fairly tale, detective story, Fantasy.'[11] Todorov's work is a landmark intervention for those concerned with the study of fantasy, but both Jackson and Butler explicitly acknowledge the limitations of his compelling thesis in terms of a wider context of fantasy as they seek to broaden the range and focus of critical and theoretical debate. These subtle shifts in describing what fantasy actually *is* engage with an underlying and enduring unease over the precise terminology that can be employed to describe critically fantasy in literature and, latterly, in film. The periodic expansion of descriptive terms by various scholars suggests that new definitions will continue to emerge in the future.

In discussing fantasy's relationship to genre, we might also acknowledge that notions of genre can vary significantly in critical and theoretical accounts. For example, on the one hand Rick Altman's landmark study, *Film/Genre*, lays out the myriad influences that impact upon on the definition of a particular genre or genres, detailing the intervention of literary theory, critical discourse, industry promotion, audience, studios, directors, producers and so on.[12] In this formulation, any understanding of genre is complex and is liable to be shaped by a number of divergent groups, institutions and/or individuals. On the other hand, the philosopher Stanley Cavell outlines what he terms the genre of the melodrama of the unknown woman in the following way: 'I claim that the four films principally considered in the following chapters define a genre of film, taking the claim to mean, most generally, that they recount interacting versions of a story, a story or a myth, that seems to present itself as a woman's search for a story, or of the right to tell her story.'[13]

Here, the convolutions of genre definition outlined by Altman are quietened as Cavell allows his debate to take place away from some of the pressures that might otherwise shape discussions of genre. That is not to say that Cavell's understanding of genre, and of his chosen genre particularly, lacks complexity. Certainly, his discussion of the melodrama of the unknown woman is both intricate and demanding. Rather, he suspends some of the broader contextual concerns in order to construct a genre based upon what takes place in the films themselves, using their content to lead debates about their generic grouping. We might regard this as an essentially subjective response, with the individual taking on the task of defining a genre without necessarily returning to the question of whether that genre exists in the same way for various other groups. Taking Cavell's work alongside Altman's, it becomes clear that genre is in itself not a fixed notion and different figures approach the subject in varying ways according to their critical investments. Such matters cannot be settled appropriately here, of course, but we should take away the fact that, whilst a study may focus upon one particular genre of cinema and debate its characteristics in detail, there are debates about genre itself that underpin any such activity and, indeed, provide opportunity for our claims to be challenged and debated.

In staying with the term 'genre', I merely state that the films I offer for scrutiny have something in common – something we might call fantasy. That is not to say that there is anything approaching homogeneity in these works' investment in and handling of fantasy within their narratives. As I have already suggested, I am committed to the notion that one strength of fantasy lies in the multifarious styles, tones and forms it proves capable of adopting. In Chapter 1 I make the modest claim that fantasy can be understood as expansion of the fictional world in film, building on the world-making principles at work in all fiction films. This assertion provides a broad understanding which requires and receives further distinction within the book, but that discussion does not necessarily make the genre of fantasy especially stable or, indeed, 'singular', to use Butler's earlier term. My interest lies in how films undertake this kind of expansion differently, rather than attempting to demonstrate only the ways in which they are the same.

Such claims for diversity and difference in my approach are emphasized in Chapter 5, which stands slightly apart from others as it details the potential for films to express characters' inner, unseen fantasies.[14] In such films, the boundaries of the fictional world are expanded only in the mind of characters, resulting in their distorted perspective on events and, consequently, their fantasized notions of existence. That discussion addresses one way that we might attempt to categorize fantasy: as the opposite of reality. In terms of film, this could translate into fantasy being seen as the reverse of realism. Setting aside the fact that 'realism' is hardly a term that has been received without difficulty by academia, the implicit suggestion that realism cannot be found in fantasy cinema seems an unusual distinction to make, given our experiences of such films. For example, we might find George Bailey's reaction to the alternative world of Pottersville in *It's A Wonderful Life* (Frank Capra, 1946) utterly convincing as a realistic response to a living nightmare. But the fact of Pottersville is dependent upon the film's fantasy of a world in which angels can interrupt the realm of the living and show to them a vision of a reality in which they had never been born. Here, it seems reasonable to suggest that fantasy and realism are entirely dependent upon one another in the film's realization of its central drama. André Bazin articulates these concerns at a more fundamental level when he asserts that:

> The opposition that some like to see between a cinema inclined toward the almost documentary representation of reality and a cinema inclined, through reliance on technique, toward escape from reality into fantasy and the world of dreams, is essentially forced …The fantastic in cinema is possible only because of the irresistible realism of the photographic image. It is the image that can bring us face to face with the unreal, that can introduce the unreal into the world of the visible.[15]

For Bazin, the technological apparatus of cinema provides the opportunity for fantasy to flourish *as a result of* photographic realism. My contention throughout this book is that reality and fantasy are not conveniently extricated and, in Chapter 5 I explore this question further by examining the extent to which an appreciation of reality is shaped by personal fantasy.

Connected to these debates is the traditional idea of fantasy as a form of escapism, something that Bazin identifies in his account. The logic behind such an assertion is clear, given that fantasy films offer a world divorced from our own where, potentially, certain tensions and constraints are temporarily suspended. But this distinction also risks carrying with it a characterization of fantasy film as lacking seriousness, of not engaging its viewers but rather providing a facile form of entertainment that relieves the complications of everyday life for a couple of hours. It may be true that fantasy can provide such an escape but no more so than any other form of cinema. The notion that we remain untroubled by what takes place in fantasy cinema does not bear up to the fact of the films themselves and in many cases these works bring with them substantial emotional and intellectual burdens. Examining our own experiences, we might legitimately challenge the idea that audience members cease to think about real life when watching fantasy on screen and, furthermore, be moved to suggest that a number of fantasy films stay with us after we have watched them, not providing a potential for reassuring escape, easily forgotten, but rather an opportunity for further thought, contemplation and even disquiet. Such notions underpin the contentions laid out in the following pages.

In ordering the book into a series of different concerns, I have tried to maintain a connection with themes and issues at work in film studies more generally. Accordingly, each chapter makes the attempt to place fantasy within the wider context of academic debates surrounding film, and many of the arguments contained in these pages rely upon the work of scholars who may have little or no connection to concepts of fantasy. My purpose here is to demonstrate the qualities fantasy has to offer the academic study of film and vice versa. I would maintain that isolating fantasy film from those broader contexts would only be an exercise in subduing its relevance and importance. As I move through the various areas of interest in each chapter I attempt to provide clear examples that support the claims I wish to make. However, for obvious reasons of space and economy, such illustrations are not intended to be entirely comprehensive, and the invitation exists for the reader to consider the book's arguments in relation to other fantasy films not contained in these pages. One way to write a book on fantasy would be to provide a list of all the films one can think of that could fall under the term and give sparse, broadly articulated details concerning their content. In rejecting that strategy, I hope to offer a more sustained engagement with particular examples of fantasy cinema, illustrating in detail the ways in which some of my arguments are manifested in the films themselves. This approach is guided by the principles of close analysis, a method of study that I will return to and rely upon throughout the book. It is worth saying that, in adopting this standpoint, I am acknowledging my investment in the practice of interpretative criticism. It is my hope that such an attempt complements the founding aims of this book and, indeed, the series to which it belongs: to provide an introduction written from a defined critical perspective.

–1–

Approaching Fantasy Film

Fantasy and the Moment

A series of critics and theorists[1] have remarked that the conclusion to Fritz Lang's *You Only Live Once* (1937) constitutes a significant and unexpected shift in the tone, mood and dramatic structure of the film. In taking this relatively brief final scene as a starting point for discussion, it is my contention that the nature of this shift and the style in which these closing moments unfold is of particular relevance to our preliminary concerns regarding the interactions between fantasy and film. That Lang's film should make an intervention into debates of this kind is perhaps as unanticipated as the events taking place in its conclusion, given that *You Only Live Once* would not be a natural inclusion in any canon of fantasy cinema, were we inclined to construct such a thing. Indeed, it is more usually described as a crime thriller or 'social consciousness' film.[2] Whilst not wishing to disrupt or challenge classifications of this kind, which in any case describe accurately the overall character of *You Only Live Once*, I am drawn to the ways in which the film's forceful departure from such generic parameters at its conclusion foregrounds issues closely fused with concepts of fantasy cinema, thus having potent implications for the themes taken up within this book.

In order to account for the tonal and structural rupture at the end of Lang's film, it is worth providing some context to events. The final action of *You Only Live Once* involves its two central characters, Eddie (Henry Fonda) and Joan Taylor (Sylvia Sydney) as they make one last desperate break for freedom after having been on the run from the authorities for several weeks. Having both sustained wounds when their car was shot at by an armed patrolman and run off the road, the couple stagger from their vehicle and make their way into the nearby woods. As they flee the car, first Eddie falls against the wheel arch of the car in pain before carrying on, only for Joan's injuries to overcome her, causing her to slump against the trunk of a tree. Eddie reacts by scooping her up into his arms and, stumbling back slightly as he takes her weight against his own wounded frame, he continues their progress slowly and painfully through the overgrowth. The sounds of car engines and the squeal of tyres in the background make it clear that a full pursuit is taking place, emphasizing the urgency of the pair's predicament and also bringing into intense focus the hopelessness of Eddie's efforts as he struggles to flee the scene with his wife. A cut away from Joan and Eddie reveals a pack of officers passing by the couple's wrecked car and swarming into the woods after them. Each man possesses a rifle.

In one sense, the pursuit of Eddie and Joan by the police officers here can be taken as a direct reference to the way in which Eddie (and, when she joins him on the run, Joan) has been hounded by the authorities throughout the film. Certainly, we are led to understand that this is the view of his fate taken by Eddie himself as, on learning that he has shot and killed a close acquaintance, Father Dolan (William Gargan), whilst breaking out of jail when ironically he was already free due to a late pardon, he responds by shifting culpability for his actions, declaring: 'They made me a murderer.' Whilst Eddie's reading of his predicament is at least precarious in that it lifts *all* responsibility for his actions from his own shoulders, we can also appreciate that a number of characters fail to give him a sincere opportunity for improvement following his initial release from prison at the beginning of the film. In one particular case Lang seems to draw a set of parallels between the dismissive attitudes of Eddie's employer on leaving prison, Mr Williams (William Pawley), and the guard who watches over him later in his cell as he awaits execution, Rogers (Guin Williams). Eddie is sacked from his job as a driver by Mr Williams when he fails to return his truck, choosing instead to delay for an hour-and-a-half while he looks around a potential new home with Joan. When Eddie returns to his office to plead for his employment to be reinstated Williams displays an almost complete lack of regard for him, turning away from Eddie to make social arrangements with his own wife on the telephone and only breaking off from that exchange to offer sharp dismissals of Eddie's entreaties. Lang makes a point of contrasting Williams' harsh treatment of Eddie with the oversweet mode of address he adopts when talking to his wife, emphasizing the tonal disparity as Williams switches between these two different styles of speech.

Rogers, the guard, replicates this dismissive attitude towards Eddie when he is charged with the duty of watching over him in his cell. Eddie has been sentenced to death after being convicted of the murder of six people as the result of a gas bomb attack and robbery of the State bank. He is found guilty of this crime based on the fact that his initialled hat was found at the scene of the crime, although whether he actually participated in the robbery is never made properly clear to us.[3] As the scene in Eddie's cell opens, Rogers sits smoking a pipe and reading a magazine and, when Eddie asks if he can see his wife, he informs him that 'It's too late now: it's against the rules.' At this, Eddie asks if Rogers will do him a favour by telling Joan that he's sorry, that he acted like 'such a heel'. The request is made with passion and is complemented by a sentimental (if somewhat heavily-asserted) string melody that rises up from the underscore. But when Eddie asks Rogers if he will do the favour, the guard reacts with a non-committal 'Mmm mmm', barely looking at the prisoner before returning to his reading and smoking. The implication of this limp response is that Rogers will not be passing on the message: that he deems it unimportant, inconsequential or futile.

Twice, then, Eddie makes impassioned pleas to characters and is turned down flat. In both instances, the effect is to strip him of his humanity, of his ability to appeal to the humanity of others, and effectively represents a dismissal of Eddie's value as a sentient human being within his world. Taken together, the responses of Williams and Rogers form a picture of a society – or at least significant and powerful aspects of a society – that take Eddie to be entirely without worth. In the final hours, Rogers sees before him a condemned man upon whom it would be pointless to reward with attention and certainly not kindness. In this sense, he interprets his job as a guard as an essentially mechanical and dehumanized procedure, perhaps regarding himself as a second barrier of protection beyond the bars that enclose Eddie in his cell. What is striking, however, is the extent to which Williams appears to view Eddie in a very similar way at a much earlier stage in the narrative, when Eddie is ostensibly a reformed criminal seeking to make a new beginning. We might implicitly take from this pattern of correspondences the suggestion that Eddie is never given a chance, from the moment he is released from prison to the moment he is imprisoned again and condemned to death. Read in this way, his declaration that 'They made me a murderer' holds value as it relates potently to an attitude of dismissal and distrust exhibited by certain authority figures in their dealings with him.

Yet it is also the case that both Williams and Rogers are somewhat justified in their mistrust of Eddie and their suspicion of his pleas to be treated as an honest man. In Williams' case, Eddie has engineered the situation to a certain extent by electing to flout the conditions of his employment in the first place, but his volatile temperament is also revealed dramatically when he responds to his boss's lack of compassion by hitting him hard in the face. Rogers' lack of regard for Eddie in fact rebounds when it turns out that his prisoner has received a note about a hidden gun in the isolation ward and proceeds to cut his wrist with the ripped edge of a metal beaker in order to secure his delivery there. Ironically, then, it turns out that Rogers' lack of attention in fact aids Eddie's deception, and so the guard is guilty not only of showing an insufficient amount of human compassion but also of neglecting to remain vigilant in watching over an apparently dangerous criminal. In both instances, however, and from a certain perspective, Eddie can be seen to be in possession of an irresponsible, violent or deceptive temperament, and so his status as a victim of an unforgiving society is at least complicated, and perhaps ultimately compromised. It is indicative of the film's subtlety in dealing with such matters of guilt and responsibility, and its commitment to keeping the lines of crime and innocence ambiguous, that we are not entitled to place the weight of blame for Eddie's predicament either with the figures of authority he faces or with Eddie himself in either instance. In this way, the film poses the conundrum of who is to blame for the crimes committed, what constitutes a crime in this fictional world, and who is guilty of which crimes – society or the individual.

The image of the fatally injured Eddie carrying Joan through the woods with a pack of armed police officers in pursuit would seem to perfectly encapsulate this moral dilemma: whose hand has brought events to this conclusion? A visual emphasis of this theme occurs in the striking point of view shot from the viewfinder of a patrolman's rifle as he apparently takes aim at Eddie and Joan. On the one hand, this seems to symbolize the extent to which the pair – and particularly Eddie – have been in the sights of the authorities from the outset, fatally marked out. But on the other hand we are also required to consider what it is the marksman sees through his lens: the back of a murderer and thief retreating into the woods with his fugitive wife. The film's social dilemma is clear as we are effectively invited to contemplate which perspective is fair: a balance of judgement that can never be properly struck. In this sense, the shot through the viewfinder corresponds with George Wilson's central contention regarding *You Only Live Once* that:

> The narration explores with elaborate care the ways in which film may enhance and complicate our difficulties of seeing the world accurately by leading perception and conviction astray with methods of its own. The film's power cannot be fully felt until the viewer recognizes that the dramas of misperception enacted on the screen have been replicated still one more time in his or her theatre seat.[4]

Here, Wilson elaborates this film's particular strategy of involving its audience closely in the potential fallibilities of vision and perception and placing at stake the ways in which these can impact upon the moral judgements we form in relation to characters and the society they inhabit, a theme that he explores fully in his landmark reading of the film. Following this lead, we might therefore speculate that the shot through the viewfinder does not simply propose a straightforward vision but instead questions the reliability of vision itself in the film's depiction of its fictional world, and the implications for interpreting images in any particular way.

Questions of vision and reliability achieve yet further significance as it is at this point that the film radically shifts its storytelling tone and, in doing so, potentially expands its boundaries of possibility. A cut away from the rifleman's point of view shot reveals Eddie reassuring Joan 'We're OK kid, we're OK' as he carries her. She touches and strokes his face, before her head falls forward in apparent unconsciousness. Eddie's calling out 'Jo' rouses her momentarily and she tells him, in an intimate close-up, 'I'd do it again, darling, all over again … glad-' and then collapses, dead. We cut back to a medium shot as Eddie cries out again – 'Jo' – but then a shot rings out and he stumbles forward, eyes closing as the bullet strikes him in the back. A moment of silence and stillness follows, before he opens his eyes once more and a male voice calls out to him 'Eddie', accompanied by an unseen choir of seraphic voices. Eddie's gaze drops down once more to Joan and he kisses her gently on the lips, but the enigmatic voice calls out once more, insistently: 'Eddie!' Eddie looks around slowly to a space off-screen, the hint of a smile forming on his face; the choral accompaniment swells and the voice continues 'You're free Eddie! The gates are open!' At these words, there is a cut to what appears to be Eddie's point of view (an assumption complemented by the invoked convention of the eye-line match between the two shots): a forest scene lit by a shard of bright daylight that falls across the woodland floor, touching the canopy of leaves and branches that enclose the scene. The underscored music and voices reach their emphatic conclusion and the scene fades to black. The film ends.

We are entitled to be unresolved in our understanding of what has occurred in these final moments. Is this a vision of heaven, and thus an endorsement of the central character's redemption? Or is it the final subjective vision of a man before he succumbs to death? The voice that calls out is recognizably that of Father Dolan, the character whom Eddie killed earlier in the film, but are we to take this to be an apparition calling out from beyond the grave, or the product of Eddie's residual guilt over his actions finally taking overwhelming hold of his physical senses? Certainly, nothing in the film up to this point can prepare us for its conclusion. On first viewing, at least, the effect of the ending approaches that of a fracture occurring in the narrative, as though a border between conventions and codes had been forcefully breached. (The moment of stillness and silence that follows Eddie's being shot in the back seems to reinforce this notion, occurring almost as a standstill between two worlds.) Furthermore, the relative brevity of Eddie's final revelation in the woods serves to heighten the impact of the event, leaving us to question whether it really took place in those few seconds, and whether it has taken place in the manner we have understood it to, or whether ultimately we have understood fundamentally what has taken place at all. The notion that the film's ending provides something of a question mark rather than a full stop to the narrative is reinforced by the major critical reactions that have been formulated in response to it. Not only do respective scholars identify the ending as odd, or at least out of step with Lang's vision of a fictional world up to that point, but there is a concerted attempt to rationalize the events taking place – a desire to come to terms with the anomaly and the terms in which it is presented to us. Continuing the themes of his general argument about *You Only Live Once*, George Wilson relates the ending to its overarching debates surrounding the fallibility of character point of view, and the unreliability of the film's narrative strategies. He concludes that:

> We have strong reason to suppose that Eddie's dying vision may only be the ultimate misperception that culminates the vast chain of misperceptions which has led him to his death. I have stressed again and again how much of the narrative development depends upon various failures of perception; how characters may appear deceptively to each other and to us. There is a compelling logic to the possibility that we are seeing in the end the past hope, the last pitiful illusion of a dying and defeated man ... Like the film as a whole, the vision is strictly ambiguous. It may be genuine or it may be horribly false, but we cannot accept without question a heavenly promise of life after death in a film whose title is, after all, *You Only Live Once*.[5]

In conceding the scene's inherent ambiguity, Wilson proposes a reading of the moment as an ironic encapsulation of the failures of vision expounded within Lang's film, centring those shortcomings upon the central character of Eddie. Consistent with this interpretation, Wilson offers the example – occurring in the film just before the final scene – of Eddie wrongly identifying a light in the woods as the morning star, when in fact Joan has spotted the reflected light of the police cars that lie in wait for them. For Wilson, Eddie's confusing an impending symbol of death with a symbol of hope and renewal proves indicative of his skewed perception of events throughout the film.[6] We might add to this example Eddie and Joan's later shared indulgence in a fantasy of their predicament when, both badly wounded by bullets, they each seek to reassure each other that they are not hurt in a blatant – and desperate – denial of the grim reality they both share. Where the incident with the morning star might be read as symbolic of Eddie's misperception of events, a misperception that he is critically unaware of, the example of the denied bullet wounds suggest both Eddie and Joan's wilful denial of reality: the extent to which they seek in desperation to resist the terms of a world that has turned against them finally and retreat instead towards a shared illusion. Wilson's reading of the film's moment places the weight of emphasis upon Eddie's vision of his world – his perception of events and his place within them. Whether or not this is a wilful or unintentional skewing of life's realities, it nevertheless makes Eddie the author of the heavenly vision at the end of the film, marking it out as a product of his imagination rather than as an event to which he bears witness. In Wilson's terms, this ultimately becomes an ironic statement concerning Eddie's fallible vision and characteristic misperception, fitting a pattern that brings him to this final predicament.

Tom Gunning also acknowledges the moment's ambiguity in his reading of the film, but in doing so proposes that the scene opens up a variety of interpretations apart from Wilson's understanding of it as an ironic statement, 'the last pitiful illusion of a dying and desperate man.' Although conceding the limitations of emphasizing solely directorial intention, Gunning asks us to consider again Lang's key claim, made in conversation with Peter Bogdanovich, that the sentiment of the closing moments was *not* designed to be ironic.[7] Gunning pursues this line of reasoning to consider what it would mean to accept the closing episode as sincere:

> Can we follow Lang and see Eddie as receiving a vision of the truth at the end of *You Only Live Once*? What would that truth be? The most obvious allegorical reading would be that Eddie and Joan are redeemed. The Production Code may demand their death, but heaven will receive them. The gates that open now are the gates of heaven. Therefore this vision would be of the sort of rebirth Father Dolan said death could be, allowing us to remember our glorious birthright. Again this is a possible reading, less fashionable than Wilson's, but also not inadequate.[8]

Although, for the purposes of his wider argument, Gunning allows this interpretation to splinter as he proposes further meanings, such as how the vagueness of
the view of 'heaven' might lead us to consider Canada as a 'promised land' across
the border for the couple (and one which remains barred from them), he nevertheless
constructs an account of the closing moments of *You Only Live Once* that runs
counter to Wilson's, proposing that the scene can be read as an allegorical expression
of freedom and redemption, rather than as a dramatic reinforcement of a character's
tragic misperception. Although taking different paths of interpretation, both Wilson's
and Gunning's claims for the unusual moment rest upon its inherent ambiguity (the
questionable point of view shot and the marrying of a heavily asserted soundtrack
with an unremarkable *mise en scène,* for example) and furthermore its obscurity
within the film as a whole. Whilst offering explanations of the moment, both critics
maintain that it can never be definitively resolved and that, within any evaluative
framework we pursue, conclusions remain somewhat precarious.

We might say that none of this is remarkable for a Hollywood film made in
1937, or anywhere else at any time, given that very few films offer conclusions
that are closed entirely to further conjecture. Indeed, the finality of closure that is
sometimes attributed to Hollywood cinema can often be a notional account of such
films, selling short the works themselves and the audience's contemplative reach.
Some of these notions depend upon a concept of the happy ending, especially as
it occurs in Hollywood cinema, yet even in the most apparently clear-cut cases,
such a classification can seem inappropriately unambitious. Few would contest the
emphatic joy felt at the conclusion of Frank Capra's *It's A Wonderful Life* (1946), for
example, but it would be an unsteady claim to suggest that the film ties up all of its
narrative threads within that happiness, to the extent that no grounds for speculation
are left open to us. As I have suggested elsewhere:

> Through the fact that Potter is never punished for stealing that money, the film resists a
> conventional narrative resolution based upon the emphatic punishment of crime. Perhaps
> similar events might occur in the future: life will sometimes be difficult again ... It is
> appropriate, therefore, that there is no easy balancing of justice through the discovery
> and punishment of Potter's crime against the Bailey's. Rather than seeing this ending
> as morally unsatisfactory, we might consider that George, in rediscovering his special
> union with Mary, embraces the fragile volatility of life that can deal out extreme joy or
> despair.[9]

In this way, a film that might be taken to be an archetype of the Hollywood
'happy ending' allows for a series of concerns to linger beyond the conclusion of its
narrative, and in doing so keeps open the potential for speculation over its fictional
world to extend beyond the closing credits. I suggest above that this tendency is
helpful to us in understanding some of the film's wider themes and issues, should we
choose that direction of inquiry. A key difference in *You Only Live Once*, however, is

that, unlike *It's A Wonderful Life*, the way in which we interpret the ambiguity of its conclusion affects fundamentally how we understand the boundaries of possibility inherent within its fictional world. If we read the film's final vision as Eddie's, following the line of argument that Wilson establishes, then we effectively accept the moment as an instance of personal fantasy 'taking over' the *mise en scène* (both visually and audibly) of the film. We momentarily share Eddie's psychological perspective. Thus, nothing in the world around Eddie has changed: the fabric of its reality remains intact. However, if we understand the vision to be an event occurring beyond the confines of Eddie's psyche, as Gunning's account implies, then the world of the film is radically changed. In one instant, a new dimension of possibility exists whereby the kingdom of heaven can be seen to impose itself upon the human realm. Rather than presenting us with a character's inner fantasy, then, the film offers a fantasy world, where ghosts magically speak out to dying men from beyond the grave.

Perhaps inevitably, I want to suggest that the ambiguity inherent in *You Only Live Once*'s conclusion relates potently to a central theoretical work on fantasy: Tzvetan Todorov's concept of the fantastic.[10] Todorov establishes three key distinctions: the marvellous, in which events can be explained and understood as supernatural; the uncanny, in which events are understood to be ultimately consistent with the natural laws of reality as we understand them; and the fantastic, which is the hesitation between those two states where events cannot be satisfactorily defined as either marvellous or uncanny. As Todorov explains:

> In a world which is indeed our world, the one we know, a world without devils, sylphides, or vampires, there occurs an event which cannot be explained by the laws of this same familiar world. The person who experiences the event must opt for one of two possible solutions: either he is the victim of an illusion of the senses, of a product of the imagination – and laws of the world remain what they are; or else the event has taken place, it is an integral part of reality – but then this reality is controlled by laws unknown to us. Either the devil is an illusion, an imaginary being; or else he really exists, precisely like other living beings – with this reservation, that we encounter him frequently.
>
> The fantastic occupies the duration of this uncertainty. Once we choose one answer or the other, we leave the fantastic for a neighbouring genre, the uncanny or the marvellous. The fantastic is the hesitation experienced by a person who knows only the laws of nature, confronting an apparently supernatural event.[11]

The 'hesitation' that Todorov describes is alluded to strongly in the accounts of *You Only Live Once* provided by Gunning and Wilson. As they maintain, the film emphatically refuses to settle upon one explanation of events or another (in Todorov's terms, 'uncanny' or 'marvellous') and so the ambiguity of the moment is never properly resolved. In this sense, according to Todorov's formulation, the fantastic is never left for a 'neighbouring genre' and instead the reasons for what has taken place are left enigmatic to us. Both Wilson and Gunning attempt, in different ways, to account rationally for the tone and nature of the film's final scene, but it is significant that, in doing so, they are always bound to its fundamental ambiguity and its indefiniteness. (I would suggest that, in both accounts, this serves as a central critical attraction for both writers to varying degrees, providing a rich opportunity for the rigours of interpretative criticism.) Lang's film is unusual in that it never allows such matters to be settled and this strategy is made the more extraordinary by the fact that the issue is raised only in the final seconds of the picture, thus potentially inviting ambiguity to become the lasting, and perhaps the *defining*, tone of the film. Moreover, the ending risks throwing into doubt all that has gone before, leaving us with the challenge of matching up such an audacious departure with the film's 'main' social consciousness narrative. For some – and certainly audiences that I have sat with when watching the film – the result of this uncertainty translates into bemusement at such an obviously moralistic or sentimental ending. For others, Wilson included, ambiguity is a wholly appropriate note for Lang's film to end on, usefully bringing into sharp focus a number of questions regarding reliability and viewpoint that have defined the director's depiction of events.

The Horizons of Fantasy

I have suggested that *You Only Live Once* is an unusual film in that it prevents explanation of its concluding moments to form properly, thus prolonging what Todorov has termed its state of 'hesitancy': the fantastic. A counter position exists, however, in that we might contend that all fiction films have the potential to expand the boundaries of possibility and plausibility precisely through their being fictions. The film maker has at her disposal an entire spectrum of possibilities that occur within the fictional world she constructs. Acknowledging that such worlds *are* fictional allows us to accept the terms of these departures; understanding that a world is taking shape that is fundamentally distinct from our own. This is a position to which I am sympathetic in certain ways, and which I have addressed directly elsewhere.[12] The potential implication of adopting this all-encompassing definition of 'fictional', however, is that fantasy becomes something of a redundant term: a film's potential as a work of fantasy is effectively curtailed by the fact of its fiction. If this configuration is appealing, it is also true that such a definition does not satisfactorily cover the ways in which we understand, at a basic level, the terms 'fiction' and 'fantasy' as they occur in cinema. To return to *You Only Live Once*, we accept that a 1937 fictional world is portrayed, which to a subtle degree resembles, and departs from, an everyday world as experienced in 1937. It contains certain features and establishments – cigarettes, coffee, baseball, guns, capital punishment – that we take to be factual representations of the period. But it also contains a host of characters – Eddie and Joan Taylor, Father Dolan, Rogers the guard – who are entirely fictitious entities, but whom nevertheless interact with the 'reality' of the world as we understand it (cigarettes, coffee, baseball, capital punishment). My assertion here echoes a key point that V. F. Perkins makes in relation to the fictional world of *Citizen Kane* (Orson Welles, 1941):

> Of course this is our world. It shares our economy, our technologies, our architecture, and the legal systems and social forms that yield complex phenomena like slum landlords, divorce scandals, and fame. Its history is our history of wars and slumps and the rise of mass media. Its notorious people (e.g. Adolf Hitler) and its decisive events are the ones we know.
>
> But of course its world is not ours. Kane is famous throughout that world, and we have never heard of him nor of Jim Geddes, his political rival. Susan Alexander's celebrated fiasco at the Chicago Municipal Opera House involves an occasion and a location without reality for us. Everyone there and nobody here knows about the construction of a new Xanadu (their Xanadu) in Florida (our Florida). These are some of the aspects that mark the world as fictional.[13]

So any fictional world in film is an intricate fusion of a world experienced as an everyday reality (or at least understood as existing historically) and a world of the filmmakers' imagination. We accept this to be the case in *You Only Live Once* and, in doing so, accept the terms of the fictional world as portrayed: like our world, but different. Our acceptance of this fictional world's conditions does not incorporate an acceptance of Father Dolan's voice as heard at the film's conclusion, however. To account for this, we have to consider an event that seemingly takes place beyond the horizons of ordinary perception, and we are asked to evaluate it on those terms: is this really happening and, if so, is this a fictional world in which the dead can speak to the living?

Fantasy, then, exists beyond the realm of the knowable and the explainable. Building upon the nature of fictional worlds to contain a series of facts and events particular to that world and distinct from our own, fantasy cinema expands the terms of credible occurrence, reshaping the world into new, and unchartered, extremes. For Lucie Armitt, writing in the context of literature, this is a key characteristic that binds together a series of texts that share in various ways the distinction of being works of 'fantasy'. She asks:

> How, then, can texts as diverse as the biblical book of Genesis, Tennyson's poem 'The Lady of Shalott,' Orwell's novel *Animal Farm*, J. M. Barrie's play *Peter Pan*, and Bunyan's allegory *The Pilgrim's Progress* all shelter under the same literary umbrella, fantasy? The answer lies in the fact that they share two primary characteristics. First, as already implied, they deal in the unknowableness of life. A reader of Doris Lessing's realist first novel, *The Grass is Singing* (1950), may find she can relive at least an element of that literary experience by reading up on or even visiting present-day Zimbabwe, but none of us can holiday in the Garden of Eden. A child who delights in Anna Sewell's

Black Beauty (1877) may try to recapture that pleasure through learning to ride, but no reader of *Animal Farm* can teach beasts to speak, any more than they can make pigs fly. To reiterate: fantasy sets up worlds that genuinely exist *beyond* the horizon, as opposed to those parts of our own world that are located beyond that line of sight, but to which we might travel, given sufficient means.[14]

The distinctions that Armitt makes in relation to these literary texts are useful as she brings the debate to the heart of fantasy's relation to the fictional. To borrow her terminology, a fictional world in film takes place within the horizons of potential action that exist within our knowable world. As with *You Only Live Once*, a couple may find themselves on a road in somewhere named America, pursued by police, very near to the border of a place called Canada. Such events are conceivable and even navigable according to the logic of the world as we experience it. The event of a voice heard from the beyond the grave lies beyond our horizons of reasonable expectation, however, and as such requires a degree of reconciliation as an occurrence within that fictional world. Put simply, is this really happening, or is it the product of character imagination?

With such definitions in place, we at least move towards a means by which fantasy in various forms of cinema can be approached and understood, and the concerns raised in this discussion will inform the following chapters contained in this book. But such conclusions also complicate the notion of fantasy as a discernible genre at all. If we take fantasy to be an expansion of the fictional in cinema, then we also have to concede that such a definition can spread across an incredibly wide range of films made up of many other genres, from science fiction to horror, from musicals to anime and so on. This lack of definition is something that has long troubled studies of fantasy and fantasy cinema. For example, James Donald's edited collection *Fantasy and the Cinema*, first published in 1989, presents a series of useful essays dealing with a multitude of genres.[15] Although designed as a reader to teach with, the challenge exists for readers concerned with questions of genre to find the connections between chapters on slasher films, German silent cinema, science fiction, the work of Alfred Hitchcock, surrealist cinema, melodrama, carnival and so on, that each explore a distinct (and frequently discrete) critical or theoretical perspective. This range complements Donald's editorial intentions. He explains in his preface that 'The framework the reader offers for teaching about film and cinema is not [...] an objective survey of the field; nor do the difference perspectives and approaches of the various articles make up a single "position" or "line".'[16] Although this may constitute an admirably broad configuration of approaches, without a unifying set of characteristics and definitions, the sense that fantasy can encompass seemingly anything can be disorientating. This point is not lost on Donald:

In a common-sense way, we can all recognise a fantasy film when we see one. Science fiction films like *It Came from Outer Space* and *Star Wars* or horror films like *Dracula* and *I Walked with a Zombie* might be the sort of thing that comes immediately to mind: films which show worlds, whether ours or not, that depart from the rules of everyday reality, often using cinema's spectacular capacity for illusion and trickery to conjure up before our eyes weird creatures and strange happenings in impossible narratives. Does this sort of recognition offer an adequate basis for defining a genre of fantasy within the cinema? My examples already suggest that the fantastic can surface in a number of genres. And apart from science fiction and horror, wouldn't we have to say that melodramas and weepies, westerns and musicals are also in some sense fantasies? Indeed, would it be possible to exclude *any* forms of entertainment cinema from the description?

Broadened to that degree, the category of fantasy becomes virtually useless as a means of distinguishing between different types of film. So is it useful to attempt a definition of a cinematic genre of the fantastic in film at all?[17]

Donald leaves these questions open, to a large extent, as the discussion in this introductory section moves to a consideration of Todorov, Carl-Theodor Dreyer's *Vampyr* then briefly history and ideology. In many respects, the points of definition are never properly asserted in the collection as a whole, given that it develops into a series of chapters that explore discrete thematic concerns. Part of the reason for this, I would suggest, derives from Donald allowing his scope of enquiry to expand beyond a disciplined set of critical, rather than only generic, boundaries. 'Melodramas, weepies, westerns and musicals' certainly do feature departures from what we understand to be everyday reality in that they provide access to a fictional world that conforms to and also departs from the rudiments of the reality that we experience and understand. However, that is not the same as defining all of these types of films as fantasy. Fantasy, as I have suggested in a continuation of Armitt's distinctions, is defined by an expanding of the fictional world's horizons beyond reasonable expectation or, as Richard Mathews describes, 'consciously break[ing] free from mundane reality.'[18] Understanding the relationship of fantasy to the fictional helps to prevent the term 'fantasy' becoming all-encompassing and therefore, as Donald points out, becoming 'useless as a means of distinguishing between different types of films.' My contention is that an appreciation of the relationship between fiction and fantasy allows for the term 'fantasy' to become a useful and productive way of distinguishing types of films. This is not only the case for film: it extends across all works of narrative fiction. It is one thing for Dickens to convince us of a world in which a character called Ebenezer Scrooge could exist, for example, but quite another for him to convince us of a world in which that character is visited by a series of ghosts that show him the past, present and future.[19] In the first instance, at stake is the acceptance of a fictional world whereas, in the second instance, it is the acceptance of a fantasy world. In this sense, expanding the term 'fantasy' across *any* forms of entertainment cinema is a limited means of critical progression. With a developed understanding in place of how fictional worlds exist and function in narrative film, however, we can begin to appreciate fantasy as an extension of and departure from the fictional.

Experiencing Fantasy

A counterpart condition in accepting that fantasy functions as an expansion of the fictional is acknowledging that fantasy can emerge in unanticipated and unusual places in cinema, as part of films that are not defined by their expanding dramatically the world's boundaries and possibilities. We have seen this expansion occur with some force and impact in *You Only Live Once*, where a departure from the rudiments of the fictional world as presented potentially throws into question the very nature and consistency of that world. But it is also true that some films draw upon fantasy in ways that create rupture with the conventions of everyday reality without necessarily breaching the conditions of their world. On this theme Robin Wood, for example, has written provocatively on the ways in which computer-generated images 'have been used quite irresponsibly to create what I see as a kind of magical unreality that seeks to impose itself as a new and better "realism."'[20] Having focussed these contentions upon an example of obvious 'fakery' in a fight sequence from *The Bourne Identity* (Doug Liman, 2002), Wood expands some of his claims in a further example from the movie:

> The film's climactic action sequence is even more remarkable. [Matt] Damon is trapped at the top of an immense spiral stairway, about ten floors up in a large ornate building; the stairs are blocked by bad guys; how can he escape (escape he must, not because of anything intrinsic in the plot but because he is the "Hero" and this is a contemporary action movie)? Well, there is a convenient corpse (a bad guy already disposed of by Our Hero), with its convenient head poking conveniently between the banister railings. Damon gives it a good shove, the railings part, and the body falls – not head first, as an unimaginative person like myself might expect, but horizontally. Then Matt 1. Hurls himself upon it, using it as a kind of magic carpet to fall ten floors or so to safety (I thought of Sabu on *his* magic carpet in *The Thief of Baghdad*, but that is signalled as 'fantasy'); 2. Finds time on the way down to turn his head and shoot one of the worst of the bad guys halfway up the stairs, and 3. Lands without even being winded. Is this what the term 'magic realism' means? No one in the audience seemed to find it as hilarious as I did; a few applauded. Today, it seems, anyone will believe anything; the whole distinction between 'reality' and 'fantasy' (always somewhat precarious in Hollywood movies) has become completely eroded, the impossible has become 'real': perfect training for life in today's culture. Compared to what we have now, the practices of Classical Hollywood seem actually to merge with Italian neorealism.[21]

Wood's critical judgement of *The Bourne Identity* – its manoeuvring of its central character into situations of entrapment and escape, its lack of tangible investment in anything that might approach 'human problems, human emotions, and human actions'[22] – is something that can be evaluated more fully elsewhere and in a discussion focused closely on that film itself. (Certainly, the spectacle of a character using the corpse of another human as some sort of vehicle for an elaborate circumvention seems particularly distasteful, even for an action film in the twenty-first century.) Of interest here, however, is the claim that Wood makes for distinctions between 'reality' and 'fantasy' becoming 'eroded' in the film to the extent that the impossible becomes 'real'. This assertion demonstrates in clear terms the instability of the terms 'fantasy' and 'reality' and the extent to which they can meld into one another in the course of any movie's events.[23] Wood's claim that the impossibility of Damon's physical exploits in *The Bourne Identity* goes uncontested by a modern audience is, in one sense, a negative appraisal of that audience's scope for critical inquiry, but it also references directly the extent to which such impossibilities are perhaps accepted conventions of the action genre in contemporary cinema: they cease to become a controversial detail. The notion of the superhuman can be found in works ranging from the Greek myths to comic books, and we recognise the fantasy of a character that transcends the limits of human existence without too much difficulty. *The Bourne Identity* (and movies of its type) departs from this convention, however, in that it neglects to include information that accounts for its central character's apparent acts of superhuman endurance. In doing so, it makes this fact a condition of its fictional world's rules and procedures, so playing upon the disparity between fictional worlds and everyday reality laid out already in this chapter. While certainly not as clearly marked out as a film such as *The Thief of Baghdad* (Raoul Walsh, 1924) – the comparison that Wood provides – we can still appreciate that the film is relying on codes and conventions associated with fantasy cinema, in that its fictional condition relies upon broadening the horizons of possibility beyond the rudiments of ordinary life.

Although he acknowledges its inherent precariousness, Wood's choice of the term 'reality' as the opposite of 'fantasy' is problematic in this context, however, in that it falls short of acknowledging the reality that the film has established within its fictional world: that the central character cannot die and can perform superhuman feats. In this sense, *The Bourne Identity* bases itself upon a fantasy of human existence, but it also presents us with a fictional reality. If we find this to be a ludicrous or profoundly unconvincing state of affairs, as Wood clearly does in his description, it is because the film has provided an account of its fictional reality that lacks credible reasoning and instead, perhaps, offers a convenient plot device to manufacture equally convenient, if spectacular, escapes for its hero. If one character is not allowed to die, death loses its meaning. At a fundamental level, however, the film presents no aberration in expanding the boundaries of its fictional world to incorporate this fantasy element. Its fallibility, if we take Wood's line, lies in its failure to account for the fantasy of its fictional world by providing credible evidence for Bourne's invincibility, or even allowing that fact to be debated beyond a broad dismissal that 'things of this kind happen in films of this kind.' (Perhaps, for some, debating the credibility of such matters may be tantamount to spoiling the enjoyment of the movie itself.) Whatever value we place upon its central conceit, the characteristics of a film like *The Bourne Identity* give prominence to the indeterminate borders of fantasy as a genre in cinema and the extent to which the fundamental narrative traits of fantasy can become transposed across a variety of film making tones and styles. On the surface at least, it would seem that an intention of *The Bourne Identity* is to suggest, even to a limited degree, that its events could take place within our reality, as part of the political and military infrastructures that exist within our world. And yet, as Wood has illustrated, the conditions of its fictional world rely upon the fantasy of an ordinary human being that can withstand unlimited physical traumas without, apparently, suffering their consequences. In this way, the contours of this particular film's fictional world are, for better or worse, shaped according to its central fantasy of human existence.

Of course, an obvious opposite of the issues Wood identifies exists in those films that *do* propose a fictional world in which superhuman abilities are a discernible and legitimate fact. In particular, the relatively recent proliferation of comic-book adaptations in cinema has brought about a plethora of superhero fantasies in which an individual's special ability or power drives the narrative.[24] The emergence of the comic book film as a dominant genre in cinema has coincided with the steady rise of computer-generated graphics brought about by rapid technological advancement. Lisa Purse has observed a tendency in some comic book films to replace entirely, at certain points in the action, the real heroic body with a virtual heroic body, asking 'what happens when the special effect *is* the action body, when the hero at the center of this vortex is completely virtual, a kind of agile digital sculpture? Can the spectator still identify – emotionally *and* sensorially – with that body's trial, exertions and successes?'[25] Working through these issues in relation to two Marvel Comics adaptations in particular, *Spider-Man* (Sam Raimi, 2002) and *Hulk* (Ang Lee, 2003), Purse arrives at a further example, *X-Men* (Bryan Singer, 2000). She suggests that:

> *X-Men* and *X-2* [a sequel, released in 2003 and directed again by Singer] seem for the most part to want to forego computer-generated bodies. Computer animation is still used extensively throughout the films, but these digital effects either depict inanimate elements of the environment *around* the pro-filmic body ... or convey powers that emanate *from* the pro-filmic body ... Whether by design or as a result of financial pressures, this recourse to the reassuring physical presence of pro-filmic actors works to allay our primal cultural fears of the mutating, transmogrifying human form that might have been mobilized by the subject matter.[26]

Purse thus identifies a stabilizing effect in the films' preference for framing the human body over the perhaps more dexterous spectacle of the virtual body found in *Spider-Man* and *Hulk*. This might hint at a certain technical restraint on the part of *X-Men* and its sequel, as a choice is made (either through creative inclinations or financial constraints) to resist the excesses of digital effects and instead provide a more identifiably 'real' human body within a fantasized – and, as Purse notes, often digitally enriched – fictional world. We might go further to suggest that the use of real people corresponds with the films' thematic intentions to portray in graphic terms the physical effect of superpowers upon the recognizably human body and, moreover, to emphasize the burden that possessing exceptional abilities can bring. (The fact that those possessing special powers are openly referred to as 'mutants' throughout the film due to a tight narrative logic of genetic mutation from human to superhuman points towards the notion that specialness can bring with it profound issues relating to social status, personal identity and segregation.) The opening scene of *X-Men* ties together concisely superpowers and suffering as it depicts a young Jewish boy, Eric Lensherr (known later as Magneto and played for the majority of the film by the older actor Ian McKellen), discovering his ability to magnetize metal as he struggles in vain to rescue his parents from death in a Nazi concentration camp. The notion that this boy's power emanates from his anguish and pain is articulated forcefully due to the unavoidably emotive scenario, defining the tone and thematic impetus of the film. This connection between superpower and suffering endures in a following scene as the film moves to a leafy suburb 'some years later' where a teenage girl, Marie/Rogue (Anna Paquin), experiences her first tentative kiss with a boy in her bedroom. The romance of the scene drains rapidly away, however, as the boy suffers some sort of massive convulsive trauma when they touch and, we are later told, slips into a coma. It emerges that this girl's 'ability' is to draw the life from ordinary humans (and temporarily absorb the powers of other mutants when she touches them).

Aside from the central association of superpowers and suffering established in these two scenes, it is also the case that they reveal the limits of the character's exceptional gifts – Eric is powerless to save his parents when he is knocked unconscious and Marie must forever avoid skin contact with anyone. Furthermore, they raise the fact that both characters must learn to wield with their powers according to ordinary human concepts of morals and values: Eric's ability is shown to be dangerously destructive as the camera lingers upon the violently mangled concentration camp gates at the scene's conclusion and, likewise, the horror of Marie's gift is intensified as we return again and again to her anguished, screaming face, hopelessly contorted in trauma and confusion. Ultimately, two groups emerge within the film: those mutants who seek to use their powers antagonistically and those who use their abilities to benignly protect others and uphold moral justice. *X-Men*'s inclination to use real as opposed to virtual bodies relates to its apparent intention to explore the human reality of characters possessing extraordinary abilities that have the potential to destruct their world and harm others. Rather than fall into the trap that Wood describes of using computer-generated graphics 'irresponsibly to create

... a kind of magical unreality', *X-Men* insists that its fantasy of mutant powers is experienced as a credible reality within its fictional world, hence it becomes imperative that we see the effects of these powers being experienced by real people. This theme is continued in the film's concentration upon the visceral physical impact of these powers upon their hosts: Marie's touch causes veins to protrude gruesomely on the face, neck and temples of her 'victims' and when another character, Logan/ Wolverine (Hugh Jackman), experiences metallic claws growing from his hands, we are shown in close detail hard metal pushing through soft flesh and are effectively encouraged to linger on the sensorial violence of that event. The disparity between human and superhuman is encapsulated in this violation and contrast of surface materials, and it is further emphasised by the fact that those possessing superpowers adopt a new name (Marie is 'Rogue', Logan is 'Wolverine') as though human identity were itself incompatible with their status as mutants.

X-Men uses this physical disparity between mutants and humans to construct a narrative dealing with issues of prejudice and intolerance. This takes the form of a proposed Mutant Registration Act, brought before the US Senate, which seeks to classify and radically restrict the activities of mutants in society. That this Act derives from the blind prejudices and fears experienced by certain groups of humans in that fictional world is made explicit when its author Senator Kelley (Bruce Davison) frames the debate with anti-mutant scare stories and propaganda. The film's emphasis upon the bodily horror of mutants' special abilities serves to illustrate in graphic terms the implicit threat posed by such powers, partially encouraging an audience member to at least appreciate what is at stake in the fears expressed by certain factions of human society. In this sense, the film is promoting an understanding of the roots of prejudice, an ethos that effectively serves to undermine the fundamental principle of prejudice itself. We might therefore suggest that, far from 'allaying our primal cultural fears of the mutating, transmogrifying human form that might have been mobilized by the subject matter' in the way that Purse proposes, the film in fact allows us to become temporarily aligned with such fears through its vivid depiction of the dangerous mutant body. As Joshua David Bellin explains: '*X-Men* is smart enough to acknowledge, indeed to cultivate, its viewers' own prejudices, to place before its audience not only villains but heroes whose mutant powers are unsettling, if not horrifying.'[27] The film moves beyond this danger, however, by insisting that the extent to which these threats are realized is entirely dependent upon the attitudes of those in possession of such powers. Each mutant is seen to possess a potential weapon, but the individuals themselves are not weapons. The film insists that they have the power of free choice, which is in turn shown to be a greater force than any special ability brought about by mutation. In this sense, we might come to regard *X-Men* as an especially ambitious comic book fantasy film, but it is worth noting that the film does not quite manage to sustain the impetus of its anti-prejudice agenda. As Bellin observes: 'by the time the final battle between the X-Men and Magneto's forces is waged, its suggestive backdrop – the Statue of Liberty – comes to seem no more than a prop or a set piece to enhance the spectacular qualities of a conventional, and tidily moralizing, scuffle between normal and freak.'[28] Perhaps this failure is attributable to the especially high aspirations the film sets itself, and such shortcomings may ultimately compromise the work as a coherent whole. Nevertheless, the *X-Men* succeeds in establishing a stable fictional world in which the powers of special individuals are not only explained but also debated with a degree of sophistication. Moreover, given that the film was released at a time when the excesses of computer-generated imagery were reaching their peak, its resistance of the virtual in favour of the real body demonstrates a commitment to creating a fictional world that is tangible and, indeed, 'real' for its audience. As a consequence, the film encourages us to treat its fantasy of extraordinary human prowess with a degree of sincerity not necessarily found in equivalent works such as *Spider-Man*, *Hulk* and *The Bourne Identity*.

From this debate, the fact arises that computer-generated images have provided a wide spectrum of opportunities for film makers seeking to construct fantasy worlds on screen. In terms of physical representation, Sabine LeBel has suggested that 'In any film, decisions about how bodies "should" look are part of production, but where CGI is involved, the possibilities for creating different bodies are endless.'[29] LeBel's assessment brings to the foreground an implicit danger that this seemingly limitless palette of options could lead to the kind of excesses that lie behind the charge of 'magical unreality' Wood levels against *The Bourne Identity*. Therefore CGI, like fantasy itself, risks compromising credibility and coherence in striving for spectacle and wonder. If nothing else, *X-Men*'s resistance to the virtual body insures against such pitfalls, resulting instead in a fictional world whose impact depends primarily upon its status as a recognizably *human* reality.

At stake here is the relationship between brands of human fantasy and the ontological stability of the fictional world in question. In this sense, we might come to appreciate a series of fundamental differences between a film like *The Bourne Identity* and *X-Men*. However, such issues are equally prominent in films that make expressive departures from the established reality of the fictional worlds they present, rather than presenting fantasy as a fundamental condition of human existence within that world. Metin Hüseyin's 2002 film *Anita and Me* is, for the most part, an unproblematic recounting of childhood memories by its central character, Meena (Chandeep Uppal).[30] Although it is made clear through Meena's narration of events and her actions within the story that she has a strong propensity for fantasy and make-believe, there is no suggestion that her world itself is imbued with these traits. Indeed, we understand Meena's imaginings to be a reaction precisely against some of the mundane aspects of her world, an escape from the monotony of everyday life as she sees it (and thus shifts in the film's style of representation, incorporating slow motion or obscure lighting states for example, are aligned with her emotional perspective). The film breaks from this pattern, however, in a scene that occurs directly after Meena has been thrown from a horse at a village fete and is recovering in bed with a sprained ankle. Her grandmother (Zohra Sehgal), affectionately named Nanima by Meena's family, visits her in her room and, although it has been clear throughout Nanima's involvement in the narrative that she speaks no English, the old woman addresses Meena in that language. The unusualness of this is highlighted as Meena interrupts her grandmother to ask how it can be possible, but she is hushed into silence and told to listen.

A series of stylistic features define this scene as unusual within the film's wider storytelling pattern: a fade to black precedes it before a fade up frames Nanima's face as she speaks, and a particular lens is used to give the scene a specific effect. As Hüseyin describes in his director's commentary for the DVD of the film: 'We use a special – I think it's called a tilt and whirl lens or something, I don't know – we use a lens that only has one plane of focus to make it look a bit other-worldly.'[31] The effect on screen is of Sehgal's face appearing distinct and sharp, whereas the space around her is rendered cloudy and blurred. The style of the moment's representation furthers a sense of uncertainty over what is taking place, a fact Meera Syal makes reference to on the same DVD commentary: 'You don't know whether this is Meena imagining this or just for this precious moment – their last moments ever together – she understands her because what she has to say is so important.'[32] The shift into this realm of uncertainty within the scene is dramatically out of step with the rest of the narrative (in which we can straightforwardly associate instances of fantasy with Anita's daydreaming) and as a consequence the moment is allowed to stand out from the texture of the scenes that surround it. Syal's reading of the sequence is useful as she points us towards the ways in which the words Nanima speaks are also made to stand out from other words spoken in the film, precisely because we cannot be sure whether she is really speaking them at all. The film thus uses a moment of hesitation between the real and the imagined to create a point of emphasis within its narrative, focussing attention upon a character's speech as the reliability of the sound and visual tracks becomes unstable.

Nanima describes the village in which she lived, its progressiveness in terms technology, culture, education and the role of women ('never did we think we were less than men – often we were more!'). The monologue is defined by Nanima's sense of pride and nostalgia for the place described and the culture that it bred, but this evaporates on her words 'then the English soldiers came ...' that bring forth a new tone of foreboding in her voice and also cause a shift in her expression from happy remembrance to painful recollection. She continues: '... and only stones rained from the sky. Nothing we owned was ours anymore, not even our names, our breath. We lost everything and moved to Delhi, your mother's schooling spoilt. We started again.' The question of character knowledge is clearly at the foreground here: Nanima describes a set of circumstances and a lifestyle of which Meena can have no insight (her parents have certainly never shared this story with her), and so the notion of her imagining Nanima's words is precarious. And yet, it seems equally improbable that Nanima should have concealed her command of the English language, communicating only in Punjabi with her family, until disclosing her aptitude to Meena, and Meena alone, now. The unresolvability of the moment is central to its ambiguity and, in its move beyond the confines of ordinary human experience, its status as fantasy. And yet, Nanima's words reflect a historical reality of cultures falling under the oppressive rule of the British Raj and becoming victims of that enforced governance. In a film that touches upon the strains between British Indian communities and the white British society in which they live (climaxing in the murder of one of Meena's family's close friends at the hands of a white gang), the highly ambiguous moment of Nanima's disclosure serves to put those tensions into a wider context, presenting some of the history behind such conflicts and the human cost of living under an Imperial regime. So fantasy is employed within the sequence to touch upon the painful memory of a real history; the jump in the film's narrative logic effectively prompting a heightening of the senses in relation to what Nanima describes. That this truth can only be spoken within such an ambiguous and indistinct scene perhaps reinforces the lack of vocal power the British Indian community have in the film: the extent to which freedom of speech is restricted for them. Within the narrative, white attitudes towards the British Indian community vary from misunderstanding of them to intolerance and then instances of overt racism, even violence. Although these are balanced to an extent by a liberal faction of that society, represented most strongly in the character of the Reverend (Mark Williams), and despite Meena's family being accepted at a Christian wedding towards the end of the film, it is still the case that these prejudices are left largely unchallenged and unresolved. Certainly, it is not made an option that Meena's family should rally against such bigotry and, in the end, they simply move quietly from the area. Nanima's precise description of the British Raj's tyranny thus encapsulates the notion that the sound of Indian protest can only be heard away from the main narrative structure of the film, in a sequence defined and bracketed as fantasy. Within the society that the film portrays, such a vocalization is by and large not permitted. In this way, the conventions of fantasy are drawn upon within the scene in Meena's bedroom to frame a political point, and so fantasy here does not function only as an escape from the real world but, rather, facilitates a re-engagement with the facts of that world by revisiting the injustices exacted upon one race by another.

Consequently, the potential for fantasy to explore darker realities of human existence is touched upon, and so any conception of fantasy as only a pleasurable escape from the world is made problematic. The small scene from *Anita and Me* opens up a debate that will inform a number of chapters in this book: fantasy's ability to form tangible connections with the realities of human existence. This is an interest I have expressed elsewhere in relation to a small collection of films whose narratives I group under the heading 'alternative worlds.' In that work, I suggest that:

> The films use the fantasy of an alternative world to debate a series of universal conditions
> associated with human experience: insecurity, ambition, loneliness, apprehension,

bravery, vanity, inarticulateness, anxiety, ambiguity, introversion, love, and so on. This kind of exploration, I would suggest, is a feature of many variations of fantasy cinema, of which alternative world films constitute a discrete group, that include an audacious or inventive narrative development in order to re-examine the human condition, forming a sincere and serious connection with everyday life.[33]

Moving on from that discrete study, it becomes apparent that such claims are linked to a wider project of taking fantasy cinema seriously, rather than using fantasy as a negative judgement – dismissing a work as being 'mere fantasy', for example, in an effort to articulate its lack of sincerity and artistic merit. The critical hostility towards fantasy is mentioned in a number of collected and individual works exploring the topic. As James Keller and Leslie Stratyner make plain in a recent work on the subject:

> Fantasy as a genre (whether in literature or film or art) has a history of being dismissed, and this is only now beginning to change. Though modernists and postmodernists have embraced texts containing non-linear narratives and linguistic experimentation, apparently many of them are not willing to embrace texts that contain paranormal rings, dragons, and elves. Magic is, of course, acceptable, but only if it is contained within a rational setting. Thus, magical *realism* is highly praised by the academic establishment. Magical fantasy is more often not.[34]

We might find opportunity to reconsider the exact terms of Keller and Stratyner's position here, not least given that a number of films featuring 'paranormal rings, dragons and elves' may be critically overlooked not on grounds of genre, but rather on quality: they may simply be works without artistic merit or distinction. (Such claims depend upon the critic's evaluative criteria, of course.) Furthermore, films like *It's A Wonderful Life* or *The Wizard of Oz* (Victor Fleming, 1939) have hardly suffered from a lack of critical attention, despite their fantasy credentials. In order for fantasy film to be taken seriously in the ways they suggest, however, it is crucial that the consequences and implications of fantasy in film are taken seriously. Thus, when a character apparently hears a voice issuing from beyond the grave (*You Only Live Once*), or another character cheats death impossibly time and again (*The Bourne Identity*), or another character's touch drains the life from her boyfriend (*X-Men*), or another character speaks words in a language they do not know to a girl who suddenly understands (*Anita and Me*), such occurrences have consequences: fantasy has real consequences. It is not adequate merely to remark that, because the films have expanded their diegetic limits and strayed into the realm of fantasy, our investment in them as portraits of human existence is ended. Rather, if we are to take these moments as sincere articulations of a fantasy, we are required to evaluate them according to the same criteria – as moments that relate potently to the human condition, for want of a better term. This position builds upon Brian Attebery's understanding of fantasy's relationship to mimesis in popular storytelling. He contends that:

> Though they are contrasting modes, mimesis and fantasy are not opposites. They can and do coexist within any given work; there are no purely mimetic or fantastic works of fiction. Mimesis without fantasy would be nothing but reporting one's perceptions of actual events. Fantasy without mimesis would be a purely artificial invention, without recognizable objects or actions.[35]

Attebery's articulation of this relationship between fantasy and mimesis is important in that it reinforces fantasy's fundamental bond with a reality that we understand and experience as humans in the world. As Attebery observes, 'We must have some solid ground to stand on.'[36] I would expand this by suggesting that fantasy relies not only upon a mimetic reproduction of the world's physical facets – its objects, languages, customs, for example – but also forges a sincere connection with the ways in which we experience and understand that reality: the facets of sentient human existence. In fantasy we discover not only fragments of our world, but fragments of ourselves.

The following chapters make this position central as they explore a series of themes related to the concept of fantasy in film. At the heart of the debate, then, lies the contention that fantasy films have something to say about the human experience, that their meanings extend beyond categorizations based around notions of escapist pleasure or a suppression of reality. Instead of facilitating only an escape from the world, I suggest that it is practical to consider how fantasy films encourage a re-engagement with the world and its conditions. In short, fantasy matters.

–2–

Fantasy, History and Cinema

Fantasies of Time and Space

There has been a marked recent resurgence in fantasy film, ranging from large-scale (and large-budget) Hollywood franchises such as the *Harry Potter* (2001–), *Chronicles of Narnia* (2005–) and *His Dark Materials* (2007–) series, to international and independent titles such as *Pan's Labyrinth* (Guillermo del Toro, 2006) and *The Imaginarium of Doctor Parnassus* (Terry Gilliam, 2009). Whilst this revival offers potent opportunities for critical discussion, there is also the inherent risk that historical perspectives on fantasy cinema might be left somewhat diminished by any exclusive emphasis upon the modern era of film making. Of course, we can hardly be unaware that the recent series of fantasy titles have their precedents and antecedents. It would not be a complex undertaking to establish a general historical account of fantasy cinema that might be based upon certain exemplary landmarks such as *Voyage à travers l'impossible* (George Méliès, 1904), *The Cabinet of Dr Caligari* (Robert Weine, 1920), *The Thief of Baghdad* (Raoul Walsh, 1924), *King Kong* (Cooper/Shoedsack, 1933), *The Wizard of Oz* (Victor Fleming, 1939), *It's A Wonderful Life* (Frank Capra, 1946) and *Orphée* (Jean Cocteau, 1950), for example. With this broad framework in place, we come to appreciate in fairly straightforward terms the extent to which certain major themes and interests within fantasy cinema have persevered over time, incorporating spectacular journeys, hallucinations, malevolent entities, tireless heroes, magic, fearsome creatures, alternate realms and lands of the dead. Even a perfunctory sense of fantasy cinema's history can yield this kind of understanding.

Rather than attempting a similarly broad historical account of fantasy cinema, examples of which are in any case available elsewhere,[1] this chapter seeks to examine more closely the very early period of film production and exhibition to outline, through a few key examples, the ways in which cinema has been bound to notions of fantasy from the moment of its birth. By containing the terms of the debate within this early historical period, I am concerned not so much with the ways in which conventions of fantasy cinema have changed and evolved to bring us to the point at which we now find ourselves, but rather with the ways in which cinema has *always* held a fundamental relationship with fantasy, even from its earliest offerings. In returning to the beginnings of cinema, an emphasis is placed upon the intrinsic relationship between fantasy and film, one that has endured from the first seconds through to the historical periods that followed.

In a short volume on early cinema, Simon Popple and Joe Kember lay out some of the key properties of the medium's relationship to fantasy, and in turn its propensity for realizing fantasy on screen. They note that:

> The cinema, initially characterised as a medium best suited to representing reality, was also a site of spectatorial disengagement. The audience was presented with a world of fantastic and often disconcerting attractions. Film had the power to picture the impossible and the improbable. It could arrest, reverse, slow or accelerate time; objects could be made to vanish, fly or change. Cinema offered bizarre perspectives, for example to 360° panoramic view, and manipulated its audience through a wide variety of technical trickery.[2]

This description refers to the ways in which the formal properties of film itself provided an opportunity for fantasy to emerge and take shape through the projection of images on screen from the earliest days of exhibition. A strip of film can be stopped, reversed or slowed down and so, when these functions are enacted in the projection of images, the world of the film is seen to stop, reverse or slow down accordingly. Thus, the reality of the film world is disrupted and altered to the extent that the images can no longer be taken as a straightforward representation of reality, but rather become a reversioning of that reality: a fantasy of the world we know and experience. For these reasons, Popple and Kember justifiably contest notions of the medium as one *best* suited to representing reality, and instead place the weight of emphasis upon early cinema's capacity for re-imagining the world it captures. We can appreciate this perspective when we consider a film like *Démolition d'un mur*, one of the first to be exhibited by Auguste and Louis Lumière as part of the famous public premiere of their Cinématographe in the basement room of the Grand Café in Paris on 28 December 1895, an occasion often credited as the birth of cinema itself. This particular film details the demolition of a wall in the grounds of the Lumière factory and, as an event in itself, can be understood to provide a clear narrative progression and even an element of suspense for the first cinema audiences as the toppling of the wall reaches its climax.[3] In the film, Auguste Lumière directs the workers in this procedure as one man extends a winch with which to topple the structure and another joins him to exert further pressure with the handle of his pickaxe. Finally the wall topples in a cloud of dust and the workers set about it with their picks, hacking bits off in an effort to reduce it to rubble. As a portrait of both human and structural action and movement, the novelty of this recorded activity to early cinema audiences is easily understood. However, in its exhibition a further intrigue was created as the film was projected once more in reverse, and so the event of the wall's demolition occurred correspondingly from end to beginning.[4] In this corrupted reality, the scene now appears to be one in which a group of workers magically reform a wall as they seemingly hack bits and pieces of debris back *onto* its structure; clouds of rubble dust re-emerging and billowing downwards to the ground as though a mystical part of some unnatural resurrection.

Here, then, the manipulation inherent in the reverse projection of the film translates into a manipulation of the reality on screen, highlighting the extent to which time almost immediately became a malleable element within the cinema. In the example of *Démolition d'un mur*'s projection, we see an early realization of cinema's dual ability to capture reality but also reshape that reality. We might say that, in the act of reverse projection, the Lumières succeed in creating fantasy from the reality they filmed, but it is also the case that *Démolition d'un mur* highlights the sometimes fractional point of division between fantasy and reality: the shifting extent to which fantasy might be taken as reality (and vice versa), and how fantasy might become merged with reality to create a coherent narrative whole. In this case, the act of fantasy – a wall being magically reconstructed by a group of men – derives from the reality of those same men performing the everyday task of demolishing a wall. Here, then, fantasy grows from reality and, more specifically, the technology of the cinema apparatus itself provides opportunity for this process to be enacted. This returns us to Bazin's founding claim, cited in the introduction of this book, that 'The fantastic in cinema is possible only because of the irresistible realism of the photographic image.' Film reveals itself, even in this earliest instance, to be well suited as much to the creation of fantasy on screen as to the capturing of reality and so, as Popple and Kember make clear in their description, the medium thus avoids easy distinction as best suited for either purpose.

If the backwards projection of *Démolition d'un mur* emphasizes the propensity for cinema to distort processes of time in its creation of a fantasy state, then another film exhibited by the Lumières at the Grand Café would serve to illustrate the ways in which space and dimensionality can become equally illusory and even misleading. *L'arrivée d'un train à La Ciotat* (Auguste and Louis Lumière, 1895) has become synonymous with cinema's origins and enjoys an iconic status as a symbol of the earliest film-making practices. The film depicts the movement of a train from the right background of the frame as it travels across the diagonal axis to the left foreground, eventually pulling into the station to allow passengers to disembark. However, apart from being an example of very early film making, *L'arrivée d'un train* attracts further notoriety due to reports from the time of audience members flinching at and even attempting to flee from the image of the train as it apparently travelled at an angle towards them. Such accounts have been scrutinized at length, often with some scepticism, and scholars continue to debate the possibility of the film having evoked a physical anxiety in its audience at all.[5] Ultimately, we are perhaps able only to conclude, as Ian Christie does, that 'We will never know how many early spectators were truly alarmed by approaching trains. Common sense suggests it may have been very few – and even these may be striving for effect.'[6] Nevertheless, even with common sense in check, it is still the case that such testimonies have survived to become one of the 'founding myths' of cinema.[7] We do not need to accept as truth the descriptions of fainting, hysterics and frenzied escapes from auditoriums in order to speculate on a shared sense of unease at the sight of an approaching train in an unfamiliar setting. Whether or not the effects were indeed experienced to such visceral extremes, it seems uncontroversial to accept that sections of early cinemagoers at least indulged in the fantasy that a train, approaching in silence and in monochrome, might somehow present a danger to them. How severely this was felt amongst individual audience members thus becomes a matter of less importance, given that even a mild reaction – or even controvertible reports of reactions – would reference the extent to which the image of the train conveyed an *illusion* of oncoming threat. Suffice to say that, although the popular magic lantern shows of the Victorian age had succeeded in giving the impression of movement through the rapid projection of slides,[8] so preparing audiences for the cinema to an extent, the newness and strangeness of projected film should not be underestimated. In this way, the spectre of the approaching train in the Lumière film would undoubtedly have been somewhat unanticipated, unfamiliar, thrilling and even frightening. It is hardly necessary for every audience member to have reacted with genuine and palpable terror in order for this effect to be acknowledged amongst them.

However strongly it was experienced, the 'train effect' illustrates the extent to which audiences engaged with – and helped to create – a fantasy of danger brought about by the style in which the train's approach was displayed to them. It is surely unlikely that the Lumières intended to create a trick film that would momentarily confuse audience belief in the image but, nevertheless, *L'arrivée d'un train* makes clear the degree to which trust in the cinematic image as an absolute 'reality' was, from the outset, a precarious investment. The train on the screen, captured in reality, turns out to be a fantasy of a train – a reproduction of its original image – and any reactions elicited within the audience come to be understood as part of that fantasy: a fantasy of impending danger. Here, the filmed image can be disorientating or deceiving through the manipulation of space – an object travelling from the background to the foreground in this instance – in much the same way that time was manipulated for a surprise effect in the reverse projection of *Démolition d'un mur*. From this perspective, the Lumière films, which we generally understand to be documentary (or 'actualities'), cross over into the realms of narrative, fiction and even fantasy, a fact dependant upon the style in which they were projected and the interpretative responses of the watching audience. This fusing together of fantasy and realism corresponds with a number of critical accounts of early cinema, crystallized by Tom Gunning when he states that 'Clearly the fascination and even the realism of early films related more strongly to the traditions of magic theatre (with its presentation of popular science as spectacle) than to later conceptions of documentary realism.'[9] To extend this, magical reversals of time and strange, disorientating spaces are features familiar to fantasy and, in these two films representing the earliest moments of cinema exhibition, we see such conventions emerge forcefully.

We might expand the terms of this debate by relating such moments of fantasy within the Lumière films to Gunning's overarching concept of the 'cinema of attractions', which he attributes to the early period of film until about 1906–7.[10] Gunning's defining claim that 'the cinema of attractions directly solicits spectator attention, inciting visual curiosity, and supplying pleasure through an exciting spectacle – a unique event, whether fictional or documentary, that is of interest in itself'[11] holds particular significance in relation to scenes of fantasy in that early period of cinema. *Démolition d'un mur*, for example, creates its spectacle precisely by providing an impossible vision of the world that defies the ordinary logic of time and space. The world is reordered into fantasy, but that reordering is dependent upon, and therefore effectively promotes, the new technology of cinema. The ability to project images in reverse creates the spectacle, 'inciting visual curiosity' in precisely the ways that Gunning suggests. If we are to concur with Gunning in seeing the cinema of attractions as the dominant conception in early cinema, we might also acknowledge the role fantasy plays in 'supplying pleasure through an exciting spectacle.' Here is a world like ours, but different; a world familiar yet strange. The unexpected, alarming, exciting, unnerving experiences found in early cinema certainly point towards spectacle as a dominant form, especially given that such experiences were brief due to the length of film available for projection. And yet, we might conclude, an engagement in spectacle was often also an engagement in a fantasy of the world on screen: a reality captured and made strange.

Fantasies of Life and Death

Cinema's ability to distort the rudiments of time and space gave rise to an even more profound fantasy in its early years. The notion arose that life preserved on screen could equate to the overcoming of death itself for as one's image is locked forever within the frames of a film, so the human presence can be understood to endure perpetually. Claims that death would no longer be final began to emerge very soon after the Lumières' first exhibition in Paris. As one reporter rather poetically suggested: 'When this device is made available to the public, everyone will be able to photograph those dear to them, not just in their immobile form but in their movement, in their action, and with speech on their lips; then death will no longer be absolute.'[12] This equating of 'everlasting life' with moving images marks a distinction from the aesthetic means by which the dead had previously been 'preserved': in photography and, before that, in painting. Seen in this way, there is almost a progression in the accurate capturing of human existence in art and so, as the report from the time makes plain, the advent of cinema was tantamount to the capturing of life on film, even when that life had ceased in reality. Writing fifty years later, André Bazin would revisit this attitude and evaluate it in more wide-ranging terms in his landmark essay 'The ontology of the photographic image.' In his introductory paragraph, Bazin tells us that:

> If the plastic arts were put under psychoanalysis, the practice of embalming the dead might turn out to be a fundamental factor in their creation. The process might reveal that at the origin of painting and sculpture there lies a mummy complex. The religion of ancient Egypt, aimed against death, saw survival as depending on the continued existence of the corporeal body. Thus, by providing a defence against the passage of time it satisfied a basic psychological need in man, for death is but the victory of time. To preserve, artificially, his bodily appearance is to snatch it from the flow of time, to stow it away neatly, so to speak, in the hold of life. It was natural, therefore, to keep up appearances in the face of the reality of death by preserving flesh and bone.[13]

Bazin continues to trace this 'mummy complex' through a series of art forms and concentrates particularly upon their failure to satisfactorily depict reality, arriving at the central assertion that 'Photography and the cinema ... are discoveries that satisfy, once and for all and in its very essence, our obsession with realism.'[14] The fusing together of artistic representation with a desire to capture life in near-resistance to the universal fact of death reveals the twin satisfactions that cinema might provide its audience. Bazin rightly relates this to the 'defence against the passage of time' that cinema offers but it is also the case that the preservation of life in film is also a spatial consideration: the physical location of human existence on screen, even after such time when that existence has ended in reality. Here, then, cinema's propensity for manipulating both time and space translates into the illusion of life preserved, dimensionally sealed from the physical laws that govern reality. As with the Lumière's reforming wall and approaching train, the rules of space and time were fundamentally different in this new world beyond the screen, allowing for certain fantasies and desires to be granted and realized. If that fantasy was everlasting life, cinema provided the opportunity to 'stow life away' from the rigours of reality: to deposit it within a realm distinct from that which we inhabit. The dead would be seen to exist within a hermetic time and space of their own.

It is significant that Bazin should choose ancient Egyptian religion as a starting point for his claims, given that the notion of life after death is as much spiritual as it is metaphysical. This much is obvious if we consider that Christianity, the dominant religion of the West, is founded upon claims of an afterlife: of death as a beginning rather than an end. But it is also the case that the late nineteenth-century society to which the cinema was born had fervently pursued spirituality and mysticism in a variety of different ways before they were presented with the image of life captured eternally on screen. Ian Christie notes that:

> ... the paraphernalia of ghosts, haunted ruins, nasty ways of dying and un-dying was already familiar by the beginning of the century that would produce such horror staples

as *Frankenstein, Jekyll and Hyde* and *Dracula*. In fact the nineteenth century was as much under the spell of the occult as of any other passion. Everyone – royalty, priests, soldiers, scientists, merchants and ordinary people – seemed caught up in a collective 'will to believe.'

What did they want to believe? Essentially that death was not final; that communication with 'the other side' was possible – from which it followed that one might see into the future, conjure spirits and even achieve immortality. So the respectable threw themselves into spiritualism, séances, tarot cards and magic of many kinds. In this climate, it was scarcely surprising that moving pictures seemed supernatural to their first viewers.[15]

Christie's emphasis upon the need to 'believe' in a spiritual realm beyond the horizon of everyday existence is vital in defining this act as a process of imagining – of almost willing the land of the dead into existence, of creating for oneself the fantasy of life after death. In many respects, this growth of interest in the occult marked a continuation beyond the confines of what had traditionally been offered (and continued to be offered) by organized religion for centuries. If the Christian faith, for example, requires at a fundamental level a willingness to invest in the concept that mortal life functions only as part of an eternal existence, then the various séances, tarot readings and conjuring acts represented an attempt to reach back across the divide from the living to the dead in order to probe some of the assurances offered by religion. What proof could be found that would justify one's faith in the supernatural? If we were to judge all of these activities from an entirely disinterested, sceptical or even atheistic perspective, we might conclude that they each represent versions of a similar fantasy: belief in a heaven, in ghosts, in messages from the dead and in psychic powers all involve a willingness to suspend disbelief, to resist the realities offered immediately by everyday existence. And each represents an investment in a fantasy that death is not absolute: that life endures in some unknown capacity elsewhere.

Cinema was born into this culture and, as much as it represented a magnificent advance in scientific engineering, this new technology became bound up with questions of metaphysics and spirituality. Images of death were certainly abundant in early cinema and took a variety of forms. The Edison Manufacturing Company, for example, commemorated the 1901 assassination of US president William McKinley by releasing not only footage of his funeral procession, but also a staged reconstruction of the moment at which his assassin, Leon Czolgosz, was executed by electrocution. The event of Czolgosz's execution is preceded in the film by a long panoramic shot of the real Auburn prison in which it took place, thus fusing together geographical fact and contrived fiction within the same dramatic structure. Elsewhere, the fantasy of life after death persisted in numerous fictional films from the early period. George Albert Smith's 1903 film *Mary Jane's Mishap* is typical of a work that combines both an extravagant death with the spectacle of an afterlife existence within its narrative. In this film, the household maid Mary Jane performs a series of domestic tasks in medium-long shot before setting about attempting to light a cast iron range. Initially perplexed by its failure to ignite, she settles upon the solution of pouring a large quantity of paraffin into the range. A cut to close-up reveals this to be a key narrative detail, capturing the word 'paraffin' written in large letters on the side of the canister whilst the actress playing Mary Jane (G. A. Smith's wife, in fact) performs a series of satisfied, knowing expressions. Dramatic irony is thus created in the scene as the audience perceives an impending danger that the character is oblivious to while she pours more and more fuel into the range. A return to the original medium-long shot reveals the moment at which Mary Jane sets light to the paraffin, and on ignition she disappears suddenly up the large chimneybreast above the range in a burst of smoke. A cut to the exterior roof of the building depicts the character rising up from the chimney with great force and disappearing out of the frame and into the sky above. After a pause of a second, fragments begin to rain downwards from the sky, and we take these to be the last remains of Mary Jane. In Smith's film, the prospect of an untimely death through misadventure is afforded a spectacular and fantastic treatment: the image of the body exploding from the chimney extending the scene beyond reasonable expectation and natural laws of physics. As a somewhat macabre piece of comic entertainment, the film achieves its aims straightforwardly and effectively. It does not finish at this point, however, as we cut again from the rooftop scene to an image of Mary Jane's headstone, replete with engraved paraffin can and the witty epitaph: 'Rest in Pieces'. The finality of this illustration might again provide a fitting conclusion to the drama, but the film moves on again to portray the graveyard, in medium-long shot, as a grounds man sweeps away leaves, pausing to direct a group of female mourners to the site of Mary Jane's headstone, positioned to the right of the frame. The assembled women pay their respects at the graveside when, to their horror, an apparition of Mary Jane rises up from the plot; they flee in terror. This ghostly figure then proceeds to search around the scene until a paraffin can magically appears in mid-air. She takes this article and returns to her resting place, in apparent satisfaction, and the film ends.

The narrative structuring of Smith's film neatly reflects certain attitudes surrounding death held in some quarters of the post-Victorian society to which it was released. The film seems to offer a conclusion in the shot of the headstone, with the punning of the phrase 'rest in peace' providing an amusing closing line. Yet, the story continues beyond the finality of death to include the graveyard scene that reveals, in explicit terms, the existence of an afterlife within this fictional world. Just as death is not the end in Smith's film, so sections of society toyed with the belief that death was not a final end to existence at all, but rather the crossing over from one state to the next; hence the significant attraction of séances and spiritualist meetings that constituted an evening's entertainment for some audiences at the turn of the century. Whilst we might suggest that this theme was inherited from organized religion, it is also the case that ghost stories had long dwelt upon such possibilities. Henry James' major work of ghost fiction *The Turn of the Screw* was published in 1898, for example, and Dickens' *A Christmas Carol*, a milestone of the ghost story genre, was over fifty years old by the time cinema had arrived. A film like *Mary Jane's Mishap* demonstrates the familiarity of the afterlife fantasy to the extent that it emerges as comedy in this narrative: a less than intelligent housemaid manages to blow herself up through the misuse of paraffin, only to return from the grave to reclaim a spectral can of the same ignitable fluid having, apparently, learnt nothing from her endeavours. In this film, the suggestion of ghostly visitation is clearly not new or frightening to its audience, but commonplace enough to be a central part of a comedy narrative.

Comedy and death would be married together regularly in other fantasy narratives from this early period of cinema. As its title indicates, Cecil Hepworth's 1900 film *Explosion of a Motor Car* features the extraordinary event of a car travelling along a quiet road, only to suddenly and inexplicably blow up in a cloud of smoke. A passing policeman appears on the scene to investigate the disturbance and finds that the shell of the detonated car is all that remains, the three cheerful occupants of the vehicle – two men and a woman – apparently having disintegrated in the explosion. However, having inspected the wreckage, the policeman proceeds to take out a telescope and looks to the skies to behold – in an effect that would be echoed in the later *Mary Jane's Mishap* – various body parts raining down upon the scene. The film moves into relatively dark comedy from this point as the policeman first takes out his notebook to begin cataloguing the assortment of human limbs, and then begins picking up various items to inspect them, before matching up torsos with arms, legs and heads in three piles around the car. The unwavering diligence of the officer in the face of this scene of carnage creates a humorous conclusion to Hepworth's story, but we are perhaps entitled to dwell upon the graphic extent to which human carnage is simulated in this short film. Aside from the fantasy of a car exploding through no clear cause, the film emphasizes the extent to which death and violence can themselves become fantasized elements within the cinema: a gruesome scene is made permissible and, furthermore, amusing due to the fact that it could never be mistaken for real-life events. *Explosion of a Motor Car* sets out its fictional boundaries precisely through having its detonation occur without discernible cause, thus distancing the narrative from any sense of documentary realism. If the film presents a fantasy of violence, death and physical laws, it concludes with a fantasy of human reaction to otherwise horrific events: the policeman dutifully yet inconceivably going about his business whilst surveying a scene of an apparent massacre. Central to an appreciation of this narrative is the basic understanding that the fictional film world is not governed by the same rules of logic that dictate everyday life: a fundamental point of fracture exists within the screen that separates that world from our own. *Explosion of a Motor Car* also seems to respond to the general perception, described earlier, that cinema could provide a defence against the finality of death. If the living could be preserved through the capturing of their image on film, what impact can death within a film have? Both *Mary Jane's Mishap* and *Explosion of a Motor Car* address this issue in different and straightforward ways: the former by proposing that death is the beginning of an afterlife, and the latter by transforming a scene of death into a site of dark comedy. Additionally, both films avoid attempting to recreate actual images of death by throwing their victims upwards, out of the frame, into off-screen space before their body parts fall to the ground. This technique may be due to obvious technical difficulties in having such dismemberment take place on screen but, nevertheless, each film effectively suspends any sense of the reality of death, preferring instead a spectacle that blurs distinction and, as a result, presents a discernible fantasy of death.

This technique of placing the moment of death offscreen is emphatically avoided in R.W. Paul's *Extraordinary Cab Accident* (1903), however, which bears strong similarities to Hepworth's earlier narrative. In this film, a jump cut is used to present the key illusion that we are witnessing a man being run over by a horse and carriage. Paul employs dramatic irony to frame this event by having the cab draw around a bend and approach the camera whilst a gentleman, in conversation with a lady and unaware of the imminent danger, steps backwards off the pavement and into the path of the oncoming vehicle. At the point of impact, the jump cut is employed and a dummy, which gets trampled under the hooves of the horse and the wheels of the carriage, replaces the actor. A policeman runs into the scene and continues offscreen in pursuit of the cab and its driver. A moment after the policeman passes the victim's body, there is a second jump cut, and a real actor replaces the dummy once more (the movement of the policeman across the diagonal axis effectively masking the cut between states). The trauma of the accident is sustained as the lady on the pavement approaches the motionless body of her acquaintance and kneels beside him; another man joins the scene and, having checked the body for vital signs, makes clear that a death has occurred by standing again and removing his hat. The man and woman stand together in stillness over the body for a considerable length of time until the guilty cab driver is brought to the scene by the policeman to witness the carnage he has apparently caused. The sombre mood of the moment is suddenly broken, however, as the 'deceased' victim jumps to his feet, gives the policeman a shove, grabs the hand of the no-longer-grieving lady and runs jubilantly away with her out of the frame.

With this twist at its conclusion, *Extraordinary Cab Accident* is clearly identifiable as an example of the trick films so popular in cinema's early years. The nature of the trick being performed is somewhat complex, however. The man who falls under the cab appears to do so accidentally, without premeditation and appears severely – indeed, fatally – injured by the impact. There is no overt collusion between this man and the woman who constructs a picture of grief at his fate and yet, inexplicably, both have been playing a trick on the assembled crowd. Even the policeman, who has attempted to seek justice for events, is rewarded only with an unforgiving push. But it is not the case that the group have been fooled into thinking a man who was apparently injured was really unhurt: the gentleman who appears on the scene confirms that he has died. Rather, the group are not in possession of the knowledge that this man can return from the dead, is not bound by the limits of ordinary human existence. Here, then, the film crosses over into the realm of fantasy as its narrative moves beyond the confines of reasonable expectation. And we are taken in by this trick too, fooled into assuming that death within cinema must be final (an assumption prompted by the film's naturalistic treatment of events up to the man's miraculous recovery). The film thus plays upon an understanding of the moving image's ability to capture life as it really is, and therefore to represent death in a form with which we are familiar. As Vicky Lebeau elucidates:

> Reproduction of life, preservation of life: the elision between the two belongs to the long, and diverse, history of naturalistic portrayal to which, as a technology of the moving image, cinema began to make its unique contribution. Far exceeding the domain of cinema, such an elision is deeply entangled with the intangible sense that what the audience is looking at in the image *is* life, the life embedded *in* the image, be it still or moving.[16]

In a direct contradiction of this 'intangible sense' that 'image is life', *Extraordinary Cab Accident* foregrounds a violation of human existence within its narrative, ensuring that we are taken in by the trick of the resurrecting man, and furthermore masking that trick by providing no means of anticipating the film's final twist. The inhabitants of the film's world who are taken in by the man and woman's 'trick' are not deceived by the straightforward duplicity of another human being but rather are confronted by the fact that the world they live in is not ordinary, is in fact 'marvellous', to use Todorov's term discussed in the previous chapter. We are similarly taken in as we too have seen the accident occur with our own eyes (although our awareness of the dummy taking the place of the actor would assure us that this is a catastrophe of the film's fictional world, and not of our own), and so vision is made an unreliable factor with the film: events are emphatically not what they seem. The duplicity that the film exhibits serves to highlight the point of fracture between the fictional world and our experience of it: the extent to which it is governed by a series of rules that we can find no equivalent for in our own existence. *Extraordinary Cab Accident* fails emphatically to meet any expectations we might reasonably hold of the physical world we experience and, in this sense, it declares itself to be fantasy.

Fantasies of Freedom and Movement

Within these debates around the broadening of perception and possibility, it is pertinent to return to the fact that cinema took its place as part of a period of mechanical invention and revolution that spanned the eighteenth and nineteenth centuries. The railway and the motorcar, particularly, were transforming urban life by reducing the burdens of time and distance, bridging those obstacles that had previously existed between people and places. Such innovations were greeted with great optimism in some quarters and, for example, when surveying the dawn of this era of progress, *Scotsman* editor Charles McClaren felt compelled to make this enthusiastic assessment in 1825: '... the inventive genius of man is creating new moral and mechanical powers to cement and bind their vast and distant members together to give the human race the benefits of a more extended and perfect civilisation.'[17]

The extent to which industrialization was changing profoundly the landscape of opportunity is encapsulated in McClaren's enthusiastic predictions for a 'more extended and perfect civilisation'. In his account, technical advancement goes hand-in-hand with societal progression and the sense that a better world was being constructed infuses his every sentiment here. And yet such optimism was not always shared among commentators during this long period of innovation. A more sceptical assessment of the age can be found eighty years later in Henry Adams' Pulitzer Prize-winning *The Education of Henry Adams*, written in 1905 but not published commercially until 1918. Adams finds himself in the midst of the kinds of changes and developments that McClaren made such bold and enthusiastic predictions for, but rather than replicate that earlier hope he observes that:

> Every day Nature violently revolted, causing so-called accidents with enormous destruction of property and life, while plainly laughing at man, who helplessly groaned and shrieked and shuddered, but never for a single instant could stop. The railways alone approached the carnage of war; automobiles and firearms ravaged society, until an earthquake became almost a nervous reaction.[18]

For Adams, the advent of rail and motorcar transport was the equivalent of tumultuous natural disaster. His expressive binding together of nature and technology in this passage creates a shared impression of volatile unpredictability: that humankind can properly harness neither nature nor technology and so we are left helpless, as both are equally prone to certain violent and destructive consequences. Here, then, we see an exact reversal of McClaren's buoyant confidence in the benefits that mechanical innovation could offer to those who experience it. Rather than regarding such modernization as a force that can enrich human society and bring cultures together, Adams instead perceives the human race to be plagued by the railway and automobile with a violence comparable not only to the firearm but to 'the carnage of war'.

The sense that technology could be an exhilarating but also an unbridled and even dangerous force is exhibited in a number of fiction films from the early period of cinema. Perhaps the most famous cases can be found in George Méliès' work spanning the turn of the nineteenth and twentieth centuries. His 1904 film *Voyage à travers l'impossible*, for example, follows in the tradition of adventure storytelling established by writer Jules Verne and depicts the invention of spectacular machinery that can take its passengers on astonishing journeys across the earth's terrain, beneath the seas and into the skies above. The spectacle of these feats within the film's fictional world is matched by Méliès' visual achievement in displaying such events through a series of special effect techniques: startling set design, pyrotechnics and editing techniques combine to create a work of ambition and impact. The film devotes itself strongly to the marvel of scientific engineering, providing scenes in which the expedition is planned and the various pieces of machinery are painstakingly constructed. Such sequences encourage a sense of trepidation as the film builds towards the moment of the voyage disembarking, and this anticipation is rewarded as Méliès presents his series of spectacular journeys by land, air and sea. Here then, technology is revealed to be a force of liberation and endeavour, harnessing the human instinct for expedition. Indeed, the figure of the professor, who conceives of and undertakes the impossible journey, comes to embody this spirit of innovation as he seeks to expand the boundaries of human experience through his ambitious inventions. And yet, it is also the case that the passengers on the voyage are entirely at the mercy of the technology that carries them, a fact that is expounded as they suffer a series of mishaps: their car is dashed to pieces when they fall from a precipice, their train crash lands on the face of the sun and they face being burned to death before being frozen in its ice truck, and finally their submarine explodes when they return to earth. Within *Voyage à travers l'impossible*, technology can be viewed equally as a liberator of but also a legitimate threat to human existence. The expansion of physical boundaries is exhilarating and captivating both for the passengers in the fictional world and for the film viewer, but this extension goes hand-in-hand with potential disaster and even the threat of death as the means for negotiating such endeavour are made extremely precarious. The film courts the possibility of fatal injury but ultimately steers its cast unharmed though the catalogue of disasters (although the sheer drop in the car does result in their confinement to hospital for a short period).

Méliès' films frame the spectacle of mechanical progress within the mutable rudiments of a fantasy narrative. There is no question that the visions contained within his work respond profoundly to the flourishing of mechanical engineering that was well underway at the turn of the century, and certainly the vehicles on show in *Voyage à travers l'impossible* (a car, train and submarine) are each taken from a reality that was recognizable and, moreover, tangible to the contemporaneous viewer. In this way, his ideas provide a reflection on the expanding parameters of possibility offered by those new, dramatic forms of transport accounted for so disparately by Adams and McClaren in the passages cited above. And yet, Méliès shapes these facts of mechanized progress so that they become fantasy machines within his narrative: a train that can fly into space or a submarine that can fall from the skies, for example. As a consequence, a film such as *Voyage à travers l'impossible* provides a clear reflection of the extent to which the boundaries of freedom and movement were being reshaped by technology but then proceeds to expand those boundaries again by effectively discarding the fundamentals of physical possibility as one extraordinary journey proceeds the next to become a succession of fantasies.

Such departures from physical reality are continued and extended in R.W. Paul's film *The '?' Motorist*, released two years later than *Voyage à travers l'impossible* in 1906 and containing a number of shared themes. Paul's film begins with a reckless automobile driver and his female passenger who plough into a policeman, attempting to stop them, and then push him from the moving vehicle, causing him to fall under its wheels. At the outset, the film appears concerned with the familiar threat posed by the motorcar to the ordinary pedestrian, a theme already identified in Henry Adams' pessimistic account of modern life and which was touched upon in any number of automobile accident films from the same period, including Cecil Hepworth's effectively titled *How It Feels To Be Run Over* (1900). The narrative of *The '?' Motorist* departs dramatically from this well-worn convention, however, as the policeman recovers from his ordeal and pursues the wayward vehicle. We cut to a shot of the motorcar heading directly towards a row of shop fronts but, rather than colliding with the buildings, it proceeds to mount the brickwork and continue driving, disappearing vertically out of the frame. When the exasperated policeman joins the scene, he can only point upwards towards the car's progress as a crowd of onlookers gather around him. From here, the film continues to widen the scope for possible eventuality in every scene. We cut to a wide shot of the motorcar flying through the skies above trees and roofs; another cut takes us into space where the car now travels along the clouds against a backdrop of vivid stars. Leaving the clouds, the motorcar circles the circumference of the moon before a comet delivers it onto the ring of Saturn, which it travels around in a circuit. This stellar journey is ended, however, when the vehicle plummets from the edge of Saturn's ring and falls through the skies to Earth, landing with a violent crash through the roof of a courthouse where a trial is taking place, before careering away again and out of the frame. A final cut reveals the motorcar drawing to a halt on a road and the driver dismounting to restart the engine manually. At this point a group of court officials and police arrive on the scene to apprehend the miscreants, only for the motorcar to transform suddenly into a horse and cart, with the driver and his passenger now in the costume of country yokels. As the gathered authorities attempt to comprehend this occurrence, the horse and cart changes once again into a motorcar and its driver steers his vehicle out of the frame and away.

Although lacking the storytelling precision of Méliès' crafted film, *The '?' Motorist* continues the theme of motorized transport being both exhilarating and alarming as the spectacle of space travel is balanced against the riotous disruption caused to society by the motorists' reckless acts. Yet Paul's film interprets the nature of such thrills and dangers somewhat differently to Méliès'. There is no sense that this miraculous technology is developed painstakingly by an expert human hand, as was the case with the professor's exploits in *Voyage à travers l'impossible*, but rather that acts of inexplicable travel and transformation occur through a mysterious and magical force: a notion introduced as the car travels up the side of the building and completed when it changes inexplicably into a horse and cart at the film's conclusion. Thus, the narrative of *The '?' Motorist* does not concern itself with fantasies of scientific endeavour and advancement, but instead creates a fictional world in which machines can be turned magically against human society without repercussion. In this way, technology is portrayed as belonging not to the ordinary world but instead becomes associated with a kind of alchemy outside of any everyday experience. Science and the supernatural thus become fused in Paul's story as the motorcar's potential for chaos and disruption is dramatically exaggerated. By equating the threat of motorized travel with a subversive, magical agency, the film highlights the perceived uncontrollability of technological advancements as experienced by society, and extends spectacularly a sense of one's inability to harness those forces that were radically reshaping ordinary human existence. In Paul's film, there is not just the sense that such technology poses a threat, it is literally realized as a chaotic force that cannot be halted or prevented. And yet, as with *Voyage à travers l'impossible*, the thrill of boundless travel is evoked and explored: if new forms of transport were reshaping perceptions of time and distance on a seemingly daily basis, then the skies and solar systems become the next imaginable arena for journeys of adventure.

Whereas other films from the early period of cinema would seek to reflect the realities of modern transport by, for example, placing the camera on a moving train or staging the act of a person being run over, titles such as *Voyage à travers l'impossible* and *The '?' Motorist* chart a different course. Rather than re-examine or re-present the facts of technological advancement, these films use such rudiments as the basis for extraordinary speculation, blending the familiar (cars, trains and submarines) with the impossible (magical flight, space travel and illusion) to create their fantasies. As with all the examples discussed in this chapter, the films illustrate cinema's early capacity for reshaping the realities of everyday life into fantasy narratives, whether that involves drawing upon themes of freedom and movement, life and death or time and space. It is tempting to see the work of an artist like Méliès as a reaction to the 'actualities' of the early Lumière films, so that fantasy and reality become diametrically opposed in examples from the period. However, in tracing certain lines of similarity between films like *L'arrivée d'un train à La Ciotat* and *Voyage à travers l'impossible* in terms of their relationship to notions of fantasy on screen, we come to appreciate that the dividing line between such works is not so deeply embedded. This is a notion taken up by Michael Chanan in his landmark study of early cinema, *The Dream that Kicks*, as he describes both *L'arrivée d'un train à La Ciotat* and *Voyage à travers l'impossible* together:

> Yet, if the first audiences saw Lumière's train as if it could detach itself from the screen, then in a way Méliès' film – in which a cut-out of a train flies through the skies and vaults

across the ravines of painted cut-out scenery – was simply the film of a train which had so detached itself and now traversed the world severed from its rails by the artfulness of the film itself. It is like a filmic metaphor for the effect on the audience of the Lumière film. (Perhaps then, we do see, after all, how films were first seen.)[19]

Chanan's potent suggestions evoke in emphatic terms the extent to which cinema did not discover its own propensity for fantasy fiction as a reaction to an establishing mode of realism but rather that fantasy was always a forceful element within the projection of film, embedded within the experience itself from the very first moments. In this way, the sky-bound train of *Voyage à travers l'impossible* complements and continues the sense of a train bursting from the screen as evoked in *L'arrivée d'un train à La Ciotat*. Likewise, the magical force that enables a motorcar to transform into a horse and cart in *The '?' Motorist* forms a connection with the magic that allowed for a brick wall to rebuild itself in the reverse projection of *Démolition d'un mur*. That is not to say that the works of film makers such as Méliès and Paul are not striking in their handling of fantasy narratives and their rearrangement of the physical world. However, it is also perhaps the case that their films matched an appetite for fantasy exhibited by the films that preceded them, and equally by the audiences that experienced them. The sight of a train rising up into the night sky *rewards* the enthusiasm displayed by an audience who might imagine, if only for a second, that a train might break out of the screened world and leave a trail of decimation in their real world. The birth of cinema heralded the simultaneous birth of fantasy cinema, fusing them together within the very first seconds of public exhibition. The various shifts, evolutions and revolutions in fantasy film making that have taken place since then only build upon the foundations laid within that first moment.

–3–

Fantasy, Authorship and Genre

Who Made What

In Chapter 1 I suggested that a series of creative decisions taken by Fritz Lang in the concluding moments of *You Only Live Once* effectively transform both the tone and narrative possibilities of the film, giving rise to a fantasy generated either by a central character or intrinsic to the world he inhabits. Such claims amount to an acknowledgement of Lang's authorship over events depicted on the screen, working on the assumption that he gave direction to the film's final minutes. In truth, suppositions of this kind rely upon a tradition of critical and theoretical investment in film directors and questions of authorship specifically, which has sustained since the 1950s within the field of film studies. Since *Cahiers du Cinéma* introduced the notion of *la politique des auteurs*, and then Andrew Sarris refigured the term to become 'the *auteur* theory', debates around film authorship have pursued a range of paths and directions, often influenced by passing theoretical trends that have impacted upon the development of film studies more generally. Such influences are reflected in the dominance of structuralism on auteur theory for a period between the 1960s and 1970s,[1] for example, or considerations of the film director's place within economic and industrial contexts that took root most notably in the 1980s.[2] It is not the place of this chapter to rehearse or evaluate such arguments anew. Rather, it acknowledges a vigorous and prolonged engagement with concepts of film authorship that has prospered within the academic study of film. It is as a result of this engagement that we can speak with a degree of confidence about Lang's choices in a film like *You Only Live Once* by drawing upon a basic assumption of authorship criticism, as described by John Caughie, that 'a film, though produced collectively, is most likely to be valuable when it is essentially the product of its director.'[3] In this sense, certain precedents for director-centred discussion of film are set, and the grounds for such a debate are made stable without requiring elaborate qualification.

It is my intention here, however, to focus questions of authorship more closely upon the films of a single director than was possible in the previous discussion of *You Only Live Once* and, in keeping with the aims of this book, to shape that emphasis around a consideration of fantasy within that director's work. Methodologies for approaching the work of a director vary but there is consistently the underlying issue of how to keep an individual artist's body of work in focus as part of a critical discussion of authorship. This matter was addressed directly and at an early stage in the pages of *Movie*, a publication that pioneered director-centred criticism in Britain in the way that *Cahiers* and Sarris had done in France and the USA respectively.[4] Ian Cameron, a founder member of the *Movie* editorial board, defines the journal's analytical stance in its second issue, published in 1962, during a discussion of critical approaches to directors' work:

> For talking about one small section of a film in great detail, whether in an interview or in an article, we have been accused of fascination with technical *trouvailles* at the expense of meaning. The alternative which we find elsewhere is a *gestalt* approach which tries to present an overall picture of the film without going into 'unnecessary' detail, and usually results in giving almost no impression of what the film was actually like for the spectator.[5]

The result of this approach within the pages of *Movie* was an emphasis upon the achievements of the director in specific examples from their corpus of films, rather than an attempt to characterize that entire body of work within a single discussion. As Cameron makes clear, the latter strategy would, for the *Movie* collective, risk imprecision in critical accounts and, as a result, represent a kind of disingenuousness to the films as screened and, by implication, to the director. Cameron's mention of the film spectator is telling because not only does the approach strive to complement the audience member's moment-by-moment experience of a film but it also ensures that, in order to understand the significance of a director's creative choices, it is not a prerequisite that the spectator should possess a comprehensive knowledge of every film that director has made. V. F. Perkins, a fellow founder member of the *Movie* editorial board, clarifies and extends this position in a later article that takes issue with Peter Wollen's concentration upon the patterns across a number of films, which Perkins contends takes place at the expense of considering those patterns contained within a single film.[6] In the course of his discussion, Perkins gives examples of walking and riding motifs from *The Magnificent Ambersons* (Orson Welles, 1942) and *Letter From an Unknown Woman* (Max Ophuls, 1948) before going on to suggest that:

> You could say that the opening of *Touch of Evil* was founded upon the opposition of walking (Mike and Susie Vargas) and riding (Linneker, the woman, the bomb, perhaps the camera). Formally the contrast is important for its contribution to the shifting rhythms of the shot. But is it a founding motif or rather a local device for the exposition of other more significant themes – like the interweaving of the random and the determined? If we can derive any help from a comparison with *The Magnificent Ambersons* we should take it, but the question will need to be pursued as one about *Touch of Evil*. Without a (provisional, as always) resolution there, the issue is not available for setting into an overview of Welles' work.[7]

In its avoidance of a summarizing position, the approach outlined by Perkins serves to accentuate the director's skill in crafting a theme or motif as a point of emphasis within a specific work – the individual film – and thus recognizes achievement in the integration of an expressive element within a film's particular dramatic boundaries. And so, whilst we might recognize certain recurrent interests or concerns within a film maker's entire canon of work, we are first attentive to how those interests or concerns are manifested within a single film: how they are expressed precisely. Crucially, Perkins does not discard comparisons across a director's work in preference for a more concentrated account of that director's technique within a single film. Rather, he suggests that a comparative appreciation of a director's films may enrich accounts of a particular work, but that conclusions will always be focused primarily within the context of that single film. Such assertions return us to Cameron's points regarding the film spectator, given that a focus upon the individual film is more likely to work in sympathy with the viewer's experience of and investment in that movie, rather than making the assumption that single films are necessarily *best* understood as part of a director's wider catalogue extending across a number of titles. Likewise, it might also be suggested that, as filmmaking is nearly always a collaborative enterprise subject to all manner of inputs and interferences, the notion of all directors in all circumstances shaping their entire body of work into a coherent whole of this kind is somewhat precarious.

Even if we legitimately query the idea of a directorial super-project being played out across a series of different films (each in any case possessing its own set of dramatic parameters), we may settle upon the common-sense assumption that the director represents the individual most likely to assert creative control over a film's production. (Of course, given the tensions that have existed historically between directors and studios, even this modest articulation of creative authority carries with it significant exceptions, especially in the case of Hollywood.) As Robin Wood has suggested in a key article debating the merits and limitations of auteur theory:

> Now that the notion of directorial authorship has become a commonplace, it should be possible to move away from the position that sees the identification of authorial fingerprints as an ultimate aim, to a position that regards the director's identifiable presence as one influence – probably the most, but certainly not the only, important one among the complex of influences that combine to determine the character and quality of a particular film.[8]

From this position, we can begin to account for and evaluate the creative decisions taken by the film maker at certain stages within the dramatic exposition of a particular film. Such an approach acknowledges the specificity of those choices within the context of the single film but, as Perkins suggested earlier, there is no practical or logical reason for resisting comparisons with equivalent examples of creative choice from other films directed by the same individual in pursuit of this focus. Indeed, it may prove helpful to draw together a series of examples in order to trace themes or motifs that a particular director dwells upon consistently within the storytelling boundaries of a number of different films. Thus, as this chapter moves on to consider a single director's approach to notions of fantasy within that director's work, we are concerned with how that element is handled and integrated within the narrative of a specific film in each instance, rather than making the case for an *absolute* continuation of handling and integration across a series of films. Likewise, we are interested in how that theme is dealt different inflections and weightings in response to the dramatic demands of each film, rather than pursuing the rather limiting argument that the same characteristic treatment is occurring across every case. In this sense, my understanding of an author is an individual working responsively and dexterously according to a project's particular creative demands, rather than one who would seek to (or would in any case be in a position to) impose *exclusively* her own attitudes and beliefs, even at the potential expense of the film's overall dramatic shape. I would go further, especially in the case of Hollywood cinema, to suggest that we can attend to directors' attitudes and beliefs in relation to the material they are given to work with, rather than material they select for themselves, and thus evaluate their perspective upon the attitudes and beliefs exhibited by certain characters within a fictional world through the nature of their representation.

It is my aim in this chapter to focus on aspects of fantasy as they emerge and are expressed within three films directed by Vincente Minnelli. The obviousness of this association is something I will address later, but it is worth acknowledging at this stage that Minnelli is hardly a controversial choice for discussions of authorship in cinema. The director's critical reputation as an artist has become more established as time has passed and, certainly, the assumption that 'the name of Vincente Minnelli could usefully serve to evoke the second-rate studio product – the film about which it would be silly to be thoughtful'[9] has been eroded, due in large part to publications such as *Cahiers* and *Movie* including his work in debates around authorship and excellence from an early stage. Nevertheless, a claim for authorship is implicitly a claim for achievement and, as a consequence, it proves necessary to articulate such claims precisely and in relation to detail from the film itself so that they should avoid becoming insubstantial or even unsubstantiated assertions of value based only upon matters of personal taste. This echoes Cameron's contention, cited earlier in this chapter, that 'talking about one small section of a film in great detail' is more profitable than the 'overall impression' generated by readings that are too vague to form a rigorous account. Therefore, a claim that Minnelli is a director whose work features strong and vital investments in concepts of fantasy would require qualification through the close critical description of examples from that *oeuvre*. Furthermore, the need for exactitude is made ever more pertinent in the context of this claim, given that the term 'fantasy' itself has a tendency to be used imprecisely and somewhat indiscriminately in accounts of the cinema – a fact alluded to in Chapter 1 of this book.

The placing together of Minnelli and fantasy also raises a series of issues related to genre, however, as the three films I will be focusing on are also musicals – a genre of film with which Minnelli was often closely associated throughout his career. In many respects, the critical status of the musical as a recognized genre within cinema is secure and, in Steve Neale's terms, takes its place alongside other categories such as the western, the horror, the war movie and the thriller as a 'major genre'.[10] Despite this relative security, however, Neale proceeds to make clear that:

> The musical has always been a mongrel genre. In varying measures and combinations, music, song and dance have been its only essential ingredients. In consequence its history, both on stage and on screen, has been marked by numerous traditions, forms and styles. These in turn have been marked by numerous terms – 'operetta,' 'revue,' 'musical comedy,' 'musical drama,' 'the backstage musical,' 'the rock musical,' 'the integrated musical,' and so on.[11]

It becomes clear that, even in the case of a 'major' genre such as the musical, classifications can become complex at an early stage due to the various permutations occurring under that very title. Such matters will be of interest to the scholar reaching for defining notions of what it means for a film to be a musical. In a book about fantasy cinema, we need hardly concern ourselves extensively with the intricacies of such a debate, but it is testament to the solidity of the notion of the musical genre that claims for definition could take place in this way without troubling the foundations of the genre itself. By contrast, if fantasy is to be viewed as a genre in cinema, we must first acknowledge that no similar claims for precise definition have been rehearsed in a sustained way and, as we found with James Donald's wide-ranging characterization of fantasy cited in Chapter 1 of this book, there is an evident danger that the term might be allowed to fragment to the extent that it potentially encompasses almost everything one might find in the cinema. This surely isn't the case with the musical, and we are reminded that the various configurations Neale draws attention to are founded upon the basic criteria of 'music, song and dance'. This points towards a broad understanding of what a musical might look or sound like, and connects with a method of viewing genre that Stanley Cavell terms 'genre-as-cycle'. Cavell explains that:

> What is traditionally called a genre film is a movie whose membership in a group of films is no more problematic than the exemplification of a serial in one of its episodes. You can, for example, roughly *see* that a movie is a Western, or gangster film, or horror film, or prison film, or 'woman's film,' or screwball comedy. Call this way of thinking about genre, genre-as-cycle.[12]

Cavell departs persuasively from this formulation in his own work, *Pursuits of Happiness: The Hollywood Comedy of Remarriage*, as he conceives a 'genre-as-medium model',[13] but nevertheless his assertion that one can more-or-less recognize certain genres of film is itself recognizable as a conventional and fairly widespread approach to genre. In the example of the musical, it may be that certain visual features indicate that genre immediately – aside from dancing this could include a vibrancy or artificiality of décor and costuming or a particularly emphatic style of performance – but it is certainly the case that, when such a film features characters regularly breaking into song, for example, we can make such a recognition firmly through what we hear. Whilst these easy definitions almost demand complication in correspondence with the musical's diversity of forms and styles, it is nevertheless the case that, when we turn to fantasy cinema, such basic descriptions are hardly even available to us. Describing what a fantasy film might look or sound like is a problematic task given the multitudinous forms in which fantasy is manifested and played out in the cinema, and also given the relative sparseness of critical literature investigating the matter.

Such issues surrounding the classification of fantasy are intensified due to its close association with other well-established genres that have gained stability through critical definition. Horror and science fiction, both included as major genres in Steve Neale's formulation, have tended to be synonymous with fantasy in critical accounts,[14] and the product of these associations are an attempt to clarify what horror and science fiction might be, whilst the notion of fantasy has remained somewhat ambiguous as it is variously applied to these other, ever more tangible, genres. As Cavell made clear in his account of a type of genre discernment, we can 'roughly see' that a movie is a horror, and this is perhaps likewise true of a science fiction. The difficulty with fantasy, as it is coupled with both horror and science fiction, is that any distinguishing 'look' might well be comprised of iconographic features from either of those genres. In similar fashion, to this fractured portrait might be added images and motifs from the musical genre, which itself has an association with fantasy at least as strong as horror and science fiction. Jane Feuer attends to this relationship a number of times in her landmark study of the musical, at one stage saying of *An American in Paris* (Vincente Minnelli, 1951) and *That's Entertainment* (Gene Kelly, 1976) that:

> Both films acknowledge levels of fantasy within musicals. Each film places a secondary, more stylized fictional world into a primary, less stylized fiction. The secondary, the unreal, the dream world holds at bay the imaginative excesses to which musicals are prone. In the musical, as in life, there are only two places where we feel secure enough to see so vividly: in the theater and in dreams. The musical's multiple levels of reality contrast the stage with the world, illusion with reality.[15]

Feuer's account reveals the musical's strong propensity for fantasy, identifying 'imaginative excesses' as a key characteristic of the genre. In the case of the two films she relates this to, *An American in Paris* and *That's Entertainment*, she contends that their positioning of a 'secondary' world into a 'primary' fictional world (signalled in both films through the use of colour contrasts similar to those of *The Wizard of Oz*) actually serves to stabilize those imaginative excesses, effectively keeping them 'at bay'. And yet, critically for Feuer, in adopting these multiple level realities within their narratives, both films 'acknowledge levels of fantasy' within musicals, that is, the extent to which all musicals demonstrate a potent investment in fantasy as a structuring element for their storyworlds. We can recognize the prescience of Feuer's claims when we consider that a great number of musicals rely upon the central fact of a fictional world in which characters can unselfconsciously sing their thoughts and emotions to an unseen audience, accompanied by an equally non-visible group of musicians. In asking us to accept these sets of laws, the musical necessarily asks us to invest in a fantasy of the world, or rather a world in which fantasy exists as a guiding force. Thus, by consequence, reality becomes a malleable element within the musical and transitions between the real and the illusory, waking life and dream, conscious and subconscious are acceptable to the extent that they become a convention of the genre. We might propose, then, that the freedom the musical displays in its transitions from speech to song and to dance derives fundamentally from its embracing of fantasy within its very conventions: its ability to challenge notions of reality and to make indistinct the borders between the real and the imaginary, which is matched by these physical shifts in performance technique.

If the musical offers itself as a somewhat obvious choice for discussions centred around fantasy, it might be said that Vincente Minnelli's work in that genre recommends itself even more emphatically. The tessellation between Minnelli, the musical and fantasy is potently realized in a range of films from the director's career, and this potency is expanded upon in Joseph Andrew Casper's critical description of the director's work:

> As an expression of fantasy, or another world where transformation and transcendence rule the day and festivity or 'genuine revelry and joyous celebration,' the Minnelli musical awakens one's primal and primitive feelings and puts one in contact with them. The Minnelli musical resounds through one, touching 'the dearest freshest deep down things,' where one also lives, moves and has one's being. It stirs and plays with one's instinctual, prereflective, intuitive side, one's locked away imagination, one's innermost hopes, one's alarming sense of awe, the child, savage, and seer within, the part that a technological, bureaucratic, scientific, secularized age forgets or ignores in fear or embarrassment. Therefore, the images and sensibilities of a Minnelli musical can be a key unlocking more of the self, affording new areas of apprehension and comprehension. The Minnelli musical expands horizons and whisks one into uncharted or lost lands.[16]

We would have little difficulty in identifying the close relationship between Minnelli's films and fantasy in the enthusiastic description Casper provides. Furthermore, one might be prepared to say that the terms of the praise he offers in relation to Minnelli's work could easily be tendered as a defence of fantasy, taking into account its abilities to open up new horizons and provide an engagement with the instinctive self: abilities shared with the Minnelli musical. Casper's contention in his account seems to be that Minnelli's musicals have the potential to expand the audience's vision beyond the constraints of their contemporary, sophisticated society to, ironically, look inwards and rediscover those qualities that have become lost to them through wilful repression or merely through neglect. In these terms, the experience is one of repelling the move from childhood to adulthood, as 'primal and primitive feelings' are allowed to surface and, indeed, take over the senses. Again, it is apparent that the type of absorption Casper claims for the Minnelli musical closely resembles arguments often circulated in relation to fantasy – of transporting one to new a realm of meaning as a means of challenging rational expectation.

If Casper's assertions mark out suggestively the intimacy between the Minnelli musical and fantasy, they fall short of turning that suggestiveness into a closely realized account of the director's work. If we are to accept Minnelli's relationship to fantasy through the musicals he made in Hollywood, it is vital to evaluate that relationship in precise detail, allowing the films' data to lead critical discussion not only to establish the fact of the relationship but also its nature. An acceptance of Minnelli as a director versed in 'expressions of fantasy' is therefore reliant upon an understanding of the terms of expression in examples from his film-making career: the weight and purpose afforded to fantasy in the films themselves. Here, the case for achievement in film-making practice – of the kind Casper makes in relation to Minnelli's film musicals – must have at its core a detailed evaluation of evidence provided by the films themselves and a close appreciation of individual scenes and moments that builds to form an appreciation of the work as a whole. Otherwise the film is allowed to remain precariously indistinct along with, in the context of this discussion, the talents of the director and the notion of 'fantasy' itself.

Finally, before moving on to a discussion of the films themselves, it is worth lingering on the issue, especially pertinent in light of these musicals made by this director, of collaboration and its relationship to questions of authorship. It is a fact that the three films I wish to focus upon are directed by Vincente Minnelli but it is also the case that each was released under the considerable influence of producer Arthur Freed, whose unit was responsible for many of MGM's musical successes, and one (*The Band Wagon*) features the supreme talents of Fred Astaire, whose creative impact is formidable. Taking this into account, we have at least three potential claimants for authority in the films, with studio and star joining the director in our critical considerations. In the cases of Freed, Astaire and Minnelli, we might venture to call these three different types of genius, intuitively suited to the rigours of Hollywood entertainment. And this is before we turn our attentions to other figures such as composers, scriptwriters, editors, cinematographers and so on: how are we to separate out these influences in any account of authorship and agency in cinema? This, quite rightly, seems an impossible proposition, and perhaps a more significant enquiry would be, why should we want to? Concentration upon a director's skill should not negate an understanding that others have contributed to the effectiveness of the film, sometimes to a very significant degree. But, although a director works in negotiation with other talents (and other agendas) any acknowledgement of this should not in turn negate an appreciation of the director's role. As V. F. Perkins observes in relation to a film's script:

> The most promising script, judiciously cast, will still fall flat if the director is unable to get all the elements of the production working together – either in harmony or in lively contrast – so that the end result flows when it is played to an audience. If it does not work on the screen, we are likely to think that there was not much of a story or that the performances were lacking. But often the fault lies in the director's inability to find a style that brings the material convincingly to life. Just as often, it is the director who should take the credit for our belief that we have seen a credible and forceful story with colourful and engaging characterization. In terms of the package and its ingredients, there is not much that separates *The Reckless Moment* (1949), *Johnny Guitar* (1954) or *Written on the Wind* (1956) from dozens of mediocre products of the Hollywood machine. The crucial factor is the direction of Max Ophuls, Nicholas Ray and Douglas Sirk.[17]

In this account, it is the director who fashions the material available into expressive relationships, crafting significance and meaning 'on the screen'. Here, Perkins uses the example of a director's relationship to the script in order to emphasize their control over the film's arrangement (and this seems especially appropriate given that one particularly unforgiving description of a director might be of an individual pointing a camera at actors whilst they say the lines that were written for them). It is an understanding of authorship that we might become sympathetic to when thinking about Minnelli, especially given that he was a director who worked with a variety of different talents and influences during his career. Managing these contributions and constraints amounts to the work of the director, an individual charged with the task of organizing the personnel and shaping the material into its most significant arrangement. In discussing a small group of films that demonstrate Minnelli's commitment to, and careful handling of, aspects of fantasy, we should not become blind to the fact that others had responsibility for dictating the nature of that fantasy as it appears on screen – be that Arthur Freed, Fred Astaire or whoever. But the placing together of such films only emphasizes Minnelli's ability to provide variations on the consistent theme of fantasy, so recommending him as an especially appropriate point of focus for debate. Furthermore, any evaluation of Minnelli's directorial accomplishments are not weakened by an acknowledgement of the strong talents he sought to balance within his film making (Astaire's magic onscreen, Freed's magic offscreen, for example) but is rather enriched by that understanding.

Cabin in the Sky

Minnelli's 1943 musical, *Cabin in the Sky*, is the story of Joseph 'Little Joe' Jackson (Eddie Anderson) who's attempts at a reformed life are compromised when he is drawn into a gambling circle and, as a result of this, is shot and wounded badly. While lying in bed, poised between life and death, he dreams that he has been granted a second opportunity from heaven to make a better life for himself and his wife, Petunia (Ethel Waters). Much like Dorothy in a similarly structured musical, *The Wizard of Oz* (Victor Fleming), released just four years previous, Little Joe is unaware that his dream is not a reality and, just as with that earlier film, this fact is also revealed to the audience only in the final reel. I want to dwell initially on Minnelli's handling of the crossover point from reality to fantasy and suggest that the aesthetic depiction of this transition strikes a pivotal contrast between those two states that effectively draws together certain key themes that guide and shape the film's narrative.

Little Joe is brought home after his shooting. A doctor visits the patient and informs Petunia that Joe should survive, but that the matter is not definitely balanced. Following this advice, she asks to be able to see him; the doctor consents and Petunia rises to enter the bedroom where Joe lies. As she passes through the doorway into the semi-darkness of the room, a soundtrack that had previously featured a tentative, wavering melody incorporates the sounds of Joe raving and murmuring from the other side of the room, 'out of his head' as the doctor had suggested he might be. (Of course, this phrase takes on an ironic resonance in hindsight when it is revealed that Joe's thoughts have indeed taken him 'out of his head' as he imagines an equivalent reality for himself and Petunia, featuring a catalogue of fictitious events and deeds.) Petunia gently closes the door as she moves across the room towards Joe, her gaze never falling from where he lies as her devotion draws her impulsively to him. As she passes the bed frame on her way over to him, Petunia touches the metal arch of the structure momentarily, as though testing it for temporary support or using its solidness to gain an element of strength as she steels herself for the spectacle of Joe in his state of unconscious fever. This suggestion is reinforced by Petunia's letting her hands rest on the handle and edge of the door in a similar fashion before she moves across to the bed frame. She keeps her arms half-raised, poised in preparation as she moves between the door and the bed, as if she were somehow profoundly reliant upon them to sustain her motion from one to the other. In this way, Petunia uses these structures for support, allowing them physically to bear a degree of the emotional strain she experiences in this moment, wordlessly expressing the effort involved in even the simple movement across the room. The affinity between the physical and the emotional in this instance is entirely consistent with Petunia, as performed by Ethel Waters, for whom emotional joy or despair is experienced so intensely throughout the film that it becomes a vibrant physical force. On that theme, it is also the case that the door and the bed frame represent slight barriers or thresholds between Petunia and Joe, presenting her with the opportunity for fleeting moments of pause before she is brought properly to his side. This fact is exemplified in Ethel Waters' interaction with these elements, as she stops to peer around the door and halts again to gaze across at Joe from behind the bed frame. Here, these physical features serve to encapsulate the apprehension Petunia experiences as she makes her approach, their spatial location allowing her to hesitate as she draws together the confidence to complete her journey and face Joe.

As she moves closer to Joe, Petunia raises her hands to caress his face and chest, a gesture that continues the pattern of her touching the door and the bed frame, suggesting that those points of contact formed parts of a sequential movement towards her finally reaching out to him. However, he stirs and tosses his head as she places her hands near him, and she instinctively withdraws, choosing instead to take a cloth from a basin nearby and attempt to place it on his fevered brow. When even this does little to ease his condition, Petunia discards the cloth and retreats back towards the foot of the bed, reaching out a hand behind her and onto the frame once more, as though instinctively returning to this earlier position (and pose) of relative security and support. The gesture is extended here, however, as Petunia clings another hand to the frame and sinks to her knees to offer a prayer for Joe's recovery. As she seeks to secure a guarantee of Joe's survival, Petunia strikes the pose of one clutching on for her own survival – to survive the pain and anguish that this event has brought to her – by gripping hard onto the metal frame of the bed as she begins to pray. The extent of Petunia's own suffering is made clear as Minnelli cuts to an extreme close-up for the majority of her prayer: this new proximity revealing in vivid detail the sweat that has formed on her brow as it glistens in the flickering light of the oil-burning lamps, and furthermore making us fully aware of the passionate grief played out across her features as she speaks. Her words are as follows:

> Lord, please don't take Little Joe from me. I know how simple he's been lately but I love him. And please forgive me for lovin' him so much. But Little Joe ain't wicked, he's just weak. And if he dies now the devil's gonna get him sure. And he don't deserve to be in a mess like that. Little Joe ain't that bad. So if you'll just let him get well again I promise you he'll mend his ways and give you no more trouble. Amen.

The nature of Petunia's speech is perhaps initially striking due to the devotion and selfless love for Joe that it expresses. Altruistically discarding her own pain and distress, she merely hopes for his recovery and, according to her own religious creed, that he should be saved from condemnation to hell. However, it is also true that the prayer furthermore reveals her knowledge and understanding of Joe, a vision not shared by other characters within the film at this stage, through her conviction that he is capable of mending his ways. Petunia is therefore guided by her faith in two ways: firstly her faith in a God that can hear her prayers and has a capacity to respond, but secondly her faith in Joe's intrinsic good, which has merely become shrouded through his weakness in the face of events.

Once her prayer is ended, Petunia slowly rises and blows out the gaslight at Joe's bedside, and then moves across to extinguish similarly the companion light placed on a small table at the foot of his bed. This action completed, she makes her way over to a modest chair by the window, sinks into it and cradles her head in the palm of her hand, a gesture conveying succinctly her exhaustion and despair while Joe's delirious cries penetrates the film's soundtrack. Indeed, these sounds break into the steady rhythm of the sombre melody that has played consistently underneath this scene. However, other interruptions of this kind have already occurred. Petunia's extinguishing of the lamps was accompanied by a briefly heard glissando of strings, lending punctuation to her act in a way that, at first, appears somewhat superfluous: the meaning of Petunia's movements is surely clear enough without the need for audio reinforcement. However, Minnelli's intentions become clear as, once Petunia has sunk into the chair, the lamp at the end of Joe's bed magically relights, accompanied by a much harsher single note played on the soundtrack. At this point, the film crosses over into fantasy – Joe's fantasy, as it turns out – and so it emerges that Minnelli has used sound and action to emphasize the fracture between the states of reality and fantasy. In Petunia's reality, the extinguishing of the lamp was marked by hearing a gentle, delicate brush of fingers on strings, but in Joe's fantasy the magical relighting of the lamp is signalled by the stark jolt of a single note played forcefully. The lamp itself becomes a symbol of the rupture between the two conditions as the light is literally put out on reality to be replaced by a new light appearing in a world of fantasy. The force and impact of the lamp relighting is extended as the sequence progresses to incorporate curtains dancing as they're caught in a mysterious breeze and uncanny shadows passing across the wall above Joe's bed. These shadows form to become the silhouette of a man who is eventually revealed to be the son of Satan, come to claim Joe's soul. The journey into fantasy is thus completed.

In its careful portrait of Petunia's dedication and care for Joe, the film sets up the dramatic issue of whether or not he will possess any awareness of these qualities in his dreaming state. Will the events that have taken place in reality – unseen by him – be matched by his unconscious understanding of events in fantasy? Minnelli's use of lamps to illustrate the break between the film's reality and its fantasy effectively sets up this comparison, prompting us to evaluate the extent to which fantasy matches up to reality. On the surface, Joe's appreciation of Petunia's profound devotion to him is somewhat ambiguous: his dream concludes with his ascent to heaven with her at his side, but this is due to them both being shot dead in a nightclub which she has visited as a direct result of Joe's lavish lifestyle after he wins $50,000 on the Irish sweepstake. Furthermore, after Joe's win is revealed to him by his former mistress, Georgia Brown (Lena Horne). Petunia misinterprets their celebratory embrace and tosses him out, yet when we next see Joe he is clearly romantically involved again with Georgia rather than attempting to win back Petunia. So, in this surface account, the final reuniting of Joe and Petunia at the end of his dream is potentially undermined.

However, it is also reasonable to suggest that these occurrences in Joe's dream may in fact derive from his own appreciation of his 'weakness' that Petunia spoke of in her prayer made earlier in the film. To accept this point we need to understand that, within the context of his dream, Joe essentially casts himself as a character within the fantasy narrative, thus creating a complex relationship whereby the dreaming Joe may possess an awareness that the 'character' Joe of the dream may not. In this way, the film shares certain characteristics with *The Wizard of Oz* and a film released a year later than *Cabin in the Sky*, Fritz Lang's *The Woman in the Window* (1944).[18] Further evidence of Joe's awareness emerges in the scene preceding the nightclub finale, and particularly his awareness of the impact his moral failures have upon Petunia. After she has misread Joe's embrace with Georgia (and his overheard promise to buy her a diamond bracelet with his winnings) and driven him from her sight, Petunia sinks down into a tattered garden chair and offers a desperate prayer to her God: 'Lord, why you let me love him so much, so he can hurt me so bad? Why?' Minnelli frames this plea in extreme close-up, mirroring the composition of the prayer said at Joe's bedside previously in the film. And, as in that first instance, the move to this position of intimate engagement picks out the tears that glint as they catch the light on Petunia's cheeks and the anguish that knots her brow into a succession of deeply set creases. A relationship is thus set up with that earlier scene, with the act of praying – and most crucially the representation of Petunia's features as she prays – constituting a theme that is continued and compared within the film's reality and its dreaming state.

After Petunia's prayer, there is a cross-fade that signals the passing of time and when the new image takes shape we find her sitting in semi-darkness, whereas in the previous shot it had been daylight. She is still in the yard of her home where she earlier confronted Joe and Georgia and, although she now sits in a different part of that space, the implication is that she has spent a long time alone with her thoughts in this environment. She rises, gathers up the groceries she dropped during her tirade against Joe, and makes her way over to the porch, stopping as she passes a refrigerator that was Joe's birthday gift to her. It is now transformed into a painful reminder of his absence but also, in her eyes, is perhaps synonymous with his lack of worth: the refrigerator is useless without electricity and has never been used just as, without honour or moral decency, Joe is useless to her. As she enters the semi-darkness of the house, Petunia makes her way over to an oil lamp on a table in the foreground and lights it distractedly with a match. As she gathers up her groceries once more, her gaze lingers on Joe's guitar lying to the side of the lamp and she allows her fingers to gently strum over its strings for a second. As she performs this action, Petunia holds the grocery bags close to her body so that, just as the guitar emphasizes the absence of Joe within the house, so the groceries become a meagre substitute for the warmth of touch she craves but no longer receives from him.

Petunia takes the groceries across to a sideboard, temporarily allowing her weight to fall against its edge as she begins to unwrap their contents (the ingredients for a meal she had intended to prepare for Joe, it seems). This temporary resting against the sideboard is transformed into a much more defined gesture as she places both hands on its surface and bows her head, allowing some of her weight to be taken by its structure for an extended period of time. From this position, Petunia begins to sing a mournful and bitterly ironic reprise of the song 'Happiness is a Thing Called Joe', which continues through to the end of this scene (she first sang this to Joe when he awoke, recovered from his gunshot wound in the dream). As she sings, she moves across the room and transfers her weight firstly from the sideboard to the small table holding the lamp and guitar, then to another table in the corner of the room, placing her hands on each surface and letting it support slightly as she moves. This pattern of movement and gesture replicates Petunia's earlier reliance on the bed frame and door for support when she visited Joe sickbed in the film's reality. In that earlier scene, this leaning on structures conveyed a need for *emotional* support, a notion that is repeated and reinforced here as Petunia also picks up certain objects – the grocery bag and one of Joe's shirts – and clutches them momentarily close to her chest, as though clinging to them for a warmth and comfort they can never provide. Finally, as the song completes, she retreats to a rocking chair and closes her eyes, a movement that rhymes with her positioning whilst keeping vigil over Joe as he raved and cried out in his fevered state after he was shot: seated in a chair and in a pose of exhausted resignation.

Minnelli imbues this sequence with certain resemblances to Petunia's earlier behaviour when she visited Joe's sickbed. The prayer said in close-up with a similar force of anguish and despair, the lighting of the lamp, the using of surface and objects for support, the final act of sinking into a chair and closing her eyes, all combine to create a bond with the tone and structure of the earlier scene. This relationship may lead us to question why, and how, Joe's dream of Petunia should match so precisely her acts in real life, which he himself had no awareness of. The implication of Minnelli's choices – the resonance he creates between reality and fantasy – is that Joe possesses an innate knowledge and understanding of Petunia even if he possesses little conscious knowledge or understanding of it. The close resemblance of his dreamed version of her behaviour to her actual behaviour in reality serves to emphasize his acute appreciation of her temperament and emotional character. That he should realize this sensitivity in an imagined moment of her grief and anguish brought about by his actions (albeit unwittingly) reveals his understanding of her pain, and his central role in contributing to that pain. He knows this woman, knows her to the extent that even in a dream containing a host of fantastic elements he imagines her with striking accuracy. It is a moment of awareness for Petunia's thoughts and feelings, but also one of self-awareness as he allows her to dwell painfully upon his shortcomings and grieve over them in his dream. This realization contributes towards Joe's immediate reform when he wakes from his dream and instructs Petunia to burn his dice and sweepstake ticket, both symbols of his former gambling life. He uses a fantasy to bring clarity to his existence, to make him alert to certain facts about his life with Petunia and the pain she endures on account of his actions. The dream makes that reality immediate for Joe, and provides an instruction on how he should live from that day on. Thus, in Minnelli's hands, the dream is not merely a dramatic or fanciful diversion but rather holds significance and poignancy within the film's structured reality.

Interpreting Minnelli's handling of events in this way perhaps risks placing a weight of emphasis upon Joe's thoughts and feelings at the expense of Petunia's. Susan Smith, for example, has suggested that the film allows a far more subversive depiction of Petunia's character to emerge, particularly through her energetic song and dance numbers ('Taking a Chance on Love' and 'Honey in the Honeycomb') and through her radical change of attitude as, having convinced herself of Joe's infidelity, she cuts a dazzling figure when she visits a nightclub, wisecracking at Joe's expense and performing an 'improvised dance sequence of her own, kicking her legs into the air (both in front and to either side of her) and shaking her full body in ways that celebrate her newfound freedom of movement.'[19] Smith equates this freedom with Petunia's rebellion against the oppressiveness of her gender situation, a rejection of her stoical, religious black persona.[20] Indeed, she insists that:

> while a narrative-based reading of the film might construe Petunia's rebellion as an act motivated solely by her mistaken assumption (on seeing Joe with Georgia Brown in the garden of their home) that he is double-crossing her, her performance during the 'Taking a Chance on Love' number crucially insists on the possibility of a more transgressive side to her character long before her break-up with Joe. Indeed, rather than viewing Petunia's angry outburst at Joe, on seeing him with Georgia Brown, as the cause of her rebellion in the nightclub, it is possible to see this moment as itself constituting a darker narrative embodiment of what was first released in more joyful, unthreatening form in that earlier number.[21]

Whilst taking heed of Smith's cautioning against a 'narrative-based reading of the film', it seems uncontroversial to suggest that Petunia's discovery of Joe and Georgia contributes substantially to her transformation, especially when we consider the emotional emphasis Minnelli affords to her sorrowful reprise of 'Happiness is a Thing Called Joe' as she moves around the house. Crucially, however, Smith does not properly account for the framing structure of the dream in her reading of the film: the fact that the events she describes are a product of *Joe's* imagination. Thus, attaching a complex psychology to Petunia's character in these sequences brings with it certain hazards: this is not the Petunia of real life and the dreaming Joe dictates any realizations 'she' may experience. This in itself may constitute a tragedy of the film, of course, that Petunia might never experience the freedom her dream-self is allowed, but nevertheless it requires acknowledgement. Indeed, if we are to pursue Smith's notion of gendered oppression being overthrown, then we must also concede that it is in truth Joe, through his dreaming, that brings about such a rebellion. Describing Petunia's actions within the dream as a product of her own consciousness is a precarious strategy and furthermore negates to an extent the importance Minnelli attaches to fantasy through his direction of sequences within the film. It may make the film a more conservative and certainly less progressive work in terms of gender, but retaining an appreciation of Joe's dream *as* a dream maintains the borderline between reality and fantasy that Minnelli constructs and utilizes.

The Band Wagon

Unlike *Cabin in the Sky*, a film that devotes a large portion of its narrative to the fantasy of one character, our interest in Minnelli's *The Band Wagon* (1953) stems from a very brief moment in which the film steps over into fantasy through its depiction of a seemingly impossible act. Although, as we shall see, this moment is not entirely incongruous with the scene in which it occurs – and with the register of the film as a whole – it nevertheless stands out as a departure from the overarching diegetic order that *The Band Wagon* sets in place. The placement, significance and impact of this moment therefore become matters for consideration and evaluation. More specifically, we might question why Minnelli chose to include a moment that, whilst leaning towards fantasy, does not immediately recommend itself as vital to an understanding of the film's story.

As one of its central themes, *The Band Wagon* debates the place and purpose of a star performer once their stardom has begun to waver and wane over time. In this sense, the film feeds into a recurrent interest of Hollywood cinema, that of the faded star, which is depicted perhaps most forcefully in Billy Wilder's *Sunset Boulevard* (1950). The star in the world of *The Band Wagon* is Tony Hunter but the theme of a spectacular career quietening after a period of intense success seems at least in some part as appropriate in relation to the star that plays him, Fred Astaire. Although having made a successful return to the screen in *Easter Parade* (Charles Walters, 1948), Astaire had returned from (an albeit premature) retirement for that picture, and the sense that he would no longer enjoy the kind of dominance experienced during his peak years when he and Ginger Rogers fundamentally shaped song and dance on film was certainly a distinct possibility, and one felt perhaps most intensely by Astaire himself, given his earlier withdrawal from the movies. *The Band Wagon* places at stake the question of Tony Hunter's fading stardom in its opening moments. Firstly when he eavesdrops on a conversation between two fellow passengers on a train as they discuss in frank terms the decline of his impact within the Hollywood firmament, and secondly when the train has embarked and he mistakes a group of reporters at the station to be awaiting his arrival, only to have them rush past him to seize upon the moment of Ava Gardner's stepping onto the platform. Whilst Astaire was certainly not at this humbling level in his career, the film coalesces the suppressing of Hunter's star persona with a withholding of Astaire's immediate screen talents as, in the number 'By Myself' that follows Hunter's embarrassment at the train station, he walks along the platform with a rhythmic sway in his step that in many other films had been the performer's trademark means of making the transition from walking to dancing. And yet no dance emerges – at least no full dance number. As Stanley Cavell notes, 'a song-and-dance man has not danced, as if dancing has been denied him, denied one whose life is dance.'[22] Indeed, the exquisite ways in which Astaire times certain moves such as the swinging of his hand, the smoking and stubbing out of a cigarette, the picking up of a book at a newsstand, are suggestive of a character – and a performer – with a predisposed impulse for choreographed movement. As Astaire allows the rhythm of his song to guide the pace and shape of his movements, we are acutely aware of dance performance being *inside* this man (or these men, Tony Hunter and Fred Astaire at the same time) – of the potential for dance being alive within him, and so the issue of whether this performance strength will emerge is placed at stake. Given the negative allusions to Hunter's career that have already been set in place and the knowledge that Astaire's own stardom was in some ways precariously placed, the question might well be whether this performance strength *can* emerge again in these men in this film.

The lightly felt melancholy of 'By Myself' is arrested temporarily when Tony is met at the station by two old friends, Lester and Lily (Oscar Levant and Nanette Fabray), who noisily greet his arrival. Their plans for a new musical, featuring Tony, are not met with enthusiasm by him, however, and when they take him along to 42nd Street, this only results in his perplexity at how changed this environment is from the theatre district he used to know and frequent as the star of various hit productions. Tony's ambivalence towards the new and his bewilderment at the dismantling of the old once again reinforces notions of a character whose achievements and thoughts are rooted in the past. Faded glory is raised once again as a central theme, and the extent to which the world has moved on from Tony Hunter is strongly evoked. When Lester becomes the hysterical victim of a stranger accidentally standing on his foot, Tony bundles him into a cab with Lily and sends the pair on their way. As he watches them depart, there is a strong sense that Tony is returning to that desire, expressed earlier through song, to be 'by himself', as though resigning himself to a view that the world as it is will not accommodate him and so he has no desire to seek accommodation within it. As he turns and joins the massed crowds on 42nd Street, Tony appears to seek the anonymity that the world, in any case, is moving closer and closer to bestowing upon him permanently.

This mood changes, however, as Tony enters an amusement arcade that was once, according to his recollections, the Elgin Theatre. He enquires about this to a man behind a grill counter when he first arrives in the arcade, but his question is met only with a hot dog being slapped into his open hand. Tony drifts away from the man and takes in some of his surroundings before finding a trashcan for his unwanted snack. Hesitating at the can, Tony notices a young boy keenly watching his every move and instead elects to hand him the hot dog, delivering a pat to his head. Casper remarks that this action lightens Tony's spirit,[23] and Cavell suggests that from the moment Tony was handed the hot dog, 'the routine has begun'.[24] It is certainly true that Astaire builds into his movements a growing sense of performance and, as he tries out a few of the amusements offered, his actions and gestures become self-consciously exaggerated (such as when he reads a tarot card dispensed by one amusement, or receives a verdict of 'gorgeous' at a 'Test Your Love Appeal' machine, or gives a slight hop and spring as he moves from one mechanical diversion to the next), as though he were performing for an audience once again. We might link together Casper and Cavell's assertions here and arrive at the suggestion that performance and spirit are intrinsically connected in Tony's world – that performance is spiritual for him – and so the opportunity and ability to perform is a product of his spirits lightening and, in turn, lightens his spirits.

The gradual development of performance technique in Tony's movements and expressions culminates in the moment he trips over the outstretched leg of a shoeshine man and thus begins the song 'Shine on Your Shoes'. Here Astaire breaks out into an energetic dance routine proper, the outbreak of sublime physical motion coinciding with a surge in his mood as he sings an opening verse that, in Cavell's words, 'declares the refrain to follow as the antidote to the melancholy he had expressed earlier in delivering "By Myself"':

> When you feel as low as the bottom of a well
> And can't get out of the mood
> Do something to perk yourself up
> And change your attitude.'[25]

The correlation between Tony's move to song and dance and the easing of his disposition is absolute in this sequence and, when he completes his mesmerizing shoeshine chair routine to launch into a routine of lyric and movement based on the countless repetitions and variations of the phrase 'got a shine on my shoes', it is as though he has become possessed by the need for dance and song as well as by the joyful mood that has overtaken him. This sequence involves his interaction with a number of different elements contained within the scene: a crazy mirror, a shooting range, a photo booth (in which he has his newly shined shoe photographed). And then he moves over to another counter, hands the attendant the photograph he has just acquired and takes aim with a ball at an arranged stack of metal tin cans. Astaire holds the ball in his right arm and points his left arm out straight in the direction of the cans, as though using it to guide the aim and motion of the ball he is about to throw. However, before he can release the ball, the tins explode into the air with a clang and clash of falling metal. And here the film seems to step over into a different spectrum of possibility. What are we to make of these tins cascading apart in this unusual way? No obvious force can be seen to control their movement, and no rational explanation offers itself for their behaviour. How are we to account for this moment? Is this fantasy?[26]

One possible explanation is that Minnelli has simply allowed himself to get carried away with the sublime pace of the action and, as a result, lost grip of the diegetic possibilities of the fictional world he seeks to present. And yet, such an assessment seems inadequately to disregard the director's skill in controlling the pace, shape and rhythm of the scene up to this point. In such a tightly coordinated sequence, in which dramatic emphasis is related so closely to the gradual emergence of Tony's/Fred Astaire's genius for performance, it seems hardly credible that such a lapse should occur within such a crucial point of the routine: the kinetic repetition of the 'shine on my shoes' section demonstrating emphatically the startling power of Astaire's performance within his role. It is this theme of power, or empowerment, that seems pivotal in understanding the moment of inexplicable fantasy as it occurs within the film. Up to this point within the scene, there has been a marked gradual rediscovering of Tony's performance strength – his natural inclination to make some sense of his world, and his own emotions, though song and dance – which takes us from his somewhat reticent demeanour at the train station to this point where he appears most comfortable and effortless in energetic performance. (And, given the context of Astaire's career, we might suggest that something similar is at work for this performer too.) As the tin cans magically explode into the air, the film seems to offer a statement about this revitalization and suggests, briefly, that such is the power of Tony's performance within his world, and Astaire's performance within this film, the borderline between possibility and impossibility might become tissue thin. The moment references the transformative potential of Tony's performance within his world, the way in which he can reshape its possibilities and potentials in accordance with the force and impact of his own sounds and movements. The piece of magic with the tin cans extends and accentuates the magic at work in this man's actions up to that point, furthermore posing questions about the limits and conditions of his power and influence within this world. Is it within his capabilities to reshape reality itself, so that the sheer force of his wilful intention can cause objects to move supernaturally? At the very least, Tony's apparent power over the stack of tin cans serves to emphasize metaphorically the extent to which he has regained his place and purpose within the world, and his ability to control and manipulate its conditions. As I have suggested, it might reasonably be said that all musicals deal in fantasy at a fundamental level: the fantasy of characters breaking out spontaneously into song and dance, for example. After all, what are we to suppose the crowd in the amusement arcade think as they witness Tony's routine? However, by crossing over temporarily into fantasy *within* the fictional world of this musical, Minnelli makes clear that Tony possesses an influence beyond that of the 'ordinary' people who stand and watch his virtuoso improvisation.

The moment of magic dramatically suggests Tony's status as a magician within his world, furthermore reinforcing his magical control over the elements that surround him. In taking this decision, Minnelli represents a character at the supreme height of his abilities precisely by pushing those powers beyond the confines of ordinary human capacity. The reversal in fortunes from Tony's performance of 'By Myself' is thus completed emphatically: the magician has realized and released his powers in a spectacular display that threatens to trouble even the fabric of reality itself. And if this is true for Tony, it is certainly true for Astaire the artist, now revealed and revitalized. The rules of this film must be set in accordance with the possibilities available within this performer's repertoire of moves. This strategy represents a risk on Minnelli's part: the inexplicable explosion of tin cans legitimately threatening the coherence and plausibility of the fictional world he seeks to construct. And yet, the event punctuates forcefully the emergence of Tony and Astaire's creative authority precisely by running against the underlying order, leaving us to question what limits can be placed upon definitions such as performance, fantasy and the musical. Indeed, Tony's act questions what the boundaries of a fictional world can be in a film and, when those borders are disrupted or made precarious, what understanding of that world can remain. And so we might conclude that the moment is one of expansion and elevation, wrong-footing a conventional understanding of the fiction film in order to foster a fundamental understanding of *The Band Wagon*'s central character and, in turn, its central performer.

Brigadoon

As a final example, *Brigadoon* (1954) offers a further variation of fantasy within the musicals of Vincente Minnelli. Distinct from *Cabin in the Sky*, which locates its fantasy as the product of one character's dreaming, and *The Band Wagon*, whose moment of ambiguous fantasy is a briefly sustained dramatic impact, *Brigadoon* composes a world in which a Highland town called Brigadoon that emerges miraculously for one day every one hundred years is a fact within its fictional reality. In this sense, it presents a world of fantasy. I have attended more closely to the aesthetic handling of this fantasy elsewhere in an extended study of alternative worlds in Hollywood cinema,[27] centring largely upon the relationships between the film's lead characters, Tommy (Gene Kelly), Jeff (Val Johnson) and, to a far lesser extent, Fiona (Cyd Charisse). In avoiding a repetition of that debate here, I want instead to concentrate upon Minnelli's representation of the Brigadoon community and, particularly, the ways in which he frames a series of contradictions and disparities that exist within that society.

The town of Brigadoon is depicted as a pastoral utopia throughout the film (and certainly accepted as one by Tommy) due to its magical presentation of a series of harmonious customs, traditions and attitudes contained within its culture. A world of song and dance, Brigadoon is represented as a vibrant and joyful community, a fact emphasized as Tommy and Jeff, two visitors from the outside realm of the modern world, are welcomed and then accepted by its inhabitants as part of a celebratory musical number. Two dissenting voices exist, however: Jeff, whose twentieth-century cynicism renders him largely immune to the charms, such as they are, of Brigadoon, and Harry Beaton (Hugh Laing), whose unrequited love for Fiona's sister, Jean (Virginia Bosler) leaves him bitter and disenchanted with the town. His position is further complicated, however, by the fact that if any one citizen of Brigadoon should leave, the spell will be broken and the entire community will cease to exist. Therefore, Harry is a to all intents and purposes trapped within the town he has grown to despise; a point not lost on Harry himself. He thus becomes an unbalancing element within the film, albeit to a fairly minor extent given the major narrative focus given to Tommy and Fiona's burgeoning love for each other, and so the issue exists of how to restore the equilibrium that Harry's disaffection threatens to disrupt. Minnelli's handling of this resolution is of interest to us here.

A set-piece number, typical of the film, marks the cause for celebration that the day has been building to: the marriage of Jean to her fiancé (and locus of Harry's resentment), Charlie Dalrymple (Jimmy Thompson). The ceremony is represented as a gala of traditional Highland Fling, replete with pipes, drums, heathers, crossed swords, tartan and flaming torches.[28] Women and men perform their respective parts before coming together in a whirling mass of interweaving bodies, hands and feet. Into this melee Harry makes a subdued entrance and, calculating his moment, joins the circle of revellers and takes position to partner Jean. On reaching her, his advances descend into wild desires as he manhandles her and attempts to force her into an embrace. Charlie rushes over and pushes Harry to the ground, at which point Harry draws a knife and is almost immediately surrounded by members of the clan, one of which points a sword forcefully into Harry's midriff. Defeated and deflated, he engages only with Jean, saying 'All I've done is to love you too much', before turning to leave the scene.

With Harry walking away through the crowds, the camera tracks Fiona's move-ment as she weaves through the wedding guests towards him. As she approaches Harry, she reaches out her hand slowly and leaves it suspended in the space between them in a gesture that suggests an offer of comfort at an almost subconscious level. However, her father, standing to her right, notices this movement and takes hold of Fiona's fingers, apparently offering her comfort but also restricting her gesture towards Harry, ensuring that her motion never reaches its intended conclusion. It is a curious moment, leading us to question Fiona's motivation as she reaches out to Harry. Certainly we might take it as straightforward sympathy for another human being, which makes Fiona a remarkable individual given that Harry has just attempted to ruin her sister's wedding day. But we might also suggest that something more fundamental guides Fiona's actions: that, beyond mere sympathy, she finds herself *empathizing* at some level with Harry's predicament. After all, we first encountered

Fiona singing 'Waiting for my Dearie' as she stared out from her window beyond the boundaries of Brigadoon, her vocalized longing extending past the borders of her world. For her, the prayer is answered in the form of Tommy, with whom she strikes up an immediate, tentative romance, but for Harry no happy resolution presents himself. He is left alone and it is perhaps this loneliness that Fiona finds herself understanding at this point, to the extent that she is drawn towards Harry in this moment at the wedding when she understands his actions to derive from his isolation and frustration: feelings that she was perhaps bordering on at the beginning of the film's interest in her. Read in this way, Fiona's act is also her acknowledgement that the world of Brigadoon can only be a utopian existence for some, whilst for others it can become a dystopia. Therefore, following this logic, there is nothing innate to Brigadoon that makes it wonderful, but rather its wonderfulness is dependent upon an individual's emotional and intellectual perspective. The enchanted world does not necessarily leave all of its inhabitants similarly enchanted. Perhaps Fiona finds herself contemplating that, had Tommy not entered her world, she too might be brought to the brink of the desperation Harry experiences now.

It becomes significant at a symbolic level, therefore, that Fiona's father should interpret her movement and, even in a gesture of comfort, should seek to repress it by taking her hand and keeping hold of it. By stopping her in her tracks, her father reinforces a brand of patriarchal wisdom and law that characterizes an individual such as Harry as sinful when he acts against the decorum of the community. The notion of patriarchy is reinforced as he assumes Fiona requires male paternal comfort, when no clear indication of this has been given, and in doing so imagines that she is reaching out to *him*. We might, without too much trouble, read this as symbolic of a patriarchal control that bears upon the town of Brigadoon, a community ruled by men and even founded in reaction to a plague of witches – 'horribly destructive women', in the words of town elder Mr Lundie (Barrie Jones). Fiona's father's response to her thus risks becoming an act of putting her 'back in her place' both physically and intellectually by signalling her reaction towards Harry as inappropriate. If we take it as an action guided by Brigadoon's patriarchal dominance, we might further read this as representative of the ways in which women in general are 'put in place' in the town as its customs and routines are divided between the genders, ruled over by the men.

Importantly, Minnelli's lingering on Fiona's movement is unnecessary to the delivery of Harry's significant line, coming seconds after, that 'I'm leaving Brigadoon! 'Tis the end of all of us! The miracle is over!' Nothing that Fiona does reinforces or builds towards that statement and its calamitous impact perhaps overshadows the dramatic interest in her act. Minnelli's inclusion of the moment requires qualification, therefore, as it is not an obvious expositional choice. It would appear that, even at a subtle or subdued level, Minnelli seeks to trouble the idea of Brigadoon as a faultless utopia in moments such as these, concurrently suggesting a complexity to Fiona's character that belies notions of an entire community blithely accepting the miracle of Brigadoon as a miracle for them personally. In the father's repressive holding of Fiona's hand there is also the suggestion that the benign surface appearance of the Brigadoon community is not entirely consistent. The restricting of Fiona's emotional response to Harry signals that a proper code of conduct must be followed, which excludes sympathizing for the wrong sort of person, if membership of the community is to be preserved. Here, then, individual freedom and personal choice are compromised within this hermetically sealed society, with anyone deviating from the prescribed order denounced as bad.

Minnelli extends this notion of something less than benign existing beneath the surface of Brigadoon in a sequence when the men of the town set out to pursue Harry as he attempts escape. This is ostensibly a musical number, with male voices describing the chase in song, but it contains none of the impulsive joy or light-heartedness of the earlier numbers performed in Brigadoon. Slipping between major and minor keys, the song has a blunt, incessant rhythm that complements the pace of the action but also lends a somewhat threatening and urgent tone to the scene. These elements are complemented and continued within the *mise en scène* of the chase, as Minnelli constructs a picture of wild and ruthless pursuit. Features of the wedding ceremony such as the torches, ceremonial swords and axes that signified Highland romance in that earlier scene reappear now but without any of the charm as men wield them as weapons. The men themselves are transformed too, no longer part of an idealized portrait of Highland wedding customs, but instead are sweating, open-shirted, some stripped to the waist, as though a frenetic brutalism had overtaken them and their appearance. Just as Minnelli takes elements of the wedding and recasts them darkly in this chase scene, so the pastoral splendour of his Brigadoon environment is transfigured to become a menacing wilderness replete with sharp rock faces, tangled undergrowth and spindly, jagged branches. Even the darkness that had gently enclosed the wedding guests in their shared revelry just moments before now becomes a foreboding element as moonshine and torchlight fall across the scene's features creating distorted, ominous shadows. Through all of this Harry runs frantically, clambering across rocks and scrambling through the branches of trees as though a wild animal pursued. Indeed, Minnelli inserts a number of shots of wildlife such as muntjac and roe buck to reinforce this point, equating Harry with creatures hunted for game. This becomes a key point, as, in both the music and the visual action, there is an excitement and zeal to the pursuit of Harry, as though the men of Brigadoon were engaged in a kind of sport almost indistinguishable from the hunting of wild animals. With their burning torches and glinting weapons, the men represent a bloodthirsty mob, intent on meting out a brand of punishment based upon primal instinct rather than procedural justice. This instinct distances them from a human understanding of Harry and his predicament, making him their quarry.

The notion of this being a hunt for sport is finally given emphasis in dramatic fashion when Jeff wanders onto the scene in a drunken haze, points his gun at a grouse in flight and accidentally shoots Harry, who had been hiding in the branches of a tree. Tragically and ironically, Jeff's confusing of Harry with a game bird reflects potently the nature of the pursuit that has been taking place: a group of men seeking their prey. With this fatal shot, the music cuts dead and the pace drains from the scene suddenly and completely. The men of Brigadoon gather around Harry's body and, unaware that Jeff possesses a weapon that can kill, attribute his death to a blow to the head. They stand around the body awkwardly, some stripped to the waist, some bearing torches, whilst the cause of Harry's death is discussed. As the energy of the chase dissipates it is as though they wordlessly confront the consequences of their own actions: that they have in some part brought about this terrible conclusion to events through their behaviour. The hunt has ended in horrible disappointment and it seems possible that their stillness and silence, which might be taken as outward signs of mournful respect, could be attributable to an acute sense of shame. When one member of the party exclaims 'He must have hit his head on a rock. The poor lad!' there is the sense that he expresses the group's relief that they cannot be held responsible for this tragedy, that their brutality and fervour has not brought about this fatal consequence. Sorrow for Harry is not sustained, however, as his own father voices his shame at his son's actions, before Fiona's father declares that Harry's death will be kept secret and no one will be told until the morning. No moment of grief will be shared among the community and, furthermore, when the women of the town join the scene and are told the lie, it becomes clear that it is the men who will keep Harry's death a secret from them, so a gender divide is reinforced and patriarchal rule endures. A decision is taken, and it is one that the women of Brigadoon have no part in. Instead, they will be made to accept a truth that the men construct, and so Fiona's father's earlier curtailing of her freedom in his physical gesture of restraint makes sense as part of a wider pattern of male suppression and control.

The dramatic transformation of tone that Minnelli undertakes between the wedding scene and the chase sequence serves to undermine concrete notions of Brigadoon as a harmonious, idyllic refuge. As characters, objects and surroundings are inflected and rendered darkly between the wedding scene and the pursuit sequence, so an ominous side to this community is brought sharply into focus. The unity of Brigadoon is shown to be delicate and fragile as it relies upon absolute adherence to a certain code of behaviour and social order. When one of its members finds that to be repressive, suffocating, or simply at odds with their own personal desires, they are dealt with in a drastic fashion bordering on brutality and, as we see with Fiona's father's restricting her show of affection for Harry at the wedding, attempts at diplomatic resolution are suppressed. In allowing these aspects to take a central role in the action for a sustained period of time, Minnelli proposes that Brigadoon can be viewed as a trap as a much as a haven, depending on the individual, so temporarily aligning with Harry's perspective when he describes the town in these terms earlier in the film. Minnelli allows the possibility to remain that this utopia possesses fundamental shortcomings that cannot easily be resolved:

Harry's wish to leave Brigadoon would indeed cause its collapse and, whilst his death ends his personal desire for escape, it only temporarily remedies the essential opposition that exists between communal harmony and personal freedom within Brigadoon. It is possible that another Harry may emerge in the future, and there is nothing to suggest that the community is equipped to prevent matters reaching the same desperate state. And so, in Minnelli's hands, what may be taken at a surface level to be a blithe adaptation of a whimsical musical entertainment becomes a more complex exploration – and critique – of the notion of social perfection embodied in Brigadoon. Minnelli succeeds in making his fantasy world uncomfortable and tense, at least in these scenes, so demonstrating the potential for fantasy films to interrogate the morals, attitudes and ethics of the characters they seek to present.

I suggested at the outset of this chapter that Minnelli is a natural, perhaps even obvious, choice for a discussion centred upon issues of authorship in relation to fantasy. Furthermore, his rendering of fantasy within the musical genre provides pertinent illustration of how those categories of film integrate and coalesce with one another. However, in focusing upon three films that represent fantasy in different ways and for varying dramatic purposes, we can also begin to understand Minnelli's skill at involving aspects of fantasy to create a range of diverse meanings and significances. Here, then, we appreciate Minnelli as a filmmaker possessing not simply an arbitrary or even rudimentary commitment to fantasy within his work, but rather an individual with a strong control over the potentials for fantasy within a film, providing different inflections for particular narrative purposes. *Cabin in the Sky*, *The Band Wagon* and *Brigadoon* all involve fantasy to different degrees and in compositionally distinct ways, so creating dramatic tones and structures that defy blanket categorizations of fantasy film or, indeed, musicals. That these films can be brought together illustrates thematic continuity within Minnelli's filmmaking, but also demonstrates his dexterity and creative agility as he avoids returning to the same version or idea of fantasy within his films. The issue of how a director manages and shapes aspects of fantasy within their work is of interest as it offers a potential means of evaluating their skill and aptitude. Minnelli is one such case for consideration, but other directors offer potential studies, with the work of recent figures such as Terry Gilliam, Tim Burton, Peter Jackson, Neil Jordan, Michel Gondry or Guillermo del Toro perhaps providing rich opportunities for debate. In any evaluation of these directors' work, however, it is the precise handling of the film's fantasy that is paramount. This is particularly important given that there exists a general tendency to characterize any director working in fantasy film as visionary or greatly imaginative, whereas it is equally the case that a director working with a reduced set of dramatic parameters is required to demonstrate just as much vision and imagination in realizing their narrative. Detailed analysis of the ways in which directors utilize and employ fantasy might help us to avoid such broad, unqualified assumptions and move us towards a stronger understanding of achievement in fantasy filmmaking.

−4−

Fantasy, Childhood and Entertainment

Questions of Value

A significant strand of fantasy cinema features a close association with and strong investment in concepts of childhood. From Cecil Hepworth's 1903 adaptation of *Alice in Wonderland* to Victor Fleming's *The Wizard of Oz* (1939) to contemporary works such as *Coraline* (Henry Selick, 2009), the figure of the child has been a consistent feature in the history and development of the fantasy genre in cinema.[1] The nature of this association may present certain obstacles to any sustained critical evaluation of fantasy cinema, however, based on general assumptions that such films are about, and therefore aimed first and foremost at, children. Thus, if the meanings in such works are so clear cut as to be understood primarily by children without difficulty, what else is there to say of them? If criticism is understood to offer sophisticated responses to works that are rich, layered, subtle and complex, what value can there be in addressing a collection of films that ostensibly lack such sophistication? Childhood can itself be a somewhat ambiguous term to contend with in a critical sense. The disparity between the experiences of children and adults can seemingly become so pronounced that articulating useful perspectives on childhood can become a somewhat precarious exercise. As Cary Bazalgette and David Buckingham point out in an introduction to their collection on children's media:

> Childhood is often seen as another world. Although it is a world we have all visited, it has become inaccessible to us except through the distortions of memory. For most adults, there is an 'essence' of childhood that is unknowable, mysterious, even magical. We can only recapture it vicariously, through the imagination and, perhaps more commonly, through accepted and conventional ideas of what constitutes childhood.[2]

Bazalgette and Buckingham's claims have particular potency in that their descriptions of childhood as 'unknowable, mysterious, even magical' succinctly convey the extent to which it can become an ungraspable concept for the adult, to the point that it resides somewhere outside of one's critical consciousness. As Bazalgette and Buckingham make clear, even as we attempt to seize it, we are only ever clutching at a vicarious recapturing of childhood, so striving towards an understanding that is fundamentally mediated and, therefore, essentially distanced.

In addition to these perceived barriers, it is also the case that children's cinema has been a somewhat underdeveloped, or even neglected, category of film studies. As Peter Krämer makes clear in relation to Hollywood:

> When it comes to research on American cinema, children's films are very low down on the academic agenda, at least in film studies. There is, for example, not a single entry for the term 'children's films', nor for the related term 'family films', in Barry Keith Grant's 1986 collection *Film Genre Reader* (as compared, for example, to three entries for 'women's films'). The recent fundamental revisions to genre theory proposed by Nick Browne, Rick Altman and Steve Neale also fail to mention children's or family films.[3]

Krämer goes on to outline some of the difficulties in defining children's film as an area of concern, given that it can incorporate a wide range of generic categories under that banner, 'from comedies to adventure stories, from fairy tales to science fiction, and, apart from the frequent presence of child or animal protagonists and slapstick humour as well as magical spectacle, they do not have much in common.'[4] However, in the course of his discussion, Krämer draws upon a series of examples that can conceivably be grouped and defined as fantasy cinema, acknowledging the work of George Lucas and Steven Spielberg as fundamentally defining the landscape of contemporary children's film, for example. The distance that is maintained from fantasy in the discussion brings to mind a more general tendency for omission and, just as children's film exists at the periphery of genre classifications, so fantasy film remains at the margins through a similar kind of critical neglect. Krämer's piece pursues an agenda away from such questions, and it would be disingenuous to argue for his neglect in any strong sense. However, it is useful to acknowledge that both children's film and fantasy film are somewhat indistinct in formulations of genre and, furthermore, that these two branches of cinema, which enjoy such close associations, can often be overlooked in critical discussion. Part of this may derive from the fact that a great number of films that may be discussed as fantasy or children's cinema can also be usefully discussed according to other genre distinctions. So, for example, *The Wizard of Oz* is unproblematically included in work on the film musical and, likewise, *E.T: The Extra-Terrestrial* (Steven Spielberg, 1982) can uncontroversially be classified as science fiction and thus incorporated into debates focussed around that genre. To suggest that children's and fantasy cinema has been neglected as a result of these points of emphasis would be somewhat misleading, however, given that such classifications are appropriately made and in any case provide a useful understanding of the films. Furthermore, such a position would neglect a key facet and interest of genre studies, namely that types of films are rarely, if ever, rigidly precise and clear cut, and that those genres of film often overlap and merge into one another. To take *The Wizard of Oz* again as an example, we might want to question whether it is a children's film, fantasy film or musical, but we must also anticipate that a reasonable answer to such an enquiry would be 'yes'.

A further significant element in the relationship between fantasy and children in cinema is the potential for films associated with notions of, and thus classed straightforwardly as, popular entertainment. In his introduction to a defining work on formulations of entertainment, *Only Entertainment*, Richard Dyer speculates on the relative lack of sales success the volume of essays enjoyed in comparison to his collection of essays on representation, *The Matter of Images*,[5] published at a similar time:

> Perhaps the essays weren't as good; certainly the cover wasn't. However I do also suspect that, amid all the current academic discussion of pleasure, desire, jouissance and carnival, entertainment is still not taken seriously as a topic. It is too social, too common-sensical, as likely conservative as progressive; it is besides a solvent of taking things seriously. Representation obviously matters; entertainment is founded on not doing so. Yet any distinction between entertainment and representation is one of emphasis and convenience. Representation is the building block of things that are entertaining and the power of much representation resides in its ability to entertain.[6]

Here, Dyer lays out what will become a key concern in many of the essays contained within the volume: the complex relationship between representation and entertainment. Of particular interest here, however, is his potent claim regarding entertainment and seriousness; the enduring perception that these topics are mutually exclusive in academic or general discussion. Taken in this way, entertainment becomes an invisible or redundant term in critical debates, something that we understand too easily to give much notice to (or at least which we assume to understand easily). Dyer's work proceeds to disrupt such assumptions by deconstructing this oppositional relationship directly, precisely by taking a series of entertainment forms seriously, and particularly in relation to crucial questions of representation. The tendency for 'entertainment' to be read as defining an inherent lack of seriousness corresponds strongly with similar interpretations that occur in relation to the use of the terms 'child' and 'fantasy' when talking about certain types of film. In this sense, such classifications risk becoming a barrier to the serious discussion of such films, resulting in the dismissal of these works as being somehow outside of the boundaries for critical consideration, or even beneath such an enterprise. Thus, the terms become conjoined and interchangeable in such dismissals, so that films are brushed aside with broad thumbnail descriptions such as 'childish entertainment', 'entertaining fantasy', 'childish fantasy' and so on. It is also the case that when films are seen predominantly as fantasy or entertainment, this amounts to a somewhat negative assessment of their artistic merit, a fact expounded in terms like 'pure fantasy' or 'pure entertainment'. The implication here is that, in their 'purest' forms, fantasy and entertainment present an almost unreadable text: we are not supposed to take it seriously and so if offered the explanation 'of course, it's pure fantasy' or 'it's pure entertainment' we are meant to understand that we are dealing with something too far-fetched or obvious to be dwelt upon for any significant length of time. (Andrew Britton, whose work we will focus on more fully later in this chapter, suggests that this might constitute a strategy of active deception in some cases, noting that 'Ideologically, entertainment yokes together, with invisible violence, the ideas of pleasure and of the superficial, the anodyne, the unimportant. We are to enjoy it but we are also to feel that it doesn't matter, that it can't be taken seriously.')[7] When such films are further associated with children, and more specifically even childishness, the temptation to assume that they are not intended for the adult critical viewer is for obvious reasons intensified. Put simply, there is no *need* to take these films seriously: we're all grownups here.

This chapter aims to take the relationship between fantasy and childhood as a central critical concern, using those themes to structure debates and conclusions. It is worth noting that this is different from claiming that these films aren't really about fantasy or children but instead hold value and significance beyond those distinctions. A view of that kind perhaps resonates with a central assumption occasionally made in relation to forms of interpretative criticism, namely that the interpretative critic seeks to uncover, deconstruct or decode meanings that are hidden, unobvious or coded in the film as it stands in its original form. This account of interpretative criticism leads to the perception that such an enterprise seeks to prise out the implicit from the explicit, to find the meanings 'behind' those proposed within the film itself. Ironically, such claims are often made in an effort to denigrate the practice of interpretative criticism precisely by suggesting that it is in possession of an elitist agenda and so is far removed from the experiences of the 'ordinary' viewer. Hence, the interpretative critic is seen to be elevating their own status precisely by formulating accounts of films that can only be appreciated by them and their (educated) peers. This charge of elitism is perhaps related to the uneasiness felt in some quarters regarding the subjectivity of interpretative criticism; the suspicion that criticism is only ever one person's perspective and therefore precariously susceptible to contestation, counterargument and challenge. Which of course is true, but to regard this as a key failing perhaps risks characterizing criticism as a search for something definitive and incontestable: the truth in a work of art. That would involve seeing interpretative accounts of films as a way of closing off future conjecture and debate, whereas the opposite may be true: that such readings invite further thought, conversation and even strong disagreement. Robin Wood attends to this by referring to F. R. Leavis' famous formulation of the ideal critical exchange: 'This is so isn't it?'/'Yes but ...'[8] In this sense, the critic's voice is never definitive or final, but it may be convincing, well-reasoned, useful or else unconvincing, poorly argued and facile. As Wood maintains: 'The critic must never set him– or herself up as some kind of infallible oracle. The relationship between critic and reader must always be one of debate.'[9]

If such an exchange is to exist, however, it is vital that the film be maintained as the central critical focus, and that conclusions derive from the themes and issues arising from that work – there for all to see, should they choose to look. Without that discipline, the process of interpretation does indeed risk becoming an elitist exercise concerned with the critic's ability to uncover 'hidden' meanings that they alone are equipped to find. In turn, such a position makes the implicit claim that an understanding based on the film as screened is a misunderstanding or failure to see what a film is *really* about. Remaining faithful to the themes as raised within the film itself avoids such a stance, whilst furthermore ensuring that any conclusions can be evaluated against a common, shared focus: the film.

With this in mind, my contention in this chapter is that certain films dealing with the subjects of fantasy and childhood have important things to say about both of those issues, rather than containing meanings that are hidden *beneath* their 'explicit' narrative structures. This is not the same as suggesting we should devote unqualified attention to a host of films simply because they are defined by the themes of fantasy and childhood, however. Whilst we might contend that children's film and fantasy film has remained something of a blind spot in critical accounts of movies, to indiscriminately pull that focus in the other direction may not help redress the balance usefully. Rather, I suggest that a more productive means of progression may be to consider in sustained terms those films that are not only defined by themes of fantasy and childhood but furthermore debate those themes actively within their narratives. Such an approach is concerned not only with these films' status as works pertaining to fantasy and childhood, but also with their value as works dealing with the issues of fantasy and childhood; the extent to which they consciously address those twin concerns.

Questions of Context

In order to frame the terms of this debate more closely, I wish to concentrate upon a particular historical period in (primarily) American cinema that is defined by an abundance of fantasy films making the child their main dramatic focus. Loosely speaking, I take this period to be from the late 1970s to the early 1990s, self-evidently incorporating the 1980s. Within those boundaries there features a profusion of such films, a brief selection of which might include *Freaky Friday* (Gary Nelson, 1976), *Pete's Dragon* (Don Chaffey, 1977), *E.T: The Extra-Terrestrial* (Steven Spielberg, 1982), *The NeverEnding Story* (Wolfgang Petersen, 1984), *Return to Oz* (Walter Murch, 1985), *The Goonies* (Richard Donner, 1985), *Labyrinth* (Jim Henson, 1986), *Flight of the Navigator* (Randal Kleiser, 1987), *Big* (Penny Marshall, 1988), *The Witches* (Nicolas Roeg, 1990) and *Hook* (Steven Spielberg, 1991). The boundaries of the time period proposed here are not intended to be taken as absolute and, for example, we can easily find films like the Roald Dahl adaptation *Willy Wonka and the Chocolate Factory* (Mel Stuart) appearing in 1971, and likewise another Dahl reworking, *Matilda* (Danny DeVito), being released in 1996, which both include children as a consistent primary focus. Nevertheless, the relative proliferation of fantasy films centred on childhood in the 1980s is significant insomuch as it features a series of titles consistently exploring shared themes and issues.

In historical terms, the prosperity of such films can perhaps be accounted for in wider debates related to the political and cultural climate of the 1980s as well as the industrial context in which these films were developed and released. For example, in asserting that the abundance of fantasy films in post-war US cinema can be understood as 'visualisations of those complicated and bewildering sources of anxiety that befell America at the close of WWII',[10] Martin Norden identifies a similar relationship at work in films made directly after the Vietnam War. For Norden, this relates certain trends in fantasy cinema closely to the national contexts in which they appeared, making them 'symptomatic of the conditions of the societies that produced them.'[11] Thus, he makes a case for historic specificity, contending that:

> fantasy films of any given society and period will usually be quite different from those fantasy films of other societies and periods. For example, the German Expressionist films of the post-WWI years, with their themes and treatments of madness, entrapment, nightmare visions, hypnotic powers and general pessimism, bear little resemblance in either form or content to the following films produced in the United States in the five-year period following the Vietnam War, which frequently featured classic good vs. evil confrontations, sophisticated special effects, space travel, and a characteristic lightness of touch.[12]

Norden understands these movements in fantasy cinema to be dependent upon issues of historical specificity and, although he is careful to acknowledge the need for delicacy so that such correspondences are not asserted too heavily, he adheres to the notion that types of filmmaking emerge in relation to, and often in response to, the socio-cultural context in which they are conceived and received. His description of the films appearing in the post-Vietnam period is consistent with a number of titles, some of which are cited, such as *Close Encounters of the Third Kind* (Steven Spielberg, 1977), *Star Wars* (George Lucas, 1977), *Superman* (Richard Donner, 1978) and *Raiders of the Lost Ark* (Steven Spielberg, 1981), for example. Norden's key assertion that such films feature a 'characteristic lightness of touch' distinguishes these works as particular kinds of reactions to the historical context in which they appear, namely that they divert attention from the realities of the war that has just been fought or, indeed, provide remedies to the anxieties and misgivings that the conflict brought about. In this way, Norden sees such films performing a similar function to those made in the post-World War II context, where films featuring 'light-hearted looks at ghosts and angels', such as *It's A Wonderful Life* (Frank Capra, 1946) and *The Bishop's Wife* (Henry Koster, 1947), in his view 'may be a reflection of the country's desire to downplay or negate the effects of the massive spectacles of death it had just witnessed.'[13] The terms of this debate propose that a particular strand of fantasy cinema emerged in the late 1970s and early 1980s in response to the end of the Vietnam crisis and that event's place within the national consciousness. Of course, such claims are not free from contention or contradiction, and Norden concedes that 'even in times of national stress the fantasy film genre usually represents only a fraction, and frequently a rather small fraction, of the films produced.'[14] Therefore, relating these films too closely to a wider social consciousness is a somewhat precarious critical activity, and we would also have to account for the surge of films dealing directly with the Vietnam conflict in the years immediately after its end, for example. It is also the case that fantasy films of the kind Norden describes were not the only type to gain prominence in the post-Vietnam period, and we might construct a counter-argument based upon the notion that films such as *Carrie* (Brian De Palma, 1976), *The Omen* (Richard Donner, 1976), *Halloween* (John Carpenter, 1978) and *The Shining* (Stanley Kubrick, 1980) sought to acquaint audiences viscerally with the trauma and violence of death in ways that were neither reassuring nor benevolent. (Finally, even characterizing Capra's *It's A Wonderful Life* as 'light-hearted' involves viewing it from a very particular perspective, and furthermore requires an obliviousness to the dark potentials that film dedicates itself to.) Whether we accept the details of his argument, Norden nevertheless identifies an expansion in fantasy cinema that took hold from the mid-1970s and into the 1980s, with a series of titles grouped around similar themes of spectacle, straightforward moral conflicts and characteristic light-heartedness.

Published in 1982, Norden's essay is unable to account for, or anticipate, the transition between the years immediately post-Vietnam and the onset of the Reagan administration in America. This development led to a culmination of what Andrew Britton has described as 'Reaganite entertainment', although the term is not intended as strictly literal as the trends Britton draws attention to predate Reagan's election to presidential office and, furthermore, he identifies elements of this film making within the period of the Vietnam War itself.[15] For Britton, Reaganite entertainment represents a cynical and repressive strand in Hollywood filmmaking of the late-1970s and 1980s that effectively portrays a series of ultra-conservative, solipsist ideologies and self-consciously resists scrutiny precisely because they are constructed as harmless entertainment, whose themes should therefore not be taken as 'real'. As he elucidates in relation to *Star Wars*:

> It leaves out everything about the existing reality principle that we would prefer to forget, redescribes other things which are scarcely forgettable in such a way that we can remember them without discomfort (and even with uplift) and anticipates rejection of the result by defining itself as a joke. Thus Reaganite entertainment plays a game with our desire. It invites us to take pleasure in the worlds it creates and the values they embody, but, because it is also ironic about them, it confirms our sense of what reality is and leaves us with the anxieties and dissatisfactions which leave a space for Reaganite entertainment. The films continually reproduce the terms of 'the world as it

is' while also a yearning for something different; if people go back to them again and again, it is perhaps because of the lack of satisfaction the films build into the pleasure: they regenerate the need for escape which they seem to satisfy, and provide confidence of a kind which leaves us unconfident. By at once celebrating and debunking the 'good old values,' and addressing them both as viable norms and the conventions of a fantasy, Reaganite entertainment perpetuates a paralysed anxiety and institutionalizes itself.[16]

The tonal and ideological contradictions that Britton identifies in Reaganite entertainment can be related to Norden's concept of a cinema that seeks to provide reassurance after periods of sustained national trauma, anxiety or insecurity. Here, the Vietnam conflict would feature as a catalyst for such a movement, but Britton identifies crucial ways in which Reaganite entertainment equips itself poorly for the project of comfort and escape from reality precisely by representing those comforts and escapes ironically or even as a joke. Thus, the terms of investment in this brand of popular entertainment are, for Britton, problematic inasmuch as the films he terms as 'Reaganite' offer the promise of engagement whilst at the same time preserving a pervading sense of distance and emotional detachment. Thus, according to his formulation, themes such as nuclear holocaust or death are raised but never resolved in relation to US culture, so the films he discusses present neither a penetrating critique of nor a reassuring rescue from issues at the forefront of the American consciousness in the early to mid-1980s. Indeed, the films can be seen to absolve themselves of responsibility in dealing with such themes, as Britton notes:

> I suggested earlier that it is the tacit thesis of *Raiders of the Lost Ark*, à propos the nuclear holocaust, that 'if you are American you cannot die,' [in reference to the moment at the film's climax where Indiana Jones (Harrison Ford) and Marion Ravenwood (Karen Allen) avoid obliteration at the opening of the Ark by averting their eyes] and I might have made the same point of the *Star Wars* trilogy. For Obi Wan Kenobi, Yoda and Darth Vader, death has no real bearing on the fact of life. While the Emperor, for all his omnipotence and omniscience, can be killed decisively merely by being thrown over the banisters, the good father, having died, proceeds to come back again.[17]

In Britton's account of these moments from *Raiders of the Lost Ark* and *Star Wars* it becomes clear that themes such as nuclear holocaust and, more generally, death are somewhat devalued due to the films' attitude towards their consequences. In a fictional world where annihilation is avoided by simply shielding one's eyes or where the 'good' return from the dead anyway, the significance and meaning of such matters is diminished, in Britton's view, to the extent that the films offer neither comfort nor disquiet in their conclusions: nothing is seen to have lasting ramifications and so a definite position can never be adopted in relation to them. Effectively, then, the films recommend not thinking at all, either positively or negatively; none of it really matters anyway. This perceived thematic and ideological blankness becomes a guiding principle for Britton's devastating critique of Reaganite entertainment. It is also significant, however, that a number of the texts to which he makes reference are works of popular fantasy, with *Raiders of the Lost Ark* and the *Star Wars* trilogy representing two such examples. By placing such fantasy films at the heart of his debate, Britton locates a movement in film making that continues the notions proposed by Norden, presenting the endurance of the fantasy genre's prominence beyond the immediate post-Vietnam era by signalling its overlap with the 'Reaganite' period. Britton and Norden depart, however, in their assessments of the films' ideological purposes and achievements: where Norden proposes that such works function as a remedy for national anxiety, Britton contends that they are so inherently banal as to lack any potential for realizing such an aim.

Underpinning the claims of both Britton and Norden are the films of two directors particularly: George Lucas and Steven Spielberg. The impact of these twin figures on the growth and development of fantasy cinema in the late 1970s and throughout the 1980s is considerable. A contributing factor here is the extent to which Lucas and Spielberg each made fantasy a legitimate commercial enterprise, epitomised by the fact that first *Star Wars* and then *E.T.* became the top-grossing films of all time in the US.[18] In their respective efforts to resurrect their memories of childhood film experiences – with Lucas reviving the B movie space adventures of his youth again as the *Star Wars* films and Spielberg revisiting the narrative structures and themes of the 'Boy's Own' serial adventures in the format of the *Indiana Jones* films[19] – both helped to provide a financial platform upon which fantasy films could not only exist but could prosper due to studio confidence in the popularity and commercial vitality of such projects. The financial strength of the titles produced by Lucas and Spielberg can be seen to lay the foundations for the progression of fantasy cinema up to and including the more recent tendency for major franchises adapted from successful literary sources, a trend encapsulated in the *Harry Potter* series of films (2001–), *The Lord of the Rings* trilogy (2001–3), *The Chronicles of Narnia* series (2005–) and the *His Dark Materials* series (2007–). Kristin Thompson has rightly drawn attention to the fact that these films mark a change in direction from the science fiction-themed blockbusters that preceded them, such as *Star Wars, Star Trek, Independence Day* and *The Matrix*, thus representing a far stronger investment in fantasy – a category that, for many years, had enjoyed a less than stable critical reputation.[20] However, it is also possible to trace a point of continuity between these fantasy series and equivalents such as *Star Wars*, listed by Thompson, inasmuch as, although Lucas' film enjoys close associations with a tradition of science fiction cinema,[21] it equally possesses a profound engagement in themes of mysticism and the supernatural that serves to blur the lines between science fiction and fantasy. With its narrative involving such themes as a hero's quest, magic, swordplay, monsters and a spiritual guide who returns from the dead, the *Star Wars* trilogy might legitimately be seen as being influenced by *The Lord of the Rings* books themselves.

Crucially, films like *Star Wars* as well as *Raiders of the Lost Ark* and *E.T.* made fantasy economically viable and also highly attractive to studios, trading on outstanding audience attendances and, in the case of *Star Wars* particularly, lucrative merchandising opportunities. Allied with the trends identified by Norden and Britton – namely the context of post-Vietnam America and the onset of a 'Reaganite' ideological position – the phenomenal box office success of Lucas and Spielberg contributed to ensuring that the late 1970s and early 1980s became a fertile milieu for fantasy cinema as a series of historical, industrial, artistic and ideological factors converged. With this in mind, a proliferation of fantasy titles in this period of American cinema is unsurprising, and instead can be seen as a reaction to one, if not all, of these wider factors. That numerous fantasy films of the period featured child protagonists can similarly be rationalized in a number of related ways. The turn away from the political realities of the Vietnam fallout, as described by Norden, can be seen to manifest itself as not only a turn towards fantasy but also a return to the perceived reassurances and comforts of childhood. Following this line of argument proposes that, given a political landscape in which guilt and culpability had become intrinsic and fundamental concerns within society, recapturing a sense of untainted innocence in works of mass entertainment provides something of an antidote to uncomfortable truths. This is essentially an extension of Norden's claims and, within such a formulation, a film like *E.T.* would seem to be a key text, detailing straightforwardly a child's struggle against dangerous, repressive adult authority figures. Robin Wood attends to this point in condemnatory fashion as he describes the relationship between the film's director, Spielberg, and its central character, Elliott (Henry Thomas), suggesting that 'Spielberg's identification with Elliott (that there is virtually no distance between character and director is clearly the source of the film's seductive, suspect charm) makes possible the precise nature of the fantasy *E.T.* offers: not so much a child's fantasy as an adult's fantasy about childhood.'[22] In suggesting that the representation of childhood in *E.T.* is essentially an attempt to return the viewer to a childish state, rather than offer a tangible connection with childhood fantasy, Wood perceives a fundamental issue within the consistent portrayal of children in Spielberg's work (with *E.T.* at its centre) namely that it is concerned more with a regressive (adult) return to childishness than a sincere exploration of childhood. This is a theme that Wood extends to his analysis of Reaganite entertainment more generally as part of an acknowledged extension of Britton's account of that film-making impulse. In relation to childishness, particularly, Wood contends that:

> It is important to stress that I am not posing diabolical Hollywood-capitalist-Reaganite conspiracy to impose mindlessness and mystification on a potentially revolutionary populace, nor does there seem much point in blaming the filmmakers for what they are doing (the critics are another matter). The success of the films is only comprehensible when one assumes a widespread *desire* for regression to infantilism, a populace who wants to be constructed as mock children. Crucial here, no doubt, is the urge to evade responsibility – responsibility for actions, decisions, thought, responsibility for

changing things: children do not have to be responsible, there are older people to look after them.[23]

Whether or not we place Wood's assertions directly into a wider context of post-Vietnam American society, whereby the desire for the evasion of responsibility can be related to a sense of disillusionment and need for security among the populace,[24] we can nevertheless identify the regression to childishness in the work of Spielberg and, equally, Lucas. Indeed, thematically their films propose, to varying degrees, that difficulties can be overcome precisely through adults behaving more like children (or the film-makers' perceptions of how children behave). Thus, in *Star Wars*, children are not required to function as protagonists at all because the role of the child has been deferred to the adult characters. Within this configuration, the mass annihilation of human life can be reduced without complication to a series of childish games – Han Solo (Harrison Ford) blasting TIE Fighters out of the sky as though they were tin cans in a shooting range; Luke Skywalker (Mark Hamill) exploding the heavily-populated Death Star in a game of skill reminiscent of the same innocent fairground attractions. In the *Star Wars* films, particularly, this rendering of the adult-as-child is also gendered, with the emphasis resting on the male's potential to succeed through childish regression: Princess Leia (Carrie Fisher) is introduced in the film as belonging to the adult world of diplomacy, subterfuge and negotiation, strategies that are shown to fail emphatically within the film's first scene as she is imprisoned by a hostile male aggressor (Darth Vader, voiced by James Earl Jones), and thus denoted as incompatible within the governing forces of this fictional world. Leia's adoption of a more physically combative role in the later films (*The Empire Strikes Back* [Irvin Kershner, 1980] and *The Return of the Jedi* [Richard Marquand, 1983]) therefore marks not her assertion of a new, more powerful status, but rather her submission to the outwardly aggressive stance favoured by her male counterparts and demonstrated to be palpably successful within the film's fictional world. Thus, as Wood points out, even when she is revealed to be Luke's sister and as a consequence a potential possessor of the 'Force' that powerfully guides the fates of characters in the films, this potential remains unexplored and instead Leia's status as Luke's sister facilitates conveniently her romantic union with Han Solo.[25] In short, in this fantasy universe, she can never become one of the boys.

Representing Childhood

The child-as-adult theme runs similarly through Spielberg's films and perhaps finds its most direct incarnation in *Hook* (1991), a film that proposes itself as a sequel to J. M. Barrie's *Peter Pan*.[26] Although closely entwining itself with the iconography of the original book, Spielberg's film makes a series of essential departures from the tone and structure of Barrie's text, particularly in relation to the distinctions the earlier work places between the adult and the child. In *Peter Pan* the disparity between adulthood and childhood is made emphatic through the character of Peter, the boy who will never grow up, and so the story creates a crucial tension between his character's fundamental resistance to adulthood and Wendy's move away from childhood. This tension culminates in the book's conclusion when Wendy, now grown up, is only able to watch Peter fly away with her young daughter, Jane, while she must remain behind, separated by her status as an adult: 'Our last glimpse of her shows her at the window, watching them receding into the sky until they were as small as stars.'[27] The defining tone of this final passage, and of the book as a whole, is of a fundamental divide existing between childhood and adulthood, and the firm notion that a person exists either in one state or the other, but never both. Certainly, Barrie makes plain that there are special qualities to childhood that cannot be re-experienced by adults ('children are gay and innocent and heartless'[28]), and so the journey can never be made in reverse: adults are forever lost to their childhood through the fact of being grown up.

Spielberg's film discards this key distinction, however, by pursuing the story of Peter as an adult (played by Robin Williams) who has entirely forgotten his years spent in Neverland, and furthermore has become increasingly estranged from his own children (played by Charlie Corsmo and Amber Scott) through his pursuit of professional success as a corporate lawyer. The dramatic impetus of the film thus involves Peter's struggle to regain *his* childhood in order to win back his children, who have been kidnapped by Captain Hook (Dustin Hoffman): effectively he is asked to cast off his adult traits in order to rediscover an innate childlikeness that once made him Peter Pan. Peter's redemption relies not so much upon his ability to understand his children's perspectives more fully as an adult and thus sincerely devote time to their interests, but rather to convince them that he can be child just like them – a fact which is repeated with force through the hyperactive performance of Robin Williams as the central character. In this way, the film's climax demands that Peter's children merely stand by and watch as he does battle with Hook and his pirates, whilst the band of Lost Boys fall under Peter's leadership and battle this shared foe. The imbalance of status between Peter and the Lost Boys – he as adult and they as children – is not made a persistent issue in the narrative, given that we are asked to accept that he has regressed to the extent that there is no point of differentiation. Yet, Peter's standing as an adult is still retained, although made ambiguous, as he battles to reinstate his authority as a father figure and when the former leader of the Lost Boys (Rufio played by Dante Basco) is fatally stabbed by Hook, his dying words to Peter are 'I wish I had a father like you.' Thus, whilst ostensibly Peter is taken to be, and perhaps takes himself to be, one of the Lost Boys at this stage of the narrative, it is still the case that he assumes a leadership role as an adult, taking this group of children to battle and, in the case of Rufio, to their deaths.

The film is not equipped to reflect upon this ambiguity surrounding Peter's status and instead moves to a point of unbridled jubilation as Peter finally brings down

Hook once and, it seems, for all. Yet, we might return to the emphasis placed upon the adult Peter as an active, rebellious leader as opposed to that placed upon his children, whose role is reduced to that of passive cheerleaders, or the Lost Boys who fall under his command. The central conflict of the film exists between two adults, Hook and Peter, as they battle over the right to claim two children. Hook has made this a literal conflict in the case of Peter's son, Jack, as he decides to adopt him and turn him against his real father. Until the climactic battle, this strategy seems effective as Jack does indeed reject his father – to the point of forgetting who he is – and takes on an appearance resembling that of Hook's. Thus, the film comes to resemble a custody battle at its climax, with Peter attempting to out-dazzle the rival father through the spectacle of physical endeavour and a series of vociferous emotional declarations of parental love. (Peter's daughter, Maggie, is not taken in by Hook and so she is not placed as a prized object in the same way. This discarding of Maggie means, effectively, that the central issue is one of fathers and sons, and so the terms of the battle become peculiarly gender-biased, given that Peter in fact has two children. Maggie's devotion remains, by and large, unquestioned and untested, however.)

Ultimately, the portrayal of childhood in *Hook* is made ambiguous precisely (and inevitably) through its blending of adult and child roles. Peter attains the status of man-as-child, simultaneously occupying the positions of protective father and hedonistic child. The lines are similarly blurred with Captain Hook's pirates, who exhibit a form of childlike behaviour throughout, particularly when they are momentarily caught in a state of innocent reverie at the sound of Maggie singing a lullaby whilst imprisoned on their ship, but also represent a threatening, adult presence within the narrative. Rather than continuing Barrie's notion of childhood as unreachable and remote for adults, as evidenced in the barrier that eventually forms between Wendy and Peter, Spielberg's film makes the suggestion that the boundaries between childhood and adulthood are mutable, so that adults can behave like children because they always keep their childhood 'inside'. Certainly, in the case of Peter, the film makes clear the shortcomings of adults as adults, proposing instead that adults should actively retain and return to elements of their childhood behaviour. The process is never made in reverse, however, as the children in *Hook* never reach a position of being able to effect change through their own choices and decisions, as adults are shown to do in the film. Peter's son Jack is certainly faced with a choice, but this amounts only to the simple selection of one parental figure over another, and the suggestion that *neither* parent is a particularly reliable proposition is never sustained, for example. It is clear, however, that children in *Hook* are not required or even permitted to perform adult roles in the equivalent ways that the grown-up characters are allowed consciously or subconsciously to indulge in child ones. In this sense, the film concerns itself definitively with adults and the freedoms afforded to them, rather than placing a weight of emphasis upon the tangible dilemmas facing the children. Jack is asked to choose between the tyrannical Hook and his dynamic father, Peter Pan, but he is never asked to appreciate that Peter's previous absences from his life were in part a necessity of the parent's role – the fact that an American bourgeois existence incurs certain financial strains that someone has to bear, for example. Instead, Jack's choice rests upon the certainty that both fathers will provide ample investment and affection, and so it is a case of who is the more attractive of the two. Here, Jack's character is reduced to a somewhat one-dimensional portrait, lacking in psychological depth and certainly not afforded the kind of self-discovery arc that Peter completes as he ultimately rejects his former life (symbolically throwing his cell phone out of a window) and apparently dedicates himself to a childlike disposition.

We might argue that this one-dimensionality extends to the film's portrayal of the Lost Boys, which at times involves constructing childhood as a kind of grotesque spectacle, particularly those scenes featuring the trading of gutter-talk insults and food fights. This theme is encapsulated in the character of Thudd Butt (Raushan Hammond). In some respects the film attempts a more positive depiction of Thudd by allowing him a special degree of sensitivity and understanding towards Peter and also by leaving him in charge of the Lost Boys on Peter's departure, thus rewarding him with responsibility and empowerment. Yet, this is severely undermined as his obesity is made a point of humour and ridicule throughout, not only in the unfortunate and crude choice of name for his character, but also in the fact that his principle role in the final battle is to roll himself up into a giant cannonball of sorts and launch himself at groups of pirates. Here, a child's obesity becomes a point of emphasis within the film's consistent association of childhood and the grotesque. Any empowerment attributed ultimately to the character of Thudd is therefore compromised as he has already become a figure of laughter and derision within the narrative. This also serves to undermine the extent to which his character is afforded any depth or texture and, indeed, as he turns himself into a human bowling ball in the film's final battle, we are reminded that he effectively functions as a one-dimensional weapon for Peter within his personal struggle, just as the other Lost Boys do, in fact.

Spielberg's revisiting of Barrie's *Peter Pan* is therefore also a revision of its major themes, with a significant point of departure being the portrayal of children and childhood. Spielberg elects to merge adulthood into childhood through an attempt to portray the adult *as* child, and to promote this as preferable to any 'adult as adult, child as child' division. The outcome of this endeavour, and its fundamental short-coming, is to privilege the adult over the child in *Hook*, and this disparity extends to a somewhat limited – or at times even unpleasant – representation of childhood. There is a recent and growing trend in film studies to attend more closely to the work of Spielberg, with some claiming that his films have been unduly overlooked by critics and scholars.[29] Of the work emerging from this movement, it is interesting that Warren Buckland's recent book, *Directed by Steven Spielberg*, should set out to 'focus on those slight differences in filmmaking, small details constituting the elusive quality that elevate Spielberg's blockbusters over other blockbusters' but should also consciously resist any attempt to 'offer interpretations of his films, in the sense of reading social, cultural, or political meanings into the stories they tell.'[30] Leaving aside the limited ambition of Buckland's project – to suggest that Spielberg's films have a quality that elevate them above other blockbusters is almost akin to damning the director with faint praise – it is significant that claims for distinction in Spielberg's work should be limited entirely to an account of film-making competence, devoid of any interpretative dimension. This approach sits uneasily with a film like Spielberg's *Hook*, however, given that it is distinctive precisely in terms of the social, cultural and political meanings which are tied up in the film's portrayal of childhood and, particularly, the status of children in relation to adults. Interpreting these social/cultural/political strategies relies upon an appreciation of the film's aesthetic choices and it is unclear how the two could be set apart in any evaluation of the work. (After all, style and meaning in film cannot be divorced from one another and, furthermore, we might contend without too much difficulty that film makers convey meaning precisely through their stylistic choices.) The fact that Spielberg's choices involve a significant departure from the themes and attitudes of the work upon which his film is based – J.M. Barrie's *Peter Pan* – emphasizes the fact that distinctive representational strategies are in place. That the meanings conveyed in Spielberg's film involve a significant neglect or disempowerment of its child characters, whereas Barrie's work sets out in the opposite direction, is a matter that has to be taken into account alongside any claims for Spielberg's film-making competence, and certainly compromise any claims for excellence. Taking this into account may result in a fairly negative appraisal of the director's work on *Hook*, therefore, but the refusal to acknowledge that Spielberg has things to say about society, culture and politics in his films risks any critical assessment becoming a myopic attempt to ignore certain negative qualities in order to construct a positive description of his technical competence and 'originality'.

In relation to these issues surrounding Spielberg as a serious artist, it is important to acknowledge that Nigel Morris devotes an entire chapter to *Hook* in his study of the director and, at times, mounts a defence of the film's artistic integrity.[31] Interesting here is the fact that Morris takes an almost opposite direction to Buckland in resisting a concentration upon directorial competence, instead placing a weight of emphasis upon symbolic meaning, dwelling upon matters such as Oedipal imagery and allegories of cinema, for example. Although his discussion of the film often verges on an elaborate retelling of its narrative at times, Morris offers the concluding value judgement that:

> Patriarchy and family values prevail. However, to argue that this is entirely conservative and occurs unproblematically would ignore the family's subterranean conflicts, that Banning [Peter's surname in *Hook*] abandons the 1980s work ethic for personally-defined, fulfilling goals, and that successful parenting – if one insists on taking this children's fantasy seriously – appears more difficult that corporate law.[32]

As a defence of the film's attempt to articulate that 'families are worth fighting for', Morris' assertions are perhaps insipid enough to defy any serious or sustained contradiction. He is correct in saying that the film does not place a 1980s capitalist ethos above family, nor does it suggest that raising families is easy. However, this is perhaps the very least we would expect from a large-scale Hollywood family film of the 1980s and it is certainly questionable whether such attributes mark *Hook* out for critical merit. I have already raised some objections regarding the 'personally-defined, fulfilling goals' of the film's central character, based upon my contention that the film privileges the needs and desires of adults over children consistently through the course of its narrative, but Morris' casual aside – 'if one insists on taking this children's fantasy seriously' – provides a final catalyst in thinking about Spielberg's interaction with, and creation of, fantasy cinema. Clearly Morris, having devoted many pages of thought to the film, would encourage us to take *Hook* seriously and so presumably his comment is intended as somewhat tongue-in-cheek. But he also, perhaps inadvertently, alludes to an earlier-cited problem that Britton identifies in Spielberg's film making and in 'Reaganite' entertainment more generally, which 'invites us to take pleasure in the worlds it creates and the values they embody, but, because it is also ironic about them, it confirms our sense of what reality is and leaves us with the anxieties and dissatisfactions which leave a space for Reaganite entertainment.' Britton's assertion relates strongly to the ambiguity Morris creates over whether or not to take *Hook* seriously: to do so might risk over-investing in this children's fantasy and, indeed, over-interpreting something untended for interpretation. It's just too obvious for that. Or perhaps it is ironic: a joke we haven't properly understood. Here we might return to Dyer's earlier thoughts on the critical status of entertainment itself, and certainly Krämer's description of the seriousness afforded to children's cinema. And yet, if we are to accept that Spielberg matters as an artist, and that fantasy matters as a genre, we are bound to ask critical questions of *Hook* and resist the notion that children's fantasy can be taken too seriously. Otherwise, the director's work is for nothing.

If Spielberg's *Hook* marks a thematic departure from the fantasy text upon which it is derived in terms of childhood and representation, an equivalent film from the same period, *Return to Oz*, is significant for the ways in which it expands upon a series of themes raised by its cinematic 'prequel', *The Wizard of Oz*. I have suggested elsewhere that Fleming's film depicts Dorothy's (Judy Garland) life in Kansas before she travels to Oz as a lonely existence in which she struggles to find a place and where others struggle to find a place for her.[33] In *The Wizard of Oz*, it is striking that, upon returning to Kansas from Oz, very little has changed and Dorothy's status within her world remains unaltered. This culminates in a lack of affection from those who surround her bedside as she wakes from her dream but also in their dismissal of that dream as being of any importance or interest to them. Auntie Em (Clara Blandick) remarks casually that Dorothy 'just had a bad dream', which not only serves to diminish the worth of the dream but also mischaracterizes its tone: Dorothy's dream of friendship among Scarecrow, Tin Man and Lion was wonderful to her, and leaving was painfully emotional for her. And so, Dorothy's final announcement that she will never leave Kansas because she loves her community and that 'there's no place like home' is undermined:

> As she declares her love for those around her, Dorothy clutches Toto close to her, hugging him in a gesture that emphasizes the lack of unabated physical comfort she has received from anyone on recovering from her apparently life-threatening injury. Once more, she turns to her little dog for affection. Her action is framed in a close-up that also partially captures Aunt Em, sitting motionless beside Dorothy, offering no warmth of contact. Contrasted so clearly with the series of affectionate, heartfelt farewells in Oz, this scene becomes a bleak, emotionally barren portrayal of Dorothy's life in Kansas. As nothing in the final scene suggests that her future there will be different, her promise to 'never leave here ever, ever again', becomes a guarantee of Dorothy's perennial loneliness.[34]

In *Return to Oz*, this disparity between Dorothy (Fairuza Balk) and her surroundings is continued and, particularly, her dream of Oz becomes a fundamental point of tension between her and Aunt Em (Piper Laurie). Talk of Oz has in fact been banned, and furthermore Dorothy is suffering from a form of insomnia that leaves her of 'no help' to Aunt Em in the morning. Whereas in *The Wizard of Oz* Dorothy's dream is a matter that is brushed over, in this later film her devotion to what is perceived as 'just imagination' becomes a far more serious matter, apparently the root cause of Dorothy's sleeplessness and certainly of anxiety for her guardians. Her lack of help to Aunt Em is a pressing issue because, in this version of the Oz story, Dorothy's family home was destroyed in the tornado and Uncle Henry's (Matt Clark) leg was broken. And so the family exist in a half-built home, scratching a living from what is shown to be a barren Kansas landscape, hampered by debts incurred through the acquiring of two mortgages for the new property. These factors are indicative of the bleak note the film strikes at its opening, discarding the stable if stifling status quo found at the conclusion of *The Wizard of Oz* and instead bestowing strong elements of insecurity and vulnerability upon Dorothy's family in the aftermath of the tornado. The desolation of this opening continues in the approach taken to Dorothy's imagination, as she is taken away for an early version of electro-shock therapy. The clinic in which this is due to take place is portrayed as especially stark and oppressive, with Dorothy kept like a prisoner in a grimy, sparse cell as she awaits her treatment. At no point is the treatment properly explained to Dorothy, with the doctor performing the procedure (Dr Worley played by Nicol Williamson) merely patronizing her visions and his nurse (Nurse Wilson played by Jean Marsh) responding to the young girl with cold malevolence: strapping her down to a stretcher and dismissing her concern for the other patients' screams that can clearly be heard. The crucial division between Dorothy and her world, established in *The*

Wizard of Oz, is thus continued and intensified. Furthermore, the conflict between childhood and adulthood is amplified. In Fleming's film, Miss Gulch (Margaret Hamilton) represented a repressive force in Kansas, but Aunt Em and Uncle Henry were united with Dorothy against her. In this later film, the same repressive forces exist, particularly in the shape of the monstrous Nurse Wilson, but Aunt Em leaves Dorothy to them, effectively sanctioning their cruelty through her ignorance.

The film thus establishes a dramatic break between adult and child in its opening, as childhood imagining is shown to be incompatible with everyday life and thus requires not only suppression but *removal*, however spurious the means. The shattering of Dorothy's dreams is exemplified when, on escaping from the clinic, she 'returns' to Oz (the film remains ambiguous as to whether she actually visits that place, or whether she dreams its existence again). Oz is now a wasteland: the yellow brick road is wrecked, the emerald city is in ruin, and Dorothy's friends have been turned to stone. The unstableness of Oz seems to relate to the similar instability of Dorothy's imagination in her Kansas world: the extent to which it might be lost to her forever. In a mirroring device inherited from the 1939 original, Dr Worley and Nurse Wilson reappear in different guises in Oz, as the Nome King and Mombi respectively, to form a repressive alliance that seeks to destroy Oz and all memory of it. The parallels between this and the actions of their Kansas equivalents are clear. When Dorothy succeeds in defeating these foes and restoring Oz and its people, we might suggest that she fully restores her memories of that place, in defiance of the adult world that seeks to prevent her visiting it through her imagination. The film reaches a point of resolution at its conclusion when Dorothy finds herself returned from Oz and lying beside a river (the same river that apparently took her to Oz, either in her dream or in reality). Toto finds her first, and the Uncle Henry follows, casting aside his walking stick and running to embrace her with a force of sheer emotion. When Aunt Em joins the scene she is laughing with joy and the three join together in an affectionate embrace. Clearly, we have a more emphatic connection between Dorothy and her guardians than was seen at the conclusion of *The Wizard of Oz* and there is a sense that, having provided such a vivid portrait of bleak desperation in its opening, the film is seeking to match this dark sentiment with equal momentum in this happy reunion. The threat from this world has also been removed, with the clinic having burnt to the ground, Dr Worley killed attempting to rescue his machines, and Nurse Wilson imprisoned in a jail wagon.

When we return to Dorothy's home once more, the house is almost fully built and she has a new bedroom at the top of the building. In this room, she catches sight of a vision of a character from Oz in her mirror (Ozma, played by Emma Ridley) and calls out to Aunt Em. But the vision puts her fingers to her lips in a clear declaration that the event must remain secret and so, when Aunt Em arrives, Dorothy does not speak of it. Effectively, then, Dorothy acknowledges the incongruity of her imagination with the adult world she occupies (she is the only child we see in Kansas) and elects to preserve the division between childhood and adulthood by keeping her visions private. Thus, the gulf between child and adult is not breached or merged in the film, but rather reinforced and made ever more pronounced. Aunt Em remarks to Dorothy 'It's nice to have room of your own' and there is a sense that the young girl's new space is not only physically removed from her adult guardians but also psychically removed: where her imagination can be indulged but never shared. *Return to Oz* inherits and extends the theme of incompatibility between the adult world and the child from *The Wizard of Oz* but balances this by allowing Dorothy to find a place within her world where imagination can exist. That this space is physically and psychically removed from the adult world only serves to reinforce the rupture that the film has sought to establish between adult and child.

Falling roughly between the release dates of *Return to Oz* and *Hook*, Penny Marshall's *Big* addresses and binds together those films' contrasting major themes: the separateness of adult and child in *Return to Oz* and the merging of adult and child roles in *Hook*. Bearing certain similarities to an earlier film, *Freaky Friday*, in which a mother and daughter swap bodies for a day, *Big* centres upon a 12-year-old boy, Josh (David Moscow), who wishes literally that he could be 'big' and, as a result, wakes up as a grown man (Tom Hanks). Once his anxieties about this sudden change are brought into check, Josh finds work at a toy company and gradually acquires the trappings of adult life, including an apartment, a girlfriend and a rewarding job. His professional success is due to the 'child's perspective' he is clearly able to bring to the workings of the organization he is employed by – a useful attribute in toy manufacturing – and the film creates a series of humorous moments based around Josh's natural, 12-year-old responses to situations being interpreted by his adult peers as sophisticated and thoughtful insights. The film seems to make two points through the treatment of Josh's character here: firstly, that it isn't so difficult for a child to function within the adult workplace (although, given that this is a toy company, a very specialized adult workplace) and, secondly, that those charged with providing entertainment for children are profoundly out of step with their target audience. This second point is emphasized repeatedly in the film, particularly in relation to the character of Paul (John Heard), who sees himself as Josh's rival on a number of levels, and whose business decisions are dictated by a series of dry statistics and industry reports. The ease with which Josh is able to perform – and outperform others – within the adult world of work is also made plain from the outset when, within minutes of starting his duties, a co-worker (Jon Lovitz) irritably demands that he slow down because he risks making everyone else 'look bad'. We are on similar ground to *Hook* with these representations of adult professional life as banal, repressive or ridiculous yet, unlike Spielberg's film, *Big* doesn't seek to rescue its grownup characters through the discovery of their 'inner child'. Instead, those characters are left to their world and the divisions between child and adult are never breached. Furthermore, this adult world is represented as being imbued with elements of childishness which Josh's behaviour actually contradicts. For example, he never reciprocates Paul's petty rivalry and, when Paul attempts to humiliate him in an impromptu game of squash it is the 'real' adult character who is reduced to childish squabbling and cheating whilst Josh's childlike enthusiasm for the sport translates into uncomplicated reason. Here, then, the film makes a strong distinction between the childish and the childlike, and in doing so undermines aspects of the adult world in comparison to the world of children.

This chasm between adult and child extends even to the more sympathetic grownup characters in the film. Josh's girlfriend, Susan (Elizabeth Perkins), is certainly shown to be beguiled by his behaviour, but never crosses the borderland between adult and child and never fully appreciates that what she finds attractive in his character is childlikeness. Thus, when defending him to Paul (who she rejects in favour of Josh) she explains in precise terms that 'he's a grownup', a statement that highlights Paul's childishness and also illustrates the depth and maturity the film affords its 'child' character, Josh. In the film's penultimate scene, Susan finally realizes and accepts that Josh is a child in a man's body, but arrives too late at a fairground pier to stop him wishing for the process to be reversed (at the same carnival attraction that granted his first wish), and for him to be a child once more. When he suggests that she join him by wishing to be a child again, Susan responds by saying 'No ... I've been there before. It's hard enough the first time' and so the film makes its border between adult and child definite once again, placing distance between the characters in the same way that Peter and Wendy, in Barrie's story, found themselves fundamentally divided through their status as child and adult. The scene concludes with Susan saying 'Come on, I'll drive you home', and these words reinforce finally that Josh is a child once more (certainly in her eyes, although physically he is still a man) and that she effortlessly adopts the adult role again, taking responsibility and providing transport that a child, clearly, cannot. For the first time in the film, she is an adult addressing a child.

This theme is continued at the film's conclusion when Susan has driven Josh back to his family home and they bid each other farewell in her car. He leans in to kiss her on the lips, as has been normal in their relationship, but she gently holds his cheek and guides his face away so that she kisses him on the forehead, as would be an appropriate gesture from an adult to a child. As Josh leaves the car and walks away, there follows a series of cross-cuts between him and Susan, still sitting in the vehicle. This technique is used to mask his transformation back to a child so that, when we cut from a shot of Susan to him, he is now a 13-year-old[35] boy walking in man's clothes. The lack of spectacle in this transition may have been a choice based upon financial constraints affecting the film's production, but the result is that Josh's changed appearance in fact delivers an impact, both for Susan and for an audience. By cutting back to Josh transformed, the film reminds us that this was always a child, that his incarnation as an adult was only ever an aberration, now reversed. The image of this boy standing in an oversized suit, shirt, tie and shoes, brings to mind forcefully the incongruity – literally the poor fit – of child and adult in the film, making sense of the balance struck in this conclusion as matters are restored. Whilst we hear the cries of joy as Josh is reunited with his mother inside their home, we are to assume that Susan merely returns to her life as it was in the corporate world. It might be that her time with Josh has altered her outlook so profoundly that she will not fall back into the role of work-driven highflyer, but the film offers no guarantees of this. And so, as the final divide is placed between Susan and Josh, between adult and child, she is left to her own world, and the contests that await her. In this way, the film insists that childhood is worth preserving, but only for children, and that adult concerns and sensibilities lie somewhat outside of its thematic focus.

Hook, Return to Oz and *Big* each display a varying commitment to, and therefore differing attitudes towards, childhood in film. Their status as fantasy affords them a certain freedom in terms of the dramatic boundaries they establish, and certainly each film debates notions of childhood against the backdrop of extraordinary narrative events. In the case of *Hook*, this amounts to the child being ultimately lost as a significant element within the story, to the extent that Peter Pan's children in fact become somewhat limited and one-dimensional portrayals in relation to their adult equivalents, as the film devotes itself to the concept of adult-as-child, and thus perhaps an adult's fantasy of childhood. In contrast, *Return to Oz* continues the themes of *The Wizard of Oz* by placing clear boundaries between the child and adult, and proposing ultimately that these must remain in place – that the two should remain fundamentally distanced from one another – in order for equilibrium to be achieved. As a further comparison, *Big* risks the issues associated with *Hook* by plainly merging the roles of adult and child, and yet makes the fundamental *incompatibility* between the two its enduring concern. In each of these cases, the topic of childhood is afforded differing inflections and configurations, thus complicating easy assumptions about what a fantasy film for and about children might involve. Indeed, across these three films various and conflicting notions of childhood are expressed, to the extent that the differences between them become a significant defining factor alongside their shared status as works of fantasy entertainment. I have suggested that the films emerge within a fertile milieu for fantasy within American cinema history, and I would suggest that the discussion could be profitably expanded elsewhere to incorporate similar works from that period. Discussing the films' representations of childhood reveals the extent to which they commit themselves to that theme, and furthermore the extent to which their varying approaches to childhood affects their outcomes. The films' status as fantasy and popular entertainment remains unchanged by this discussion, of course, but this in no way negates the extent to which they offer potent representations of childhood that have lasting repercussions for how we view and evaluate them.

–5–

Fantasy, Imagination and Interiority

The Invisible Dream

Where previous chapters in this book have concerned themselves primarily with the somewhat broader questions that can be posed in the context of fantasy film (entertainment and representation; authorship and genre; history and style, ontology), the final two chapters set out a slightly different course. Preceding discussions have addressed certain issues that tie notions of fantasy cinema to overarching interests within the field of film studies. Such academic investments have endured as the discipline has evolved, withstanding the trends, movements and revisionist directions that have, from time to time, provided new impetus to critical and theoretical debates. Their inclusion, therefore, has a logical purpose within this book. Although not designed to provide a radical shift from the ideas represented thus far, the final two chapters of the book are intended to sketch out positions that offer new or alternative perspectives on fantasy film. The closing chapter seeks to achieve this by, in fact, returning notions of fantasy cinema to questions of coherence that are central to a consideration of all fiction film yet are not always sustained in critical accounts. In the present chapter, however, the focus rests upon an aspect that is not necessarily pronounced in understandings of fantasy film, perhaps through its intrinsic lack of visibility: the question of characters' interior fantasies that, unlike overt representations found elsewhere in examples ranging from John Ballantyne's (Gregory Peck) famous Dali-designed dream in Alfred Hitchcock's *Spellbound* (1945) to Lester's (Kevin Spacey) erotic reveries in *American Beauty* (Sam Mendes, 1999), we have little or no 'direct' access to. They remain hidden. The question persists of how films manage the fantasies we can't see. How are the thoughts, desires and dreams of individuals conveyed without a conventional stepping over into fantasy realms? How is the intangible given shape, significance and meaning in a film?

Self-evidently, this direction places fantasy in the more familiar context of an everyday reality recognizable to and experienced by us, the viewer, whereas many of the films discussed thus far in this book seek emphatically to expand the borders of reality in the course of their narratives. The composition of fantasy as a facet of ordinary existence is crucial here, so dissolving in part the potential opposition between fantasy and reality that we might feel inclined to construct: fantasy as the *opposite* of reality. Distinguishing strongly between fantasy and reality in terms of the means by which we experience our world makes the implicit claim that there are ways of viewing existence that are 'real' – objective, unbiased, non-emotive – and ways of seeing that are blighted by their 'unrealness' – subjective, biased, emotive. In this formulation, there would be a type of experience that was based in reality and one that was conditionally based in fantasy. Such divisions appear at first alluring – it is common to suggest that an individual is living in world of fantasy or, indeed, has become somewhat detached from reality – but it is also inherently disingenuous. The way that we interpret the events that shape our lives, the environments we encounter and the individuals we interact with, is dependent to a large extent upon processes of fantasizing – of imagining a portrait of our world that lends coherence to what is essentially the chaos of existence. Clearly we do not record information objectively, without bias or emotion, but instead bring our own perspectives – our own fantasies of our world and ourselves within it – to play in any understanding we might hope to reach. Supposition, hypothesis, assumption, presumption, ignorance, prejudice, optimism, insecurity, anxiety – all of these features and countless others can shape our view of the world. We piece together fragmentary knowledge to *create* a picture of the whole. No two pictures can be identical in any two minds and so what we take to be reality is based, to a large extent, upon a fantasy we have wilfully constructed. These points are articulated with force by Stanley Cavell when he suggests that:

> It is a poor idea of fantasy which takes it to be a world apart from reality, a world clearly showing its unreality. Fantasy is precisely what reality can be confused with. It is through fantasy that our conviction of the worth of reality is established; to forgo our fantasies would be to forgo our touch with the world. And does someone claim to know the specific balance sanity must sustain between the elaborating demands of self and world, some neat way of keeping soul and body together?[1]

Cavell centres these claims on a discussion of Hitchcock's *Vertigo* (1958), an especially apt choice for debating the interrelation between reality and fantasy given that the film features a character (Scottie, played by James Stewart) who effectively attempts to reshape reality to fit his fantasy of a woman, Madeline (Kim Novak), who never was. As Cavell contends, 'no other movie I know so purely conveys the sealing of a mind within a scorching fantasy.'[2] Scottie's obsession makes any sense of reality and fantasy indistinguishable to him, to the extent that they become conflated. As he orchestrates Madeline's reappearance through his remodelling of Judy's appearance (the girl who bears a striking resemblance to Madeline precisely because, as it turns out, she is one and the same) it becomes clear that he overlaps reality and fantasy so that the borderlines no longer appear to him: Madeline is alive again.

But the examples do not need to be so keenly felt for us to appreciate Cavell's point that fantasy 'is precisely what reality can be confused with.' Rather, in the context of films, a number of works investigate the fundamental concept that a character's perspective on their world is guided profoundly by the intersection of fantasy in any understanding of reality. A crude and literal way of depicting this might be to structure a film to include a series of point-of-view shots whereby the character whose view we are temporarily aligned with is shown to be emphatically divergent, skewed or distorted, from the 'objective' reality the film depicts elsewhere. This strategy is not without interest: in Richard Kelly's *Donnie Darko* (2001), the eponymous character frequently sees a vision of a giant, sinister bunny-costumed entity and, rather than simply ask us to accept that Donnie is in a delusional state, the film leaves open the possibility that what he sees is real, and that other characters simply fail to see the 'truth' that he witnesses. At the film's conclusion, it is this possibility that turns out to be correct. Elsewhere, *Fight Club* (David Fincher, 1999) performs its famous cheat ending by revealing that Jack (Edward Norton) has unwittingly allowed his fantasy of the world to supersede almost entirely any rational understanding of reality: a fact epitomized by his imagining an entire person (Tyler Durden, played by Brad Pitt) who is invisible to everyone else. At times in the film, Tyler is Jack's alter ego: nobody sees Tyler; they see only Jack. Here, an apparently 'objective' *mise en scène,* which shows Jack and Tyler existing together in the same world, is revealed to be inherently 'subjective': Tyler is Jack's fantasy and Jack in fact performs all actions that we take to be *interactions* between the characters.

The role that fantasy plays in guiding characters' understanding of their reality is the central concern in this chapter. The films offered for discussion propose fantasy to be a constituent feature of everyday life, rather than something that is divorced from or an opposite to reality. As a result, these films draw attention to the fragility and unreliability of human perception: the extent to which our views and insights can be determined by the intangible, fanciful and delusional. By insisting on this inherent fallibility of awareness, the films demand that we consider their characters as complex, complicated and even contradictory individuals whose ideas of their world may be mysterious, difficult and perplexing – even to them. As a result, it is these characters' involvement with fantasy that makes them real.

Framing Fantasy

Max Ophuls' *Letter From an Unknown Woman* (1948) is regarded as a masterpiece of cinema and has been the subject of a particularly refined and expressive body of criticism.[3] In the most straightforward terms, the film depicts a man, Stefan Brandt (Louis Jourdan), receiving a letter from a woman, Lisa Berndle (Joan Fontaine). The reading of the letter reveals to him the significance he has had in her life over a number of years, as the object of her affection, as her brief lover, and as the father of their son, now dead. These facts appear to have been unknown to Stefan and, in the film's concluding moments we are told that he cannot act upon the revelations: Lisa too is dead and the letter is but a posthumous record of her life and love for him. Indeed, her life and her love for him become inextricably fused in her written account. Given the sustained and fluent accounts of the film's value and achievements already provided by some of the finest critics of cinema, it is appropriate to acknowledge that Ophuls' depiction of this melodrama make such brief and crude summaries of its plot inadequate. Returning to the film reveals the nature of those inadequacies in every moment of its progression.

In line with the aims of this chapter, I want to focus on a series of observations George Wilson makes about the film in relation to fantasy. Wilson suggests that Lisa's 'perception of herself and her situation is filtered through a complex structure of fantasy and desire' and, furthermore, asserts that:

> In a way, Lisa is a fairly conventional heroine of a certain type of 'woman's picture': the woman who sacrifices everything for an unworthy male. But this film is probably unique in its sharp definition of that sacrifice as the result of a partially willed obsession with an object of love who is largely the product of a passionate imagination. The film is doubly unique in that its disturbing heroine is viewed throughout with tact, sympathy, and serious affection. In *Letter* and in other Ophuls' films, love is held to be based necessarily on illusion, but the capacity for love is valued as a state of quasi-religious detachment from the self and from the world.[4]

Wilson's account guards against a view of Lisa as a hopelessly delusional character whose downfall is primarily of her own making. This assessment would constitute a particularly unforgiving portrait of the film's central female character, but might also attest to the ambiguity and inscrutability of her actions, emotions and intentions. Such qualities might leave us perplexed. Why does this seemingly intelligent and emotionally articulate woman continue to allow herself to be drawn towards this man who, from a number of perspectives, can be seen to offer only intense suffering to her? By taking her desires and drives seriously and treating them with sincerity as Wilson proposes, the film ensures that Lisa's illusions of her world are treated with equal seriousness and sincerity. The film provides a portrait of a character whose imagination does not set her apart from us, but instead provides a fundamental connection to the ways in which our own fantasies can shape our view of reality, even to the extent that they cloud and obscure our rational senses. We are revealed in the film's truths. In *Letter from an Unknown Woman*, love is not rational and devotion lies beyond the confines of logical calculation.

Ophuls' method in exploring fantasy's potential to shape profoundly a character's perceptions of reality is both subtle and delicate. A key early instance is found in the event of (the teenage) Lisa and (adult) Stefan's first meeting. We join the scene as Lisa sits on a swing in the courtyard below Stefan's open window (they share an apartment block) listening to his virtuoso piano playing (Stefan is a concert pianist). The composition of this scene succinctly accentuates the notion of a young girl on the threshold of adulthood: the idle swinging representing a mode of behaviour connected to childhood but her rapt dedication to Stefan's performance (and, by implication, to Stefan) suggests a desire and sexual awakening that moves her towards adulthood. To her clear annoyance, a somewhat vulgar acquaintance of Lisa's (played delightfully by Carol Yorke) interrupts her moment of reverent appreciation. But Lisa is physically disturbed and propelled into action when, a few moments later, Stefan's playing ends abruptly as he attempts, and misses, a particularly intricate run of notes. Matching his vexation, Lisa runs with some urgency away from the courtyard and arrives at the glass-panelled doors that front the apartment buildings. Lisa's actions here provide an indication of the ambiguity inherent in her character and her motivations. It is singularly unclear what prompts her to hasten towards the doors. Has she heard movement that suggests Stefan might be making his way out of the apartment? Does she simply move to that position in the hope that he could appear, his practice having ceased abruptly? Has this happened before? We cannot know, and so it becomes one of those details that is particular to the character, rather than one in which meaning is made overt and so universally explicit.

Certainly, Lisa appears apprehensive when she reaches the doors, first peering through a corner of the framed glass, then walking away and out of sight of the apartment's lobby, as though suddenly conscious of her visibility, before finally returning to her position at the glass, where she can see whether Stefan emerges and, in turn, she can be seen by him should he appear. Indeed, when Stefan does descend the steps into the lobby (our awareness of his presence cued by the sound of his voice as a reverse shot captures Lisa looking through the glass) she does not retreat again but instead holds her position, watching his arrival as though the member of an audience admiring a performance: distanced and safe. As we return to a shot from behind Lisa looking on, this effect of her distance and separation from the environment of the lobby is reinforced, her positioning placing her in temporary alignment with us, the film audience. This momentary allusion to Lisa as audience and Stefan as performer perhaps prefaces the nature of their union as the film progresses, referencing a fundamental awareness of him on her part, and an equally fundamental lack of awareness on his: in these terms, he is the star who fails to acknowledge his public. We can hardly fail to recognize that the balance of the relationship is compromised profoundly from the outset. But the alignment of Lisa's positioning with that of an audience member should not lead us to overlook the fact that she is also active in this scene, forming an impression of this man at a distance which she will then act upon, in a way that a passive spectator could not hope to replicate. If Lisa views Stefan's introduction in a manner that alludes to a theatrical experience, it is a performance she inserts herself into, interacting with the object of her admiring gaze: Stefan.

Stefan continues his journey out of the building and, before he reaches the door, Lisa reaches across and opens it for him, matching her movement with his progress in a smooth, fluent gesture. As a result of her action, Lisa is positioned behind the opened door that Stefan passes through. He stops to acknowledge her, and so we are given a moment to reflect that Lisa inadvertently constructs a means by which they might view each other, framed in the glass as if on public display, but also establishes a barrier between them, the door demarcating a boundary between them and confining them to their respective zones. Here, then, a play on intimacy and distance is inherent in Lisa's act, whereby a moment of apparent closeness can in turn reveal the gulf between two characters. This theme will prove to be central to their relationship, so that even as they appear to be moving closer to one another (from Lisa's perspective especially), they remain profoundly distanced. The pattern is continued in their very last meeting, where Lisa mistakes Stefan's advances to be verging on his genuine recognition of her, only to discover that he has no such recollection forming, and instead fits her into a routine well rehearsed with other women. The door in the earlier sequence becomes a point of access to each other, viewed and viewable through the glass, but also sets them apart, a tangible visual barrier between them.

As Stefan pauses to acknowledge Lisa, Ophuls cuts to a shot that resembles, if not replicates, Lisa's point of view: Stefan framed in a glass pane of the door. He is literally framed as the four sides of the panel compose his features as though in a portrait. At first we might take the shot to be an arbitrary intervention, the cut to close-up corresponding with the delivery of a line of dialogue – Stefan says 'thank you' to Lisa. In this sense, we might regard it as a basic film-making technique. But the framing of Stefan's features in this way also serve to accentuate Lisa's idealized view of him at this stage in the film. His portrait-like appearance reveals her infatuation with an image, a surface: a fantasy of a man. (The image of Stefan here resembles the photograph of him on a playbill later in the film, which Lisa furtively borrows from a man's pocket, apparently not to keep, but rather to steal another look at Stefan's framed image.) The move to close-up also serves to convey the emotional weight Lisa places on this moment between them: his simple utterance of thanks becoming a framed, composed event that is elevated beyond its immediate significance. To emphasize this point, Lisa will go on to say: 'From that moment on, I was in love with you', an extraordinary admission given the sparseness of their interaction in the scene. Crucially, we are not given access to Stefan's direct view of Lisa as they meet at the doorway but, instead, only share his perspective when he is leaving her, turning back to see her holding onto the door, as though she were still cherishing the site at which their paths crossed by staying close to this object. Again, this might read as a straightforward choice on Ophuls' part, the clichéd glance over the shoulder as a character leaves a curious encounter. However, the timing of the point of view shot means that Stefan's view of Lisa is only made apparent when he is moving *away* from her, in fact achieving a *lesser* appreciation of her. Furthermore, Lisa's proximity to the door renders her part of the scenery, as though she recedes to become a physically diminutive element within the scene's composition, a fact that potentially compromises her individuality and distinctness. Choosing this moment to reveal Stefan's view of Lisa has clear repercussions: just as she objectifies him in order to elevate his status and appeal, so he objectifies her in order to denigrate those features, allowing her to fade in his mind and, ultimately, in his memory. In the film's final moments, Stefan will walk through this doorway again, this time to his certain death as he travels to a duel with the man that Lisa married. He stops and turns, just as he did in the original scene, and is rewarded with the same view of Lisa: a ghost in his memory now. As he looks back, she fades from the scene. We might interpret this as a symbolic reference to her death, her fading from reality. However, if we relate it to the earlier scene in which Stefan actually had this view, we might take it to be his final, tragic acknowledgement that he did not see her properly even in that first meeting: allowing her to fade from view as she literally does in this ghost vision.

This first meeting between the characters establishes in clear terms the extent to which Lisa allows her fantasy of Stefan to become her guiding view of him, enduring as a myopic infatuation as she moves from teenage to womanhood. The brevity of the meeting and Stefan's distanced appreciation of her demonstrates the incongruity between her fantasy of the world and the realities it contains. We might conclude that, in the film's representations of their views, neither Stefan nor Lisa sees the world properly: he overlooks her as much as she idealizes him. And yet, the possibility that Lisa's conviction is *truth* remains suspended in the scene. It is intriguing to note that, before her irreverent friend interrupts her, Lisa's swinging was almost perfectly in time with Stefan's playing. Are we to take it that she orchestrates this difficult synchronicity in order to manufacture a relationship between them (which she alone could appreciate)? Or is the film proposing a subconscious synthesis between the characters, symbolized by the fact that their actions take place harmoniously in this way? The latter suggestion is certainly in play when the friend's crude interjections not only disrupt Lisa's swinging but also seem to disrupt the tempo of Stefan's playing, to the extent that his performance falls apart and he is left frustrated. It is as though the same interruption breaks both characters' concentration. In leaving these questions open, the film emphasizes the notion that fantasy and reality are not inseparable: that Lisa's fantasy of a life with Stefan may conceivably touch upon a real life that they might have shared. The film's tragedy is that such a life can never be realized as death and tragedy draws them finally away from one another, and from their fantasies of one another.

Containment as Concealment

Just as straightforward accounts of *Letter from an Unknown Woman*'s plot provide only surface appreciations of its intricacies, so Nicholas Ray's *Bigger than Life* (1956) similarly cannot be reduced to a brief synopsis. Ostensibly, the plot involves a husband and father, Ed Avery (James Mason), who is a schoolteacher struggling to meet the financial demands of bourgeois domestic life, and so is forced to take a part-time job working in a taxicab office. He hides this fact from his wife, Lou (Barbara Reed), although certain features make lack of money a clear issue, especially the Avery's faulty boiler, which is a source of muted agitation for her. He is prescribed the (then) experimental drug cortisone to relieve a crippling pain that he has been suffering from, a further fact that he has kept hidden from his wife. Ed's medicine spirals out of control, however, and his ever-increasing doses cause his behaviour to become ever more erratic, leading to wild delusions of grandeur. Eventually he convinces himself that he must correct God's preventing Abraham from sacrific-ing his son, Isaac, in the Old Testament story ('God was wrong') by sacrificing his own boy, Richie (Christopher Olsen), and then taking his and Lou's lives ('I hadn't planned to go on living. Do you?') The inflation of Ed's ego is encapsulated perfectly by the film's title: he indeed becomes bigger than life, thinking himself above the morals and reasons of 'ordinary' human beings. The link between Ed's psychosis and the drug cortisone is proposed as an explicit connection in this brief account of the film, leaving us to suppose that it is a dangerous excess of medication that disastrously affects his sanity, making him delusional and volatile. And yet, something of a consensus has formed among scholars writing on Ray's film that the use of cortisone doesn't exactly provoke a reversal in Ed's behaviour and attitudes but rather provides the means for certain tensions, frustrations and anxieties to rise dangerously to the surface.[5] This point is made explicit in Robin Wood's early account of the film:

> *Bigger Than Life* is not really a film about psychosis, any more than it is an Awful Warning about cortisone. Ray is concerned with the tensions inherent in life in contemporary society; or, more basically, with the tension between aspirations and environment which is perhaps fundamental to the human condition. The structure of the film draws its strength from the way in which all of Ed's excesses under the influence of the drug are subtly anticipated before he has taken it, without at any point overstepping the bounds of recognizable 'normality' – a normality that is, with which all of us can (to whatever varying degree) identify.[6]

Wood's description here relates Ed's distorted view of his world, and the fantasy of his status within it, to fundamental attributes of everyday existence. The tensions he refers to can be seen to manifest themselves in subtle aspects of Ray's stylistic rendering of Ed's world. Ray expresses these fundamental strains through the film's *mise en scène,* drawing upon an 'architectural awareness' that Wood detects as a guiding factor in his work, suggesting that it is 'there not only in the extreme sensitivity to décor – in the way the structure of rooms, apartments, houses is used for purposes of dramatic expression – but in the structure of the images, in which the actors themselves are often used architecturally: Ray's treatment of the human body is closer to Cézanne than to Renoir.'[7] As Wood goes on to acknowledge, *Bigger*

Than Life's CinemaScope format provides the director with arresting opportunities to express this interest in *visual* relationships.

From an early stage, Ed's (as yet) private fantasies are referenced in aspects of the Avery's home and the characters' interaction with those features. We are nearing the end of a scene in which Ed and Lou have hosted a bridge party for a number of friends and professional acquaintances of Ed's (those found in the school, not the cab office, so complying with the illusion he wishes to maintain). Layers of tension are introduced as Lou grows suspicious over Ed's reasons for arriving home late from work (he gave the excuse of a board meeting at the school, whereas in reality he was working at the cab office) and she connects this to another suspicion she holds about Ed's attraction to a female colleague, Pat (Kipp Hamilton). Once the guests have departed, Lou closes the front door and walks past her husband without any form of acknowledgement or engagement: her emotional coldness made explicit, something she undoubtedly wishes her husband to register. In the front room she begins to tidy away, but Ed switches out the light. She moves to the next room and he does the same thing. She enters the kitchen and begins to fill a kettle for hot water to wash dishes (the fault with the boiler leaving them without an instant supply) but he reaches across her and switches off the tap, saying 'Leave them honey.' He moves to a small utility room and flicks another light switch. We move to a shot depicting Ed as he enters the hallway, slowly unfastening his bowtie. As he moves, he speaks: 'Wouldn't it be great for both of us to really get away one of these days?' His thought is perhaps provoked, in part, by his friend Wally's (Walter Matthau) suggestion that he, Ed, Lou and Richie go fishing at the weekend. But Ed's mention of a vacation is prompted directly by his catching sight of a poster, framed on the wall, of Bryce Canyon National Park. That he should equate this image to the notion of 'really get[ting] away' suggests a distinction that Ed makes between the modest proposal that Wally puts forward and his own ideas of a grand vacation, reflected in the size and scale of the canyon image. At stake in this separation is Ed's perception of a fishing trip as small and humdrum as opposed to travelling to visit sites of importance, beauty and – significantly for this film – magnitude. His proclivity for large-scale travel is complemented and furthered in other posters that line the walls of the Avery household depicting distant locations – France, London, the city of Bologna – that are synonymous with notions of European cultural landmarks. There are maps on some walls of entire countries and even of the world, further indicating a breadth and scope of potential voyage.

As Ed and Lou make their way upstairs after Ed's remark about getting away, they pass a number of these framed images. Their journey is also punctuated by a conversation that sees the couple misinterpret emphatically each other's responses: she suspects his attraction to Pat, and perhaps that he has acted upon this desire; he misreads the nature of her questioning and further inflames the exchange by suggesting, with an apparently light-hearted intention, that their life together is 'dull'. When Lou responds 'Have you found someone that isn't?' Ed looks at her with genuine confusion and surprise, James Mason's performance indicating successfully that the character simply could not anticipate his wife's response, such is the gulf in comprehension that exists between them in this scene and in their marriage more generally. Although we might hazard a sympathetic response to Ed's remark in light of his sincere reaction to Lou's question, this is compromised by an appreciation that his classing them as dull, even if intended as a joke, speaks of a underlying – and repressed – perception he holds of their domestic life. The posters on the walls that depict culturally refined and, due to their intangibility, exotic locations represent a lingering desire on Ed's part to escape the 'dullness' of his current existence. That is not to say that he wishes to escape Lou, or their son Richie, necessarily but rather to escape the life that they have built and hemmed themselves into. The posters embody a fantasy of a life elsewhere, of a life more befitting of his intellectual capacities (television is 'always the same story' to him; his friends are incapable of articulating anything that is 'funny, startling or imaginative') and, crucially, of a life that is bigger than the one they currently lead. The scale of the posters – the Bryce Canyon, a cityscape of London, a map of the world – taken together suggest Ed's belief that he can measure up to a world far larger than the one he currently inhabits. The posters represent a safe and contained way of exploring borders and horizons that extend beyond the confines of his professional and domestic environments. Connected to the earlier discussion of *Letter from an Unknown Woman*, we are again struck by fantasy existing within frames for characters: captured and held but representing a wealth of possibilities and desires.

If the pictures in the Avery household help to sharpen an appreciation of the suppressed desires inherent in Ed's throwaway description of his and Lou's life together as dull, we might also extend that to understand his actions prior to that exchange. His following Lou around the house may be suggestive of a wish for her to relax, an acknowledgement of her work in preparing a successful social gathering in their home. And yet, Ed does not wait for her to finish her small jobs before extinguishing the lights. Rather, he plunges her into darkness mid-task, making the gesture assertive and manipulative rather than considerate and careful: she is left with no choice but to leave the now-darkened room in each case. By throwing the rooms into darkness, Ed also extinguishes the vision of his domestic environment, dispensing with each room as he switches off the lights. Furthermore, he casts a shadow over the domestic tasks that Lou performs, so cutting off his engagement with the chores that must be performed before and after entertainment and enjoyment can take place: the 'dull' aspects of everyday life, we might say. If the posters represent a fantasy on Ed's part to escape his domestic constraints, his actions in switching off the lights complement this notion, encapsulating a rejection of domestic reality by casting it in shadow, removing it from his sight. Even Lou's attempt to wash a couple of dishes is curtailed as he lays a forceful hand across her and prevents her from filling the kettle for hot water. This particular instance of him forbidding Lou to perform her domestic tasks may crystallize a couple of other simmering issues related to Ed's status in the world. Firstly, that the filling of the kettle may remind him of the broken boiler that will not heat water but cannot be replaced due to money and, secondly, Lou's performing duties of this kind underlines the Avery's position as a financially stretched middle-class family in which the wife must carry out such work, rather than a higher class, more affluent household in which chores of this kind would be performed by staff. His emphatic restraining of Lou as she attempts to clear away perhaps indicates a truth of which Ed is acutely aware: her actions demonstrate that, while he may wish to escape his dull domestic existence, its dullness is at least in part due to his perceived inability to provide properly for his family in financial terms, a fact that leads to his second job in the cab office and so leaves him furthermore resentful of his lifestyle. The broken boiler acts as a central motif of this frustration (and Ray makes it an ugly, spatially obtrusive feature of the kitchen's *mise en scène* as if to emphasize the way in which it causes the characters a degree of unease) and Lou's performing of the chores serves to illustrate the point. Ed's responses in this sequence express his agitation with his domestic environment; the pictures on his walls express his fantasy of a life elsewhere.

Ed's suppressed fantasies of escape register as an unsettling element that threatens to unbalance any sense of harmony that might exist within the Avery household. However, Deborah Thomas suggests that Lou's fantasies are also revealed when the couple are upstairs and the argument about dullness has taken place. Lou leaves her husband to check on Richie in his room; Ed is overcome with an attack of pain and collapses. This breakdown is registered by a thud on the film's soundtrack while we remain with a shot of Lou at Richie's door, turning around and towards the noise. A strange visual connection is made between her and the event of Ed's sudden collapse, an effect that is furthered as his attack cuts off the speech about the dullness of their existence which had so agitated his wife. As Thomas elucidates:

> Ed's devastating attack of pain after the bridge party – which leads to his hospitalisation – can be understood not just as the final surfacing of Ed's previously repressed resentment, but as a punishment directed towards him from the outside, that is, from Lou ... The idea that Lou wills Ed to fall gains further support by the throaty sensuality of her initial response – 'Ed?' – as she turns around after he has fallen, and the way she seems to savour the moment as she stands in the doorway for an instant, framed by the bedroom's darkness behind her, before remembering herself and rushing to his side, repeating his name in a more appropriately worried tone of voice.[8]

Revisiting Ray's lingering on the moment of Lou hesitating at the doorway reinforces the strength and persuasiveness of Thomas' reading. Of course, there is no suggestion that Lou *causes* Ed's collapses through force of will – such an event would certainly place the film as a far more extreme strand of fantasy film. Rather, an event taking place in reality coincides with a dark desire that Lou harbours, if only for a brief moment. The uncanniness of reality matching a character's fantasy is encapsulated in the strangeness of Lou's behaviour and the film's depiction of it. Her hesitation at the threshold of Richie's doorway equates to her hesitation between two responses to her husband's apparent breakdown: concern and anxiety for his wellbeing or relief and satisfaction at his enforced lapse into silence and stillness.

Ray's skill in bringing out the underlying tensions associated with Ed and Lou's interior, repressed fantasies makes fragile any claims for later, highly melodramatic, ruptures being solely caused by Ed's abuse of the cortisone. It is true that Ed's fantasies of his place within the world expand beyond any reasonable scale but, as Robin Wood makes clear in his account of the film, those delusions derive from a perspective he holds before the course of drugs is begun. Likewise, Lou's fantasy of Ed's absence from her life is revealed in slight details during his decline under the influence of the medication, such as when she tells Ed that he must stop taking the cortisone: a course of action that would lead to a worsening of his attacks and death. Inadvertently, Lou is once again wishing harm against her husband, just as she did *before* his cortisone-induced episode. Ray's depiction of his characters' troublesome and suppressed fantasies in the film's early stages also ensures that *Bigger Than Life*'s conclusion – ostensibly a happy ending – is made precarious and, we might contend, ironic. After suffering a massive attack after attempting to 'sacrifice' Richie, Ed wakes in a hospital bed with his family around him. Lou is to administer his medication from now on, and the doctors are satisfied that he has made a recovery from his psychosis as he realizes the harm he almost caused his son and is ashamed. They leave the room at Ed's request and, once outside, one of the doctors casually switches off a red emergency light to the side of the doorframe. This action signifies the end of their concern over Ed's mental health and reinforces the notion that they are satisfied a balance has been restored. Yet, the doctors place their judgement solely on the cortisone drug being under control in Ed's system. The film's projections of the characters' inner fantasies reveals tensions and disturbances that cannot be so conveniently fixed – as in the flicking of a light switch – and will continue to manifest themselves within the Avery's marriage. To accept the film's conclusion as a definitive resolution would involve blinding ourselves to the fundamental conflicts Ray draws attention to in his depiction of the couple's 'normal' everyday life together. The fantasies that Ed and Lou harbour are real and, potentially, destructive to their marriage. To believe that such profound discrepancies can be brushed away is to indulge in a fantasy that the film offers no tangible evidence to support.

Interior Fantasy as Reality

If *Letter from an Unknown Woman* and *Bigger Than Life* make the overlap between fantasy and reality a key implicit theme within their narratives, *Harvey* (Henry Koster, 1950) proposes such a connection as both explicit and fundamental to its fictional world.[9] The film tells the story of Elwood P. Dowd (James Stewart) who claims, quite casually, to have befriended a rabbit, standing at six-feet three-and-a-half inches tall, by the name of Harvey. This causes much consternation amongst his family – sister Veta (Josephine Hull) and niece Myrtle Mae (Victoria Horne) – and Veta elects to have Elwood committed to a sanatorium. After a series of complications, Elwood is due to receive an injection that will rid him of Harvey once and for all. However, by this point in the film we have been made aware that, far from simply being a figment of Elwood's imagination, Harvey exists – an invisible, magical entity described by Elwood as a 'pooka' (from the Celtic term Púca) – and this fact is communicated straightforwardly to us as he is seen to open and close doors. At the last minute, Veta hears from a cab driver how the injection can lead to a loss of innocence and wonder in patients, causing them to behave cynically and aggressively, and she pleads with Elwood not to have the injection: she wants him to remain as he is. We have been heavily persuaded throughout the film that her course of action is well chosen: Stewart's depiction of Elwood invests the character with a benign charm and geniality that forms the film's emotional centre. The performance builds on the actor's earlier accomplishments in films such as *Mr Smith Goes to Washington* (Frank Capra, 1939) and, particularly, *It's A Wonderful Life* (Frank Capra, 1946), which help to prepare the way for his portrayal of Elwood as an extraordinary man without agenda, personal ambition or any kind of dishonesty. As we witness the magic of his influence over others, raising their perceptions of themselves and each other, the prospect of *this* Elwood being lost to the world registers as a genuine loss. Veta's intervention prevents the injection being administered and so Elwood's relationship with Harvey is kept in place.

Until the point at which Harvey's presence is indicated by the opening and closing of two sets of doors, we might well be led to believe that the film is suggesting the six-foot rabbit to be Elwood's hallucination – a fantasy of his world caused by some of kind of mental illness. By making Harvey's existence real, the film creates a fantasy world in which such mysteries are a reality. And yet, at the film's conclusion only Elwood and the director of the sanatorium, Dr Chumley (Cecil Kellaway) are definitely able to see Harvey. Veta had earlier indicated, in a moment of private disclosure, that she occasionally thinks she catches glimpses of the rabbit (a confession that leads to her being mistakenly incarcerated in place of Elwood). But in a penultimate scene she only suspects that Harvey had hidden her coin purse, she cannot see whether he is responsible or not. In short, he is still invisible to her. This extends to every other character besides Elwood and Chumley, as no one else lays claim to sharing their vision. Proof of existence is therefore an inconsequential factor in the world's acceptance of Elwood's visions that leads to his release from the sanatorium. Chumley's associates, Dr Sanderson (Charles Drake) and Nurse Kelly (Peggy Dow), seem to have disbanded all concerns over Elwood's sanity or otherwise as they happily shake his hand when he departs. Indeed, these two make a group with Elwood and Veta against the more cynical Judge Gaffney (William H.

Lynn) when he suggests that Veta's actions are misguided and that she really wants rid of Harvey for good. In this visual composition, they form a united barrier against Gaffney's accusations, and his insistence upon a restoration of 'reality' proper, providing a background support to Veta when she passionately defends herself, her brother and a giant invisible rabbit: 'Well what's wrong with Harvey? If Elwood and Myrtle Mae and I want to live with Harvey, what is it to you? You don't even have to come around. It's our house!' Her words make clear the divide that is being erected: those who wish to stand alongside Elwood and those that would wish to rid the world of his apparent fantasies. None of the individuals that take their place beside Elwood in the defence of his fantasies has a proper sense of the truth: that Harvey really does walk among them, silent and invisible, seen and heard only by Elwood (and, latterly, Dr Chumley). The importance of separating fantasy from reality, of separating the visible from the invisible, has receded entirely so that Veta's unusual phrasing – 'If Elwood Myrtle Mae and I want to live with Harvey' – is not strange to anyone, even though it suggests that Harvey is a rightful inhabitant of their home, and that these family members should choose to live with him, rather than permitting 'him' to live with them. When Veta delivers the line 'It's our house', the clear implication is that she not only means her, Myrtle Mae and Elwood, but has added Harvey to that grouping: it is his house too. The power of Elwood's fantasy, for it is still a fantasy for everyone else (bar the absent Dr Chumley) has overwhelmed conventional logical thought and reason to the point of blissful obliteration. The effort to rid Elwood of his fantasy has allowed each character to see him properly, to see each other properly, and to form a temporary solidarity with one another. And so, through fantasy, the characters see the reality of their existence properly. This point is emphasized not only through Veta appreciating Elwood and insisting that he never change but also in Dr Sanderson and Nurse Kelly rediscovering their love for one another through Elwood's direct intervention (he persuades them to dance together earlier in the film) and even in spinster Myrtle Mae finding her romantic union with the hospital porter, Wilson (Jesse White), as a result of the latter pursuing her uncle. Without the knowledge that Elwood's vision is truth, the characters allow fantasy to co-exist with reality in their world, appreciating the value in its intersection. The film further insists that fantasy and reality are not easily distinguishable and, more specifically, that sanity and insanity can be easily confused. Hence, Veta is incarcerated in place of her brother by mistake and the head of sanatorium, Dr Chumley, shares the 'insane' Elwood's vision of a six-foot rabbit. This latter reversal of roles is made even more explicit when, in the process of describing his fantasy of a life in Akron with a pretty woman and a cold beer, Dr Chumley reclines on his psychiatrist's couch and Elwood sits attentively in the doctor's chair. Patient and physician effectively reverse their roles.

The conclusion to *Harvey* rests on the optimistic promise that, for the characters to whom Elwood forms an emotional bond, fantasy and reality are able to co-exist without concern. (Veta's slipping of Harvey's name into her family group illustrates the extent to which illusion can effortlessly become tangible fact.) The question of whether a fantasy can be proved as fact or not is left as an immaterial concern: the truth of Elwood's claims remains a suspended issue. Such an affirmative resolution clearly is not available in *Bigger Than Life* or *Letter from an Unknown Woman*, where the fantasies harboured by characters carry with them implicit threat and tragedy. In *Harvey*, Elwood is left to his fantasy (for that is what it is must be perceived as by all other than Dr Chumley) with benign support from his immediate community. And, within a logic of fantasy as reality that those other characters cannot be aware of, fantasy chooses Elwood again: Harvey elects to return to his friend, rather than Dr Chumley. As the truth of Harvey's existence becomes an incontrovertible fact for us, even as his physical appearance is still hidden from us, the fictional world is revealed as fantasy.

As a means of bringing together the issues raised and discussed in this chapter, it is useful to consider a film that I take to be a contemporary reversioning of the *Harvey* narrative: *Lars and the Real Girl* (Craig Gillespie, 2007). The film centres upon Lars Lindstrom (Ryan Gosling), an emotionally reticent man whose shy reclusiveness causes his immediate family and wider community degrees of concern. Their fears are not allayed, however, when, on declaring that he has a girlfriend, Lars introduces a mail-order life-sized mannequin named Bianca to them. When initially presenting her to his brother, Gus, (Paul Schneider) and sister-in-law, Karin, (Emily Mortimer), Lars first warns them that Bianca does not speak very much English and is wheelchair-bound, thus effectively explaining away her silence and stillness to them. Seeking guidance, Gus and Karin are advised by their local physician (Patricia Clarkson) to indulge Lars' delusion indefinitely until such time as he no longer needs to maintain the fantasy of Bianca. In the words of their doctor: 'Bianca's in town for a reason.' The exact catalyst for Lars' invention of Bianca is not provided, although during the course of the film he is seen to forge a closer bond with Gus and Karin, whereas before he purposely distanced himself from them, and also to take the first steps towards a romantic relationship with a co-worker, Margo (Kelli Garner). Previously physical contact with anyone caused Lars real physical pain but, in a key scene, he takes Margo's hand in his and holds it, sustaining the moment of touch and reaffirming the emotional evolution he experiences. These reversals indicate a lack in Lars' life up to this point and the film moves to a point of resolution when it becomes clear that he no longer needs his fantasy of Bianca, in no small part due to the relationships he has formed with those other characters during her time with him. Lars develops the story of her having a travel-related illness – an invention of the doctor's to monitor Lars' wellbeing without him knowing – and discloses, or rather invents, the fact that Bianca is dying to Gus and Karin. Eventually Bianca dies and, supported by Gus and Karin, Lars organizes her funeral. The film's last image is of Lars standing next to Margo at Bianca's graveside. They are alone and, before travelling back to the house, they agree to go for a walk. Thus Lars is seen to move on from his fantasy of Bianca to the reality of Margo.

Lars and the Real Girl presents an unusual and ambitious story centred upon the power of delusion and personal fantasy. It bears clear similarities to *Harvey* in terms of its depiction of a benign fantasist who is convinced that his vision of the world is correct. Unlike *Harvey*, however, the suggestion never emerges that Lars' view of events could in any way be accurate. The film settles upon a realistic tone that sets it apart from that earlier work and prevents it from becoming another version of *Mannequin* (Michael Gottlieb, 1987), which features the spectacle of an alluring shop dummy (Kim Cattrall) that really does come magically to life. But *Lars and the Real Girl* departs yet more emphatically from *Harvey* in terms of its community's response to a character's inconvenient and bizarre fantasy of their world. *Harvey* details Elwood's family's embarrassment and anxiety as they struggle to deal with his fantasy of a giant benevolent rabbit. As a result, Veta's eventual defence of Elwood and, indeed, Harvey possesses great dramatic emphasis as it represents a reversal of her previous overtly stated position. In *Lars and the Real Girl*, however, Lars' family and community elect to indulge the fantasy of Bianca to the extent that they make her a central element in the town's day-to-day life as she performs such activities as helping out in local stores, visiting children in hospital and sitting on the school board. To a great extent, Bianca is allowed to become a *functioning* member of the local community and, more extraordinarily, that community forms an emotional bond with her that resembles the love Lars feels for his invented girlfriend. Far from dismissing the notion that she can bring any quality to Lars' life, it becomes the case that Bianca brings significant qualities to theirs. As Nicole Markotic suggests: 'By introducing Bianca into his community, Lars escapes the need to avoid community contact and is able to present himself as "dating". It is almost as if *he* is taking care of *them* by getting this mail-order doll and treating it as his girlfriend.'[10]

The effect of this unanticipated affection for Bianca is a series of surprisingly tender moments as characters interact with the fact of her existence in Lars' life and in theirs. These instances are often understated or briefly held in the film. For example, Lars' brother Gus voices perhaps the greatest hostility to Bianca's presence but, on the night when it is established that she is 'ill' he gently opens the door to her room and checks on her. The action is entirely futile: there can be no possible change in Bianca's condition and furthermore she requires no vigil: she is lifeless to begin with. Yet, Gus' gesture demonstrates the extent to which a burgeoning love between Lars and his community has displaced rationality and reasoned logic. To illustrate this further, after Gus has checked on Bianca he even averts his eyes by letting his gaze drop to the floor, as though conscious that he is looking at another person while they sleep. Logic is temporarily displaced as Gus sees not a doll but a person due to Bianca's place in Lars' life. The fact of what Bianca is materially becomes irrelevant as the fact of what she can represent between people takes dominance. The film presents a poignant study of human compassion as it depicts a community embracing a fantasy for the sake of one of its members: Bianca is real to Lars, therefore she will be treated as real by everyone else. The force of this fantasy seems to overwhelm the community, however, as they grow to experience genuine feelings of affection and love for Bianca, in Markotic's terms, it is as though Lars' fantasy were taking care of them somehow. And so, when it emerges that Bianca is 'dying' – that Lars has invented her imminent death – we are presented with a short, slowly conducted montage of community members sharing the news with one another: sharing confusion, shock and sadness in the way that the news of a real death might be received. In this film, of course, the death is real: the death of Lars' fantasy of Bianca. The death of a fantasy is mourned. In common with *Letter from an Unknown Woman*, *Bigger Than Life* and *Harvey*, *Lars and the Real Girl* emphasizes the potential for personal desire and imagination to shape the conditions of a fictional world, to affect profoundly the attitudes and actions of its characters. In centring intensely affecting emotional scenes upon the absurd fantasy that Lars creates, the film illustrates the capacity for fantasy to take on powerful meaning in the lives of individuals and communities. As with the previous films discussed, drawing strong distinctions between fantasy and reality becomes only an exercise in futility. In *Lars and the Real Girl*, a community takes on one man's fantasy absolutely and completely, allowing it to shape their reality for the better. Fantasy *becomes* reality and when it is gone they mourn because the fantasy was real to them.

–6–

Fantasy, Style and Coherence

The Value of Coherence

This final chapter seeks to crystallize a notion that has underpinned a number of the debates taking place within the book: coherence within fantasy film. At a basic level, concepts of coherence have clear prescience in the context of fantasy films, given that these works attempt not only to compose a world that is conceivable but also to expand the boundaries of conceivability beyond the confines of ordinary experience. In this sense, they seek to shape a world that is credible from elements that are unfamiliar, strange and unrecognizable to us. The make-believe must still make sense. And yet, a series of critical and theoretical accounts outlined in this chapter propose coherence to be a more complex matter than simply whether something makes sense to us or not. Indeed, any stringent insistent upon absolute sense-making in film might carry with it certain risks and drawbacks. For example, we may dismiss a film that is difficult to comprehend in terms of plot structure but, when revisited and reviewed, emerges as a work of coherence and significance. Furthermore, we might be quick to discard films that are troubling, enigmatic and ambiguous based upon the assumption that they do not adhere to a clearly observable logic. On reflection, this seems to be a somewhat inadequate set of criteria for formulating value judgements, particularly in relation to fantasy cinema where trouble, enigma and ambiguity might be the very qualities that draw us to the films: the things that capture our interest and hold us. The counter position is to suggest that, when films propose new configurations of sense and reason, they must also find a way of establishing new coherent relationships within that arrangement, ensuring that creative audacity is matched by significance and meaning. Thus, the extent to which coherence is achieved within this narrative structure becomes a potential measure of the fantasy film's value, concurrently shaping our sense of its aesthetic achievement.

The criteria for achievement in film are not fixed, however, and different points of emphasis can emerge even across readings of the same film. As a consequence, it is neither desirable nor practical to offer one evaluative criterion as a universal marker of accomplishment in film. Nevertheless, it is also the case that a number of expressive critics and theorists have given prominence to the concept of 'coherence' in their accounts of cinema, and particularly in relation to notions of achievement. It is this theme that I wish to dwell upon here.

In one sense, coherence is a structural matter of overarching reliability that extends across narrative works of art. George Wilson has written usefully on this concept in relation to classical narrative structure, explaining that:

> The macrostructure of classical film narration does offer a guarantee of global reliability, a type of reliability that both presupposes and extends the shot-by-shot reliability of that which is directly shown. As in many other traditional forms of narration, there is a promise to depict a set of events, acts and situations which will turn out to have an internal *explanatory coherence*.[1]

Wilson proceeds to emphasize that this promise of 'explanatory coherence' is not tantamount to having every element of a film's fictional world explained to the point of redundancy and he makes the key distinction that 'No film narrative is solely a function of what, in some narrow sense, is literally shown on the screen.'[2] Nevertheless, explanatory coherence provides an assurance that individual moments within the narrative of a film combine to form (and conform to) a broader fictional world, the dramatic force of which is dependent upon the manner in which the film maker discloses those moments to us. In this way, and in relation to classical narrative particularly, an understanding exists between audience and film maker that an overarching coherent world is being adhered to, and so events are balanced and unified within that framing logic. This extends beyond linear stylistic concerns such as when a character is seen to enter the door of a building in exterior shot this is matched by an interior shot of them inside the building, to a more general understanding that a character's actions and attitudes are consistent with the potentials and possibilities of the fictional world they inhabit, so forming a coherent whole.[3]

In this formulation of coherence, our understanding of the complete work is intrinsically dependent upon the style in which certain details from a fictional world are portrayed for us, and so the particular and the general become inextricably related. Robin Wood's definition of coherence is instructive here, as he understands the term to mean 'the internal relations that give a work its structure.'[4] To return to Wilson's terminology, we might say that Wood's account emphasizes the relationship of the microstructure of elements within a film to the macrostructure of the film as a whole, and furthermore accentuates the interrelationships between elements of the microstructure that in turn form the whole. This notion of interacting elements within a film is continued by Gibbs in his work on *mise en scène* when he concludes, in relation to coherence, that: 'This paradigm has sometimes been described as organicism, because of its emphasis on an 'organic' relationship between the parts and the whole – that is, the relationship between elements in the admired artwork seems natural and mutually beneficial rather than being too obviously constructed or negatory. The whole formed is greater than the sum of its parts.'[5]

Gibbs progresses an understanding of coherence to incorporate a sense in which the interrelationship between elements within a film might be achieved with subtlety and dexterity, so that the resulting structure appears seamlessly formed and, indeed, organic. In this way, film making skill is closely associated with the achievement of coherence or organic unity within a work of art. This emphasis reminds us of the fact that the film maker attempts to create dramatic *significance* out of the elements she constructs, rather than striving only to create a work that is internally coherent. Here, we arrive at some of the concerns laid out by V. F. Perkins in *Film as Film*, a theoretical work central to concepts of coherence, credibility, balance and unity in film. One passage from the book describes in clear terms the creative dilemma facing the filmmaker: 'The movie is committed to finding a balance between equally insistent pulls, one towards credibility, the other towards shape and significance. And it is threatened by collapse on both sides. It may shatter illusion in straining after expression. It may subside into meaningless reproduction presenting a world which is credible but without significance.'[6]

Following Perkins' reasoning, we come to appreciate that coherence within a film is not simply a matter of the dramatic world making sense to us through the credible arrangement of elements. Rather, it involves a complex of significant relationships that conveys meaning in a style that is neither obtrusive nor over-assertive. As Perkins outlines: 'Meaning may exist without internal relationship; but coherence is the prerequisite of *contained* significance. By this I mean significance which we find within, rather than attached to, the form of the film.'[7] The relationship of coherence to significance is crucial if it is to have any value as a criterion at all. One can conceive of very limited and unambitious works that succeed emphatically on the grounds of making credible sense in terms of their internal dramatic structures but lack expressiveness, fluency or refinement in completing those aims. Indeed, as Perkins confirms elsewhere: 'Coherence is only interesting when it's an achievement, when you've actually managed to bind into one piece a range of different potentially conflicting [items of] eloquence.'[8] This assertion is useful as it helps to avoid making the assumption that there is a formula or set of criteria that a film maker can follow in order to achieve coherence in a work. The film maker may choose any element as a point of dramatic emphasis, but the challenge lies in establishing that emphasis without threatening the balanced unity of the fictional world as a whole: to retain the coherence of that constructed world whilst at the same time accenting a feature or features within it. On this theme, Gibbs provides a useful distinction between coherence across the work and coherence between the different elements of a single film moment.[9] That the coherence of a moment in a film is related fundamentally to the coherence of the work as a whole is clear and coherence is achieved precisely through the moment-by-moment progression of film art, as individual sequences link and interact to form the whole. The relationship between moments results in the patterning of representational strategies within a film, so that points of significance emerge, which, in combination, shape an understanding of the world depicted on screen. Again, to follow the contentions that Perkins and Gibbs raise in their accounts of coherence, such patterning requires careful handling if the film maker is to avoid certain elements protruding from the film's fictional world in an effort to assert their significance and meaning. Perkins addresses this in clear terms when he suggests that 'Asserted meanings, crude juxtapositions, tend to be both blatant and unclear, like over-amplified noises bellowing from a faulty loudspeaker.'[10] The notion of over-amplification succinctly encapsulates a failure on the part of the film maker to integrate meanings within the texture and patterning of the film as a whole, and so the unity of the fictional world is left unsatisfactorily balanced.

Perkins' interest in contained significance, 'which we find within, rather than attached to, the form of the film', furthermore presents a clear connection between the evaluation of coherence within a work of art and the methodology of close analysis. If significance is achieved within the internal structuring of a film's stylistic elements, then detailed reading of moments, sequences and scenes comes to represent a particularly apt means of judging the extent to which this is achieved. Crucially, Perkins views significance as emanating from the world of the film itself, rather than becoming reliant upon matters external to that world. Here, then, coherence depends upon the inner consistency of the fictional world and significance is achieved through the expressive arrangement of elements within that world by the film maker. Taken in this way, no external criteria that we bring to a film, whether based on broad social, historical or even theoretical knowledge, can lend coherence to a film's fictional world: it is reliant upon those meanings constructed and contained within that world on its own terms. In this way, close analysis of the medium is vital in determining the achievement of coherence within a particular film. The concentration upon the interaction of elements within a work of art encourages proximity between the critical viewer and the film itself, necessitating a heightened level of observance and engagement. In short, close attention is required so that the subtlety and complexity of a coherent work might be properly accounted for and judged.

Fracturing Coherence

Perkins gives a useful account of the issues surrounding internal relationships, coherence and credibility when discussing Alfred Hitchcock's *The Birds* (1963). Hitchcock's film, adapted from Daphne Du Maurier's novella of the same name, famously features a sustained attack on the residents of Bodega Bay by flocks of malevolent birds. Hitchcock, in characteristic style, heightens the tension of the birds' apparent maliciousness by building upon small, seemingly isolated incidents, until we reach the point of outright violence committed against humans in swathes. Perkins offers a series of pertinent comments on the spectacle of the birds attacking Bodega Bay:

> A very basic demonstration of the two levels of credibility is provided by Hitchcock's *The Birds*. On the first level, we can make no difficulty about the fact that the feathered

kingdom is seen to declare war on humanity. That is given. But it is also given that the attackers are ordinary, familiar birds. Nothing in our experience or in the film's premises permits them to develop intermittent outlines of luminous blue as they swoop, or to propel themselves in a manner that defies the observable laws of winged flight.[11]

Perkins' points here outline a central undermining of the film's point of emphasis, effect and, indeed, horror: that the force attacking those residents of Bodega Bay is an ordinary facet of everyday life. As with so many Hitchcock films, the power of this fact lies in its implication that danger and violence can emerge precisely from the benign and the familiar. In Perkins' terms, however, the effect is compromised not only by the appearance of the birds exceeding the boundaries of that ordinariness but also in that their luminous outlines and impossible propulsion should occur unprompted by anything signalled in the film's story. The premise that birds can attack humans is perfectly acceptable within the film's fictional propositions but the further supernatural aspects to their appearance and behaviour, due to special effects, are not motivated in the same way, and so they risk becoming incoherent features within the film's expression of its ideas. How the film handles such elements within its framing narrative logic therefore becomes a compelling matter.

Perkins' assertions are of interest as they speak directly to notions of coherence in fantasy film. Hitchcock gives us the fantasy of a world in which ordinary birds attack people, but that fantasy is potentially undermined – or a least risks losing its full effect – through a series of visual aberrations. In Perkins' description, it is clear that we cannot reject a film's fantasy out of hand, as in 'the fact that the feathered kingdom is seen to declare war on humanity' but that, having accepted such a fantasy, we reasonably anticipate a film to behave according to the rules of the fantasy it proposes. From this we can appreciate that, regardless of the audacity or ambition of the fantasy set in place, it is paramount that a film maker works to preserve the coherence – the 'inner consistency' – of the fictional world she depicts on screen. Perkins sums this up eloquently when he explains that: 'As an illusion-spinning medium, film is not bound by the familiar, or the probable, but only by the conceivable. All that matters is to preserve the illusion.'[12]

The attributes of the birds' appearance and flight in Hitchcock's film are technical issues that threaten the consistency of the fantasy being proposed. In striving to convince the viewer that an attack by 'the feathered kingdom' could occur in this fictional world, the film inadvertently introduces visual elements – special effects – that may cause us to doubt the conceivability of such an occurrence. How far this affects our sense of the film's value is a matter to be weighed against the achievements of *The Birds* as a whole work. It may well be the case that such inconsistencies in the representation of its narrative world carry less significance when taken in combination with the overall accomplishments of Hitchcock's film. This view would certainly seem to be supported by the strong body of favourable critical work on *The Birds*.[13] We may find the difficulties over the special effects employed to represent the birds' movement and demeanour are features that demonstrate Hitchcock's creative ambition, but elements upon which he was unable to fully exert his characteristic directorial authority. As Perkins points out, 'it was scarcely Hitchcock's fault if his movie's central hypothesis was weakened by the fallibility of Special Effects.'[14] In turn, Hitchcock's reputation as a director is perhaps enhanced through such a discussion.

If we can excuse the difficulties of visual representation in *The Birds* as unrepresentative of the film's overall achievements, it is also the case that certain films seek to wilfully rupture the coherence of their fictional by, for example, introducing fantasy into a world otherwise bereft of such elements. We saw this in the brief discussion of *You Only Live Once* and *Anita and Me* in Chapter 1 but in both of those cases explanations were sought for the significance of such departures within the films' overall sets of intentions and ambitions. Furthermore, within such explanations, it was proposed implicitly that the films' fictional worlds were not necessarily thrown out of balance by the intrusion of the impossible. Jia Zhangke's *Still Life/San Xia Hao Ren* (2006) pursues a different direction in its handling of fantasy within a fictional reality.[15] The film takes place in the city of Fengjie, which is due to be flooded as part of the massive Three Gorges Dam project. We follow the story of Han Sanming (a character sharing the name of the actor playing him) as he searches for his estranged daughter, and then an unrelated story of Shen Hong (Zhao Tao) who is searching to find her estranged husband. The film returns to Han's story in its conclusion. The film is shot entirely on location and blends professional and non-professional actors. These features, along with a style reminiscent of Italian neo-realism, suggest a work attempting a sincere connection with the reality the people of Fengjie experience. And yet, two unprompted and inexplicable events threaten to tear through this fabric of reality.[16] Firstly, in the cross over between Han and Shen's stories, a travelling object is seen glinting in the overcast sky. It is first seen as Han stares out across the lake (we do not see whether he notices its) and, as the object comes more clearly into view through its forward propulsion, we see that it is a conventional depiction of a UFO: a glowing, shiny craft travelling smoothly through the sky and emitting only a quiet, low humming. As the camera tracks the left-to-right trajectory of its progress, we cut from the scene with Han to a new scene where Shen is seen similarly looking out over a lake. The UFO continues its progress in this new shot, and Shen appears to notice it, turning her head and body to trace its progress before it disappears behind nearby hills. The second interruption to the film's realist style occurs when, in a later scene, Shen stands on a balcony at night, hanging an item of clothing on a line. She pauses and then walks out of shot to the left. As she departs, an unusual-looking building in the immediate background of the scene slowly rises into the sky, 'lifting off' in a cloud of orange flame and smoke like a space shuttle. This goes unnoticed by any character, and no further explanation for the event is offered.

The insertion of computer-generated images into an otherwise naturalistic aesthetic treatment registers with a jolt, especially on first viewing. Have we seen what we think we have seen? What are we to make of these excursions into fantasy? The director himself makes a case for these instances constituting allegorical expressions of central issues within the film's narrative. Jia explains:

> People tend to think that moving will bring them greater happiness and prosperity, but then they usually find themselves trapped anew. The UFO that appears in the film is an allegory of happiness: it's as elusive as their dreams of benefitting from the 'great changes' ... With the speeding up of the transformation process, especially in the last two years, many aspects of Chinese life have become absurd, surreal. I used the special effects precisely because my conversations with friends kept turning to how unreal things had become. The monument that flies off was designed by a classmate of [prominent Chinese artist] Liu Xiaodong's. That means that our generation is implicated in the absurdity too; we can't just blame the older generation! The people there explained to me that its shape is based on the Chinese written character 'Hua' – which means both 'China' and 'flowering.' I took one look at it and thought it was just begging to fly off.[17]

As a means of expressing the emptiness of change and the growing sense of surrealism in Chinese life, Jia's depiction of the Unidentified Flying Object and launching building represent ambitious and highly precarious creative choices. In one sense, the boldness of his strategy might be an effective way to engage audiences with the issues he wishes to foreground, making them consider the meaning of the two events due to their violent break from the diegetic texture of the film. It might be that the viewer will arrive at the same points the director wishes to make regarding transition and change in contemporary China. However, Jia also shatters the reality of his film in order to achieve this effect, which may create an effect so perplexing that it renders the events impenetrable to interpretation: we struggle to make sense of his creative choices within the film's internal logic. In this way, we might be led to suggest that Jia imposes meaning onto the scenes through his inclusion of those extraordinary and unmotivated events, rather than allowing meaning to emerge from the film's internal structures. In Perkins' terms, these might well be viewed as examples of asserted meanings. The effect of the UFO, particularly, is made more complicated by the fact that Shen sees it and watches its progress across the sky. Here, we are led to believe that the UFO is not only an allegorical symbol inserted by the director, but also representative of a world in which UFOs exist and can be seen by its inhabitants. Are we to understand this to be a world like ours, which we take to be reality, or a world once removed, which we would define as fantasy? The question remains tantalizingly open and unresolved in the film, which may excite or frustrate. If nothing else, Jia's creative choices demonstrate the fragility of coherence within fiction films and, whatever conclusions we reach about the balance he strikes between directorial statement and integral credibility, it is certainly the case that the director forcefully and irreparably shatters the reality of his world in an effort to make his points.

Expressive Relationships

Whereas *Still Life* introduces CGI elements that threaten the inner consistency and coherence of its fictional world, Nicholas Roeg's *Don't Look Now* (1973) by contrast establishes the strange coherence of its world precisely through a pattern of inexplicable relationships created through the fragmented style of its opening sequence.[18] As its central dramatic impetus, the scene depicts a young girl, Christine (Sharon Williams), drowning in a small pond in the grounds of her family home. Her father (John Baxter, played by Donald Sutherland) rushes out of the house and attempts to save her, but his efforts are in vain: he pulls her out of the water but she is dead in his arms. Roeg captures the horrific trauma of this event: he withholds Christine's fall into the water until the moment of her sinking below its surface, dreadfully peaceful in slow motion, and draws out a brutal, raw performance from Sutherland as John desperately attempts to save his child. When he emerges from the pond clutching her lifeless body to his, the film moves to slow motion again, capturing in terrible detail John's anguish. The scene continues as we watch him awkwardly trying to breathe life into her little body – wet mud clinging to their clothes, pondweed tangling in their hair – and then pick her up, stumbling and groaning as his grief swells and threatens to overpower his very being. The ordeal is only ended (for us at least) when John's wife Laura (Julie Christie) emerges from the house and, looking casually in their direction, catches sight of this appalling spectacle. Her scream violently pierces the soundtrack, continuing into the next scene and merging with the sound of a drill being operated, as though the power of her reaction transcends the boundaries of space and time.

As an opening sequence, Roeg's introduction is both powerful and shocking. As a film undergraduate ten years ago I found the scene disturbing; as a father now I find it almost unbearable. Little wonder that this film is often regarded as a masterpiece of British horror cinema, for here is an attempt in its first moments to depict the horror of a child's death in unflinching detail. In thinking about *Don't Look Now* in the context of fantasy film, I want to dwell upon the ways in which this opening section of the film encapsulates the nature of its fictional world, and how a series of apparently inexplicable relationships in the framing and editing of the sequence can be seen to function coherently in establishing the terms of that world. Roeg arranges a succession of enigmatic audiovisual resonances that lend an uncanny tone to events, suggesting connections existing beyond our understanding of ordinary life. Such resonances are slight, but significant. The director includes a number of shots at the beginning of the sequence showing Christine's reflection on the surface of the pond as she moves around it, as though somehow pre-empting the moment when she will be fatally submerged in its waters. As John views slides of a Venetian church indoors, his eye is drawn to a figure seated in the pews, faced away from the camera and dressed in a red hooded mackintosh that closely resembles the one Christine is wearing outside. The film makes an explicit connection between these two individuals by cutting from a close-up of the red-robed figure in the slide to Christine outside, creating a visual resemblance by matching their size within the frame. Immediately afterwards, a close-up of Christine's foot splashing in a puddle is followed by her brother Johnny (Nicholas Salter) riding over a pane of glass, shattering an equivalent reflective surface, and back in the house their father looks up momentarily from his work, as though disturbed. When Laura gestures that she wants a cigarette by putting her hand to her mouth, we cut to a matching image of her daughter replicating the gesture outside, as though mirroring her mother without seeing her. John's throwing of a cigarette packet to his wife follows Christine throwing a ball into the air: the two characters brought together in a shared act. John knocks over a glass of liquid after his throw, and we cut to Christine's ball landing with a splash in the pond: impact and water brought together in both events. John's spilt drink has caused the red of the hooded figure in the slide to run, and so a pool of scarlet ink forms and oozes across the image. He looks up from the slide with an expression of alarm and profound concern, which clearly extends beyond the potential ruining of the image he was viewing. We cut to a shot of Johnny running towards the house and then back to John's face, as though this were somehow, impossibly, his point of view. John seems to follow this vision and leaves the house with increasing urgency. We cut to an overhead shot of Christine disappearing beneath the surface of the water – is this a view that John also shares somehow? When he finally finds his daughter and pulls her from the pond, we cut to another overhead shot of the two, her lifeless body curled around his as he holds her. We cut to the image of the slide again, where the bleeding red has formed into a curve that mirrors the shape of Christine's body in her father's arms. The red of the slide and the red of Christine's body in her mackintosh is further mirrored in the blood that flows from Johnny's finger – he has cut himself on a shard of glass caught in his bike tyre – and an arrangement of red flowers visible behind Laura's head when she finally arrives at the scene, still in frame when she screams. Even the image of the drill, whose sound her scream becomes merged with, has a red section on its body, as though the stain of Christine's death spreads far beyond the Baxter's home.

The series of visual resonances that Roeg establishes through his framing and editing introduces an ominous tone to the opening, suggesting that there is a reactive logic at work that we cannot properly understand. Are the resemblances coincidental or is a fundamental pattern of choreographed circumstance at work here? These questions are pursued throughout the film. When, some time after Christine's death, Laura and John make the acquaintance of two mysterious ladies, Heather (Hilary Mason) and Wendy (Clelia Mantania), in Venice, we are left to speculate on whether Heather can 'see' the Baxters' dead daughter sitting with her parents in a restaurant. The matter is complicated as certain facts are given by her – the colour of Christine's hair and the red coat – but only Laura believes Heather's claim to be true. However, it is the sceptical John who appears to possess extrasensory perception, a fact that culminates in him catching sight of his own funeral barge at one point in the film (although he naturally does not recognize it as such). And so, when he repeatedly sees a red-coated figure appearing in the backstreets of Venice, we are perhaps encouraged to believe that he sees his dead daughter. In fact, the figure turns out to be a serial killer who brutally murders John at the film's conclusion.

The strange psychic resemblances that the film establishes visually in its opening minutes index a coherence particular to *Don't Look Now*'s fictional world. Making sense of its world involves acknowledging that visual relationships take their place as part of a clairvoyant force that runs through the film, but a clairvoyance that is uncontained, disordered and tragic. John sees his daughter's peril too late to stop her; Heather sees John's death too late to keep him from it. The unsettling peculiarity of the connections Roeg makes between events is suggestive of a world that is like ours but significantly altered, whereby psychic powers exist and are experienced by individuals. A world of fantasy. And so the relationships between certain visual elements in the film's opening moments represent coherence innate to the film's fictional world, and become significant as an indicator of the underlying forces guiding the characters. For Christine and John, these forces drive them to their deaths, and so the film becomes saturated with a mood of stifling grief and mourning. Even Venice looks dead. Psychic ability is not represented as a quality that can prevent disaster and save, but instead a frustrating and unwieldy power that cannot be harnessed advantageously. It can only reveal the world's connections and coherences in retrospect. Premonitions of death permeate the film's narrative, but characters lack the power to act upon those visions and, instead, they only underscore an inevitable pattern of fate and fatality.

Watership Down (Martin Rosen, 1978) shares with *Don't Look Now* an interest in psychic episodes and motifs of death. The film is an animation, charting the troubled progress of a group of rabbits as they struggle to find a new home after the destruction of their warren. At a basic level, *Watership Down* needs to convince an audience of its fantasy that a group of rabbits are able to talk, plan, reflect, deceive, show loyalty, act courageously and even, in the case of Fiver (voiced by Richard Bryers), experience premonitions. Against the backdrop of film animations featuring anthropomorphic talking animals stretching back decades, with Disney a notable contributor, perhaps this pressure wasn't greatly felt by the film makers. And yet, the film insists upon its fantasy as a reality with a degree of inventiveness and economy. Again, as with *Don't Look Now*, it is a question of the fictional parameters the film establishes in its opening moments. *Watership Down* begins with a stylized, abstract animation depicting the evolution of the animal kingdom from the dawn of time. The sequence tells of how a God, Frith, made the world and all of the creatures within it. The story focuses on El-ahrairah, prince of the rabbits, whose people multiply and run out of control, eating the food of other animals. When El-ahrairah refuses to control the rabbits, Frith punishes him by transforming the other animals into fierce creatures and bestowing upon them a desire to hunt and kill the rabbits. But Frith also gives to El-ahrairah and his kin an ability to run faster than any other creature and an alertness that would allow them to escape their hunters. The stylized opening sequence ends with this status quo in place, and laid out in Frith's words: 'All the world will be your enemy, prince with a thousand enemies, and whenever they catch you, they will kill you. But first they must catch you ...'

The animation in this sequence is unsophisticated, line drawn, self-consciously cartoonish in its two dimensionality. It has a child's picture-book quality, a feature complemented by the casting of Michael Horden as Frith, his voice recognizable as that of the excellent narrator of the British *Paddington Bear* television series for children (first broadcast in 1975). Furthermore, there is a simplicity and thematic neatness to the language of this opening section that matches the animation style and suggests it to be the reading of a straightforward genesis fable for children, much like a Bible story adapted for a young audience. Like those Bible stories, however, some of the violence is unavoidably retained, and so the ferociousness of the other animals and the eternal plight of the rabbits are not concealed from the telling. Once the story is ended, we cross-fade from the depiction of the beaming sun god Frith to a watercolour image of green meadows with flowers tottering in the foreground of the frame. The abstract depiction of Frith is replaced by a realistic portrait of a real sun, low hanging in a hazy sky and, as the camera pulls out and pans left, a similarly realistic tree marks a contrast with the stylized forests of the opening animation. This new state is also a hand-drawn animation, but the attempt at naturalistic depiction marks it out as a reality in comparison to the abstract drawings of the previous section. This simulating of the natural world will endure throughout the film as an effort is made to not only represent the visual appearance of nature and animals accurately but also to lay bare, with some force, the brutality of the animal kingdom and the violence that takes place between its members. The transition between the non-naturalistic style of animation in the film's prologue and the naturalistic rendering of the fields, trees, sun and flowers is crucial in proposing the latter state as a reality, as opposed to the story book depiction inherent in the former. Although both sequences are animated, the opening section announces itself as animation far more blatantly, drawing attention to its craft and construction, whereas what follows conceals the fact of its animation, instead attempting a close depiction of reality. Here, then, the rest of the film is designated as a fictional reality, and the fantasy of talking animals is subdued as it takes place in a more 'realistic' context than the opening prologue, which was clearly marked as a fantasy of creation.

The prologue also provides a frame of fantasy for the film's reality, preparing for the fantastic interventions that occur from time to time later in the narrative. When Fiver psychically predicts imminent doom for the colony, he sees the fields turn blood-red and the black shadows of the trees extend ominously. The images seem to close in on him as the tree branches become a tangled mass of confused shapes until they spin and form a circle, closely resembling the pulsating image of Frith from the film's prologue. Later, when it seems as though his brother, Hazel (voiced by John Hurt) might be dead, Fiver follows a vision of El-ahrairah, prince of the rabbits, mentioned in the opening sequence, which leads him to Hazel. The course of this journey is marked by Fiver experiencing a series of abstract dream-like visions in which objects become vivid, two-dimensional hallucinations that merge and fall apart to become impressionistic patterns and shapes. Often the shapes combine to form a representation of a sun, again echoing the earlier depiction of Frith. This detail, combined with the appearance of El-ahrairah and the overall stylization of Fiver's visions, ties the sequence together with the prologue's tone and form. The interjections of an abstract animation style into the naturalistic 'real' world of the film is suggestive of Fiver having innate access to the elements of fantasy described in the opening sequence: a god called Frith, a prince called El-ahrairah, and a prophecy that guides the fate of all rabbits. And so two layers of fantasy emerge in *Watership Down*: the fantasy of rabbits exhibiting human behavioural traits, and a spiritual fantasy of gods and apparitions that are channelled into the characters' immediate reality through Fiver's psychic vision.

As the visions of a spiritual realm are exclusively experienced by Fiver, we might find cause to doubt their reliability, given their close stylistic association with his point of view at times. This argument would involve regarding his accurate premonitions as coincidental luck: he predicts the demise of the original colony, he finds the injured Hazel and, later, he senses that a dog is on the loose. However, even if we were to accept this sceptical position, the film's conclusion makes it clear that Fiver's spiritual episodes are genuine: that he glimpses a divine kingdom existing beyond the world he inhabits. Hazel, in his old age, is visited by the spirit of El-ahrairah, taking the form that Fiver saw earlier, and is invited to join him. Hazel lies down in the grass and breathes his last. His spirit leaves his body and he runs through the air with El-ahrairah, the two finally disappearing together in the sky, hidden by the sun's glare, which we might take to indicate their joining Frith, the rabbit's sun god. Here, then, the film secures its portrayal of an animated reality in which rabbits exhibit the intellectual traits of humans, and where a world beyond – a world of the dead – can be glimpsed and, ultimately, passed into. By establishing this as a plausible reality in its opening moments, *Watership Down* binds together fantasy and coherence within its fictional world.

Scale and Significance

Peter Jackson's *The Lord of the Rings Trilogy* (2001–3) places spatial coherence as a central concern in its narrative, making use of geographical relationships in order to tie together and integrate disparate storylines. As David Butler points out:

> *The Lord of the Rings* films are packed with reference points which aid the spatial orientation of the spectator. Throughout *The Return of the King* [the final film in the trilogy] there is an outstanding attention to geographical detail and spatial consistency,

which is essential if key elements of the narrative's multiple strands are to realise their dramatic potential. Space is crucial to *The Lord of the Rings* – we need to have a clear sense of the expansive landscapes at work and the distances between the significant landmarks in order to fully appreciate the heroic tasks being undertaken.[19]

In these terms, coherence is a familiar matter of the world making sense to us, of its arrangement giving clarity to the dramatic impetus of the story. In the case of *The Lord of the Rings*, the actions of characters are not only followed but also *plotted*, as Jackson places an emphasis upon distances and proximities for dramatic effect. The films are successful here in mapping the space of their world to provide a coherent sense of its dimensions and scales. Many examples of this exist in the films, but of particular note is the lighting of the beacons sequence in *The Return of the King*.[20] Within the film's narrative, this moment signals a climax to the question of whether the kingdom of Rohan will aid the kingdom of Gondor, laid under siege by the massed forces of Mordor. When the beacon is lit in Gondor, a request is made for Rohan's help, and a line is traced across a series of mountain ranges as beacons are lit in sequence, beginning at Gondor and ending at Rohan. Here, the expanse of Middle Earth is shaped into a series of linear spatial relationships, as a path is literally traced in fire from one summit to the next. We gain a sense of the distance and also the terrain that separates Rohan from Gondor, mapping their relationship to one another. An actual drawn map of Middle Earth is in fact provided in editions of Tolkien's books, from which the films are adapted, and Jackson's attention to the spatial coherence of this world performs an equivalent function, allowing us to appreciate its geography and navigate between different strands of narrative action. On this theme, Kirsten Moana Thompson notes that:

> Throughout the many journeys across Middle Earth, repeated zoom-out, aerial and high angle photography, and extreme long shots punctuate the beginnings and endings of each narrative sequence as the fellowship move from one kingdom to the next. All through the trilogy, topography and maps are central in demonstrating the progress of the fellowship ... but also in orientating the viewer to the fellowship's spatial placement in the furtherance of this narrative goal.[21]

As Moana Thompson suggests, it is the case that this attention to spatial relationships translates into a succession of aerial shots that sweep over landscapes and place a prominence on the spectacle of sheer scale at work in the film. The magnitude of natural features such as mountains, forests and vast plains as well as manufactured landmarks such as towering structures of stone and metal is emphasized as the camera passes along their surfaces, capturing their enormity and vastness. The films skilfully integrate location shooting in New Zealand with CGI landscapes to create a consistent fictional world through a balanced visual style. One of the particular pleasures when watching the films (and one that I would suggest endures beyond an initial viewing) is the spectacle of viewing a world from above, at speed, with apparently limitless freedom of movement and vision. This exhilarating effect is intensified by composer Howard Shore's grandiose orchestral scoring of such moments, providing a sensation of elevation in both sight and sound. Freed from the restraints of ordinary human movement (by means of a camera positioned within a helicopter in these instances) we occupy an empowered position over the fictional world we survey, seeing it stretch out before us in a size and range unavailable to the characters that occupy it. Or most characters, at least. For the roving camera also bears a resemblance to the piercing glare of Sauron, the film's principal antagonist, who takes the form of a giant eye surrounded in flame, able to focus on any area of Middle Earth at will. As Saruman (Christopher Lee), a powerful wizard and servant of Sauron, describes at a point early in *The Fellowship of the Ring*, the first film of the series: 'Sauron has regained much of his former strength. He cannot yet take physical form, but his spirit has lost none of its potency. Concealed within his fortress, the lord of Mordor sees all. His gaze pierces cloud, shadow, earth and flesh.' Ultimate power, in Saruman's terms, is dependent upon ultimate sight – the ability to survey the world without borders or barriers. As we swoop and glide over the world's surface by means of Jackson's mobile camera, we become temporarily aligned with that power, sharing in Sauron's ability to see Middle Earth spread out before him, its occupants reduced to mere specks moving across its terrains.

The relating of Sauron's awesome visual command to the spectacle of the films' aerial cinematography might be regarded as a difficult aesthetic detail, creating an uncomfortable union between the style in which events are presented to us and the narrative's central villain. We could be led to say that Jackson's desire to show the magnitude and splendour of the world he has created is at odds with the films' insistence upon limitless vision being equated to despotic power. And yet, these films also give weight to the notion of broad-spanning, unfettered vision being essentially fallible, leading to a paradoxical failure of insight into the minutiae of the world. There is a consistent attention to the potential for small actions and details to carry great narrative weight. It is precisely these less pronounced aspects that can become lost in the scale and magnitude of the aerial shots and, indeed, in Sauron's view of the world. The miniature may be regarded as trivial or insignificant given the grandeur of Middle Earth's landscapes and structures, but such trivialities exercise a dramatic impact on the shape and progression of narrative events. An example can be found in a sequence from *The Fellowship of the Ring* where Saruman has imprisoned Gandalf (Ian McKellen), a heroic but as yet less powerful wizard, in the uppermost turret of his immense fortress. An aerial camera moves across the fortress' territory, which has been plundered and opened up into cavernous subterranean factories dedicated to the manufacture of an army to serve Sauron. (My description here is based upon an understanding of these objects existing within the film's fictional world whereas, of course, the extensive use of CGI in such sequences means that such sights do not derive from the real world, but are created. A camera therefore does not exist above the scene in the conventionally physical sense. Moana Thompson provides a strong discussion of the technical aspects of the film's aesthetic spectacle in her chapter 'Scale, Spectacle and Movement: Massive Software and Digital Special Effects in *The Lord of the Rings.*')[22] As we pass across this landscape, we are presented with a view into that immense underground fissure, glimpsing colossal struts and stairways, huge heavy machinery, the glow of furnaces and endless numbers of workers dedicated to the operation of this industrial monstrosity that has been carved into the rock. Views such as this one take their place in the film's dedication to spectacular display, the extreme height encouraging us to marvel at the multitudinous layers of activity that make up this vast scene.

As the camera continues to travel, however, a small moth flutters into shot, high above the heat and action below, and continues its journey from right to left, matching the panning movement of the camera. The industrial sounds of metal on metal and roaring furnaces are left behind as the moth makes its way higher, a single soprano voice becoming the central focus of the soundtrack, the strident orchestral rhythms softening into a more subdued arrangement. As the top of Saruman's tower comes into shot, we realize that this moth is making a purposeful journey: to Gandalf. We arrive at the bedraggled, exhausted wizard as he looks up, catches the moth delicately in the cradle of his palm and whispers to it before letting it fly free. The moth sails into the air, but we are dragged down further and further along the fortress walls and into the fiery trenches below until we reach a red-hot blade being hammered vigorously on an anvil: a virtuoso display of the camera's unbridled movement and the dedication to scale and depth in these films. The mass exhibition of labour and industry is contrasted with the slight, fragile appearance of the moth: a natural element existing in contrast to the brutal manipulation of an organic environment. If the film did not make its progress so pronounced by tracing the moth's flight in close-up, changing the tenor of the soundtrack, and having Gandalf communicate with the winged creature, it is a detail that would surely be lost in the frenetic commotion of the scene. It will emerge in the course of the narrative that the moth leads to Gandalf's rescue from the fortress tower on the back of a giant eagle: the tiny insect was a messenger.

This pattern of small details leading to larger consequences is a central motif in the three films, realized most emphatically perhaps in Sauron's defeat at the hands of 'halfling' Hobbits or, indeed, in the fact that the future of an entire world rests upon a delicate band of gold: 'One ring to rule them all.' It is significant that Sauron's gaze should miss the Hobbit's progress as they deliver the ring to Mount Doom and destroy it, causing his ultimate demise. Just as the progress of the moth takes place amongst the chaos of Saruman's kingdom – a detail likely to go unnoticed – so the two small figures of the Hobbit pass beneath the range of Sauron's eye among the chaos of war. Sauron's concentration upon widespread domination prompts him to view the world on a grand scale, taking in vast landscapes, armies and kingdoms. Yet, as the sequence involving the moth and the fiery pit emphasizes, such a broad perspective risks overlooking slight details that, over time, have drastic ramifications. The aerial shots of Middle Earth replicate Sauron's overarching sight, but they also emphasize the limitations of that vision: the extent to which the importance of smaller elements might easily be missed. And, of course, a distanced, sweeping view does not appreciate the subtle loyalties and friendships that exist between characters – qualities that allow them to complete their quests. The moth's bond with Gandalf is made clear as it orchestrates his escape from Saruman's clutches; likewise, it is Sam's (Sean Astin) profoundly strong friendship with fellow Hobbit Frodo (Elijah Wood) that finally secures the delivery of the ring into Mount Doom. Sauron's ruthless perspective holds little interest in such details, just as the sweeping aerial shots are unable to pick them out, and so they remain hidden from sight. But it is these subtle alliances that will provide the foundations for the characters' victory over a colossal force. And such alliances are often captured in pared-down, less frenetic passages with the camera settled as it records the intricacies of character interaction. An example of this occurs in *The Return of the King* when Sauron's armies are about to break the defences of Gondor and swarm into the kingdom. Jackson places, in the midst of this struggle, a quiet conversation between Gandalf and Peregrin Took (Billy Boyd) regarding the existence of an afterlife, Gandalf's words bringing comfort to the Hobbit in the face of war and likely death. The sounds of battle are diminished and the film adopts a conventional shot-reverse-shot pattern to complement the pace and quality of the two actor's words, with McKellen's performance delivering particular impact. Once their conversation is ended, we are swept back into the chaos of battle but, for a moment, we appreciate the friendship, respect and trust that has grown between the two characters. There is no grandiose spectacle here but, without such moments, the allegiances that lead these individuals towards victory would surely not be felt so strongly by us.

Rather than seeing the films as being blindly obsessed with capturing the magnitude and grandeur of a created Middle Earth, a notion alluded to by Butler as he describes the '(sometimes excessive) elaborate helicopter shots',[23] we might suggest that the *Lord of the Rings* trilogy sets up a series of contrasts in size and scale, combining highly structured aerial photography with a quieter, more subdued, style to bring out those differences. In this way, the films insist upon the existence of a broad, overarching perspective alongside a more intricate, focused understanding of the world. Furthermore, it proposes that the small, humble and seemingly insignificant elements are inextricably connected to the grander scale, taking a role of great significance in the shaping of events. In many respects, this becomes a defining theme within the trilogy and, as Moana Thompson points out, 'These contrasts are epitomized by the culminating scene in *The Return of the King* when Aragorn [Viggo Mortensen] and the city of Minas Tirith bow to the Hobbits for saving them ("My friends, you bow to no-one").'[24] Here, then, the value of diminutive stature and scale is made emphatic.

Through a few varied examples, this chapter has sought to demonstrate the ways in which coherence within fantasy films is not simply a matter of those works making sense in terms of narrative progression and orientation, but rather how significance is achieved through the expressive presentation and arrangement of elements within their worlds. As I have indicated earlier in this chapter, such concerns can be seen to branch out across the whole of fiction cinema, but I would again contend that these issues have a particular importance in understandings of fantasy film. The parameters of reasonable expectation are set especially wide in fantasy, and our willingness to accept the strange and the magical is perhaps heightened. Yet, these facts bring with them a responsibility on the filmmaker's part to handle those elements and shape them into a work of significance, creating not only a work of fantasy, but of fantasy that matters.

Conclusion

What is fantasy film? This study has sought to provide at least some answers to that question by tracing a series of central themes and issues through the course of its chapters. The breadth of topics covered in this investigation is indicative of the diversity we might find to be inherent in fantasy film. Beginning with Fritz Lang's *You Only Live Once* and ending with Peter Jackson's *The Lord of the Rings* trilogy, the multifariousness of fantasy in the cinema has been at the centre of any conclusions reached within the book. It is certainly the case that its extraordinary range can make the subject of fantasy somewhat unwieldy, perhaps even intangible to those wishing to articulate its merits. Indeed, it may well be the case that the concerns represented in these chapters are simply ways of keeping fantasy in temporary focus, containing aspects in order for certain assertions to be made regarding its nature and potential. But that attempt is only ever achieved for a moment, as fantasy is always in flux.

If we are to avoid the elusiveness of fantasy causing frustration and throwing us into critical silence, we might embrace the fact that fantasy takes on a broad spectrum of forms in film and that any discussion will only account for some of those incarnations. There is always more to say, and different things to say about the matters discussed here. One of the key advantages of fantasy film's divergent forms, it would seem to me, is that they open up especially wide opportunities for debate to take place from a variety of critical perspectives and investments. This is a process that is sure to continue and develop, with new voices adding themselves to the discussion and providing new insights. To my mind, this encapsulates some of the vibrancy and vitality of fantasy film, its ever-changing, ever-shifting nature constituting a key attraction and excitement. Related to this is fantasy's capacity for surprise as it emerges, sometimes unexpectedly, in different films. Like the children in C. S. Lewis' *The Lion, the Witch and the Wardrobe* who discover a whole magical world waiting behind a mass of coats in an old wardrobe, we are caught in a moment of awe and enchantment as a world of fantasy opens out on the screen. Sometimes the doors are thrown open from the outset, as in the case of the *Lord of the Rings* trilogy; sometimes we are offered only a glimpse through the cracks at the very latest opportunity, as is the case in *You Only Live Once*. Entirely disparate in terms of their style, tone and dramatic aims, these two films nevertheless are joined in fantasy as they speak of world beyond, and of codes and conventions existing beyond the fictional worlds we regularly experience on film. And this is fantasy: the fictional world expanded, sometimes even exploded. On occasion it is there for all to see, at other times it lives only in the mind of an individual character.

Irrespective of such distinctions, fantasy is always experienced by film characters as fact, becoming their reality to all intents and purposes. Fantasy therefore brings us back to facets of human nature, returning us to the foundations of our existence. Fantasy may draw us away into worlds of wonder, spectacle and impossibility, but human behaviour is always at the centre of these revelations. The question of how characters respond to the conditions of their world is paramount regardless of whether we recognize that world, or whether it is one we can never experience. Once the film has ended, we are left only with a sense of the fictional world's reality, and of ourselves.

Annotated Guide to Further Reading

The following titles are of particular relevance to the study of fantasy film. The list is not exhaustive but instead offers some opportunities for further reading and a brief introductory note on each entry. Full details of all titles are listed in the bibliography.

Tzvetan Todorov, *The Fantastic: A Structural Approach to a Literary Genre*

For many, this is an essential starting point for any discussion of fantasy. Todorov's book is a landmark in the study of fantasy as he elaborates a general theory of the fantastic that is founded upon a close consideration, from a structuralist perspective, of particular case studies. Although subsequent scholars have noted the limitations inherent in his central thesis of the fantastic as the hesitation between the uncanny and the marvellous, this formulation nonetheless holds a strong degree of potency in considerations of fantasy. The book is centred upon the fantastic as a literary genre, but its arguments are made with a clarity and precision that makes them translatable to the study of fantasy film.

Rosemary Jackson, *Fantasy: Literature of Subversion*

Another landmark in the study of fantasy, Jackson's work builds upon Todorov's earlier thesis and makes a number of significant departures. Jackson places a much greater emphasis upon the relationship between the fantastic and modern life, suggesting a series of resonances between fantasy and modern industrial civilization and regarding fantasy as a reaction to a lack brought about by the constraints of cultural life, for example. Jackson also acknowledges that the spread of works is too broad to be arranged into a stable genre, and so departs form Todorov's structure of a genre in order to describe fantasy as a mode of writing. Finally, Jackson's work is further defined as she emphasizes the key role of perception in understandings of reality and fantasy, proposing a reliance upon psychoanalytic theory missing from Todorov's earlier, structuralist, work.

Lucie Armitt, *Fantasy Fiction: An Introduction*

Armitt's book is a comprehensive and confident introduction to fantasy literature, written in clear terms and possessing a strong, coherent structure. As a result of these characteristics, it is particularly useful for anyone wishing to gain their bearings in the study of fantasy. The book takes a broad approach to fantasy, bringing together a range of different titles from various periods and movements. Armitt moves through areas of concern such as spatial theory, dream theory and psychoanalytic approaches, historical context, gender, cultural studies, definitions of genre and so on. An overview of existing critical literature is also provided, but one of the book's main strengths is the author's rigorous attention to the detail of the texts she offers for discussion, providing clear evidence for the claims she makes.

James Donald (ed.), *Fantasy Cinema*

This is one of the first titles to place fantasy and film together in a single work. Describing itself as a reader to teach with, Donald's book, first published in 1989, can more accurately be viewed as an edited collection of influential essays that deal with fantasy from critical standpoints that are notably (post)structuralist, semiotic and psychoanalytic in their approach, in line with the editor's stated intention to return to the theoretical frameworks of 1970s film discourse. There is a consistent focus upon the fantasy of horror cinema in the collection, although this interest dovetails with science fiction and surrealist works in certain chapters. The individual arguments presented in each essay are certainly of value and interest to students of fantasy film, but definitions of fantasy cinema are elusive within the collection and a coherent exploration of the genre never quite takes shape.

Joshua David Bellin, *Framing Monsters: Fantasy Film and Social Alienation*

Bellin's book is an engaging study, moving through a number of examples of fantasy film and considering them within their particular social, cultural and historical contexts. His outlining of fantasy's potential to reinforce negative and, indeed, alienating attitudes through its representations is of particular value to the study of fantasy, and a range of different titles are covered in discussions of race, gender, class, mental illness, and so on. Some readers may find that a limited number of the book's arguments have been rehearsed already elsewhere, such as the relationship between *King Kong* and negative racial stereotyping. But elsewhere the work provides original insights into films, as with the author's re-reading of *The Wizard of Oz* in terms of its technological context. Bellin also demonstrates a keen knowledge and understanding of issues surrounding the study of fantasy cinema, and the book's introduction is of particular value here.

Leslie Stratyner and James R. Keller (eds), *Fantasy Fiction into Film*

This collection deals with the topic of how ideas translate from page to screen in fantasy, and the essays contained within the book cover a range of examples drawn, mainly, from contemporary Hollywood cinema. There is an intention, stated by the editors, to treat fantasy seriously as a focus of academic study and also to place film and literature on an equal footing in the critical discussions that ensue.

The first aim is clearly met, as authors engage sincerely with the topic of fantasy in their work but, quite often, the debate descends into an illustration of how film makers (and Hollywood film makers especially) adapt literary texts to the detriment of the original work. Perhaps one reason for this attitude derives from the fact that none of the contributors list film studies as their main critical concern and, while this is hardly an issue, it does seem to have skewed the collection's concerns somewhat. It might also explain why any sustained analysis of the films offered for discussion rarely takes place. The high point of the collection is Janet Brennan Croft's fascinating essay on the various scripts for *The Lord of the Rings* that were prepared before Peter Jackson filmed his definitive version.

James Walters, *Alternative Worlds in Hollywood Cinema: Resonance Between Realms*

This study characterizes and analyses a type of film that presents characters with an alternative to their world. Although dealing with a narrowly defined set of examples, the book covers a number of prominent fantasy films from the classical and contemporary periods of Hollywood, such as *The Wizard of Oz*, *It's A Wonderful Life*, *Groundhog Day* and *Pleasantville*. The title debates the seriousness and sincerity of fantasy cinema, placing these issues within a broader understanding of the fictional world in film.

David Butler, *Fantasy Cinema: Impossible Worlds on Screen*

This recently published book provides a valuable introduction to fantasy film, moving through a number of pertinent debates in clear, concise terms. Butler demonstrates a critical and personal investment in the films he offers for discussion and, while the title is clearly designed to provide an accessible overview for students, there are a number of original insights, such as his handling of violence in fantasy, his discussion of the lost concept of *film blanc*, and an extended analysis of John Boorman's *Excalibur*, a film that must surely have slipped beneath most people's critical radar. Butler has a strong command of the topic, and guides the reader through a series of issues with assurance. The length and aims of the book mean that discussion is kept relatively brief and there is a sense that, given a wider scope for expression, Butler's potent and persuasive assertions will be developed with further depth and precision.

V. F. Perkins, *Film as Film: Understanding and Judging Movies*

Perkins' book, like Cavell's below, is not a study not of fantasy; however, a number of its themes and concerns can help to inform our critical understanding of that genre. In particular, his eloquent concentration upon issues of coherence and credibility provides an exemplary framework for understanding a series of issues at work in fantasy film. Likewise, his understanding of the fundamental relationship between realism and illusion in the cinema has clear relevance to issues surrounding the limits and potentials of fantasy in film. Although dealing with concepts that are often complex and intricate, Perkins' writing is especially clear and lucid, making this an accessible book, free of the jargon that can often clutter academic discussion.

Stanley Cavell, *The World Viewed: Reflections on the Ontology of Film (enlarged edition)*

By no means a straightforward book for the uninitiated, Cavell's work nonetheless concerns itself with the formal properties of cinema that in a way that is strongly relevant to concepts of the fictional world, and returns to the notion of fantasy both directly and indirectly on a number of occasions. His central idea of cinema's ontological status relates potently to the ways we experience fiction, and especially fantasy, in film. An expansive and idiosyncratic work, *The World Viewed* is of significance to anyone wishing to underpin his or her understandings (or even have them challenged) by a fresh theoretical perspective.

Notes

Introduction

1. Deborah Thomas, *Beyond Genre: Melodrama, Comedy and Romance in Hollywood Films,* Moffat: Cameron Books, 2000, p. 15.
2. Lincoln Geraghty and Mark Jancovich (eds) *The Shifting Definitions of Genre: Essays on Labelling Films, Television Shows and Media,* Jefferson, NC: McFarland, 2008.
3. Ibid., p. 2.
4. George Lakoff and Mark Johnson, *Metaphors We Live By,* Chicago, IL: Chicago University Press, 1980, p. 71.
5. Brian Attebery, *Strategies of Fantasy,* Bloomington, IN: Indiana University Press, 1992, p. 12.
6. Ibid., p. 14.
7. Ibid., p. 13.
8. Tzvetan Todorov, *The Fantastic: A Structural Approach to a Literary Genre,* Cornell University Press, 1975.
9. Rosemary Jackson, *Fantasy: The Literature of Subversion,* London: Routledge, 2003, p. 35.
10. David Butler, *Fantasy Cinema: Impossible Worlds on Screen,* London: Wallflower, 2009, p. 43.
11. Eric Rabkin, *The Fantastic in Literature,* Princeton, NJ: Princeton University Press, 1976, p. 118, quoted in Jackson, *Fantasy,* p. 13.
12. Rick Altman, *Film/Genre,* London: British Film Institute, 1999.
13. Stanley Cavell, *Contesting Tears: The Hollywood Melodrama of the Unknown Woman,* Chicago, IL: University of Chicago Press, 1996, p. 3.
14. Chapters 5 and 6 are designed to provide new or alternative perspectives on fantasy film, whereas Chapters 1 to 4 concentrate on a series of broader issues.
15. André Bazin, 'The Life and Death of Superimposition' in B. Cardullo (ed.), *Bazin at Work: Major Essays and Reviews from the Forties and Fifties,* London: Routledge, 1997, p. 73.

Chapter 1

1. Lotte Eisner, *Fritz Lang,* New York: Da Capo Press, 1976, p. 190; Tom Gunning, *The Films of Fritz Lang: Allegories of Vision and Modernity,* London: British

Film Institute, 2000, pp. 258–60; George M. Wilson, *Narration in Light: Studies in Cinematic Point of View,* Baltimore, MD: Johns Hopkins University Press, 1986, pp. 16–38.

2. Thomas Leitch, *Crime Films,* Cambridge: Cambridge University Press, 2002, pp. 92–3; Steve Neale, *Genre and Hollywood,* London: Routledge, 2000, p. 115; Wilson, *Narration in Light,* p. 22.

3. The extent to which the fact of Eddie's innocence or guilt is left suspended by the film is interpreted differently within two major analyses of *You Only Live Once.* George Wilson takes this ambiguity to be a central facet of the film's unreliable structuring of point of view, making firm judgements at least precarious if not impossible (Wilson, *Narration in Light,* pp. 17–22). However, Tom Gunning queries Wilson's 'inventive gymnastics to try to keep open the possibility that Taylor *was* involved in the robbery' as he constructs a reading based upon Lang as enunciator leading the audience deliberately and playfully towards the conclusion of Eddie's guilt in order to finally reveal the 'withheld information' about the bank robbery (that Eddie was not in the crashed armoured getaway car) at the point when we have withheld our own complete sympathy for Eddie due to our lingering suspicions of him (Gunning, *The Films of Fritz Lang,* pp. 244–5).

4. Wilson, *Narration in Light,* p. 38.

5. Ibid., pp. 36 and 37.

6. Ibid., p. 37.

7. Peter Bogdanovich 'No Copyright for the Director' in *Fritz Lang in America,* London: Studio Vista, 1967, p. 35.

8. Gunning, *The Films of Fritz Lang,* p. 259.

9. James Walters, *Alternative Worlds in Hollywood Cinema: Resonance Between Realms,* Bristol: Intellect, 2008a, pp. 130–1.

10. Tzvetan Todorov, *The Fantastic: A Structural Approach to a Literary Genre,* New York: Cornell University Press, 1975.

11. Ibid., p. 25.

12. Walters, pp. 15–40.

13. V. F. Perkins, 'Where is the World? The Horizon of Events in Movie Fiction', in John Gibbs and Douglas Pye (eds), *Style and Meaning: Studies in the Detailed Analysis of Film,* Manchester: Manchester University Press, 2005, p. 19.

14. Lucie Armitt, *Fantasy Fiction: An Introduction,* London: Continuum, 2005, p. 8.

15. James Donald (ed.), *Fantasy and the Cinema,* London: British Film Institute, 1989.

16. Ibid., p. 1.

17. Ibid., p. 10.

18. Richard Mathews, *Fantasy: The Liberation of Imagination,* London: Routledge, 2002, p. 2.

19. Charles Dickens, 'A Christmas Carol' in *Christmas Books,* London: Wordsworth, 1995.
20. Robin Wood, *Hollywood from Vietnam to Reagan ... and Beyond,* New York: Columbia University Press, 2003, p. xxx.
21. Ibid., pp. xxxi – xxxxii.
22. Ibid., p. xxx.
23. Here it is appropriate to reference *The Bourne Identity*'s widely acknowledged indebtedness to the James Bond series of films (1962–), which themselves feature an indestructible titular character and actually extend this theme as Bond is 'reincarnated' in different forms as new actors are cast in the role.
24. For a sustained consideration of this trend in cinema see Ian Gordon, Mark Jancovich and Matthew McAllister (eds), *Film and Comic Books,* Jackson, MS: Mississippi University Press, 2007.
25. Lisa Purse, 'Digital Heroes in Contemporary Hollywood: Exertion, Identification and the Virtual Action Body', *Film Criticism* 32(1) (2007), p. 8.
26. Ibid., p. 17.
27. Joshua David Bellin, *Framing Monsters: Fantasy Film and Social Alienation,* Carbondale, IL: Southern Illinois University Press, 2005, p. 198.
28. Ibid., p. 199.
29. Sabine LeBel, '"Tone Down the Boobs, Please!": Reading the Special Effect Body in Superhero Movies', *CineAction* 77 (2009), p. 58.
30. The screenplay is adapted by Meera Syal from her book, Syal M., *Anita and Me,* London: Flamingo, 1996. Syal also plays the part of Meena's Auntie Shaila in the film.
31. *Anita and Me,* DVD release, Icon Home Entertainment, 2007.
32. Ibid.
33. Walters, *Alternative Worlds in Hollywood Cinema,* p. 213.
34. Leslie Stratyner and James R. Keller, *Fantasy Fiction into Film,* Jefferson, NC: McFarland, 2007, p. 1.
35. Brian Attebery, *Strategies of Fantasy,* Bloomington, IN: Indiana University Press, 1992, p. 3.
36. Ibid., p. 4.

Chapter 2

1. Increasingly, the Internet has become a source providing useful historical overviews of fantasy film for the uninitiated, as well as critical descriptions of the titles contained within the periods described. Two such examples can be found at the peer-edited site Wikipedia (http://en.wikipedia.org/wiki/Fantasy_film) and at Filmsite (http://www.filmsite.org/fantasyfilms.html). The appearance of historical outlines on such fansites suggests – and helps to construct – a collective knowledge of fantasy cinema's heritage that is shared among audiences.

2. Simon Popple and Joe Kember, *Early Cinema: From Factory Gate to Dream Factory,* London: Wallflower, 2004, p. 61.

3. For an account of how the early Lumière films can be understood in terms of narrative, see André Gaudreault, 'Film, Narrative, Narration: The Cinema of the Lumière Brothers' in T. Elsaesser (ed.), *Early Cinema: Space Frame Narrative,* London: British Film Institute, 1990, pp. 68–75.

4. Barry Salt, DVD commentary for *Early Cinema: Primitives and Pioneers,* London: British Film Institute Video Publishing, 2004.

5. Stephen Bottomore, 'The Panicking Audience? Early Cinema and the "Train Effect"', *Historical Journal of Film, Radio and Television,* 19(2) (1999), pp. 177–216.

6. Ian Christie, *The Last Machine: Early Cinema and the Birth of the Modern World,* London: British Film Institute, 1994, p. 15.

7. Ibid.

8. David Parkinson, *History of Film,* London: Thames & Hudson, 1997, pp. 11–12.

9. Tom Gunning, '"Primitive" Cinema: A Frame-up? Or The Trick's on Us' in Elsaesser, *Early Cinema,* p. 96.

10. Tom Gunning, 'The Cinema of Attractions: Early Film, It's Spectators and the Avant-garde', in Elsaesser, *Early Cinema,* pp. 56–62.

11. Ibid., p. 58.

12. *La Poste,* 30 December 1895 quoted in Paul Arthur, 'The Living Dead', *Film Comment* September/October (2007), p. 18.

13. André Bazin, *What is Cinema?* translated by Hugh Gray, Berkeley, CA: University of California Press, 1967, p. 9.

14. Ibid., p. 12.

15. Christie, *The Last Machine,* p. 111.

16. Vicky Lebeau, *Childhood and Cinema,* London: Reaktion, 2008, p. 32.

17. *The Scotsman,* 22 December 1825 quoted in Christopher Harvie, Graham Martin and Aaron Scharf (ed.), *Industrialisation and Culture 1830–1914,* London: Macmillan for the Open University Press, 1970, p. 82.

18. Quoted in Leo Charney and Vanessa R. Schwartz (eds), *Cinema and the Invention of Modern Life,* Berkeley, CA: University of California Press, 1995, p. 74.

19. Michael Chanan *The Dream that Kicks: The Prehistory and Early Years of Cinema in Britain* (Routledge, 1996), p. 34.

Chapter 3

1. Peter Wollen, *Signs and Meaning in the Cinema,* London: British Film Institute, 1967.

2. Thomas Schatz, *The Genius of the System: Hollywood Filmmaking in the Studio Era,* New York: Pantheon, 1988.

3. John Caughie (ed.), *Theories of Authorship,* London: Routledge & Kegan Paul/ British Film Institute, 1981, p. 9.

4. Ibid., p. 50.

5. Ian Cameron, 'Films, directors and critics', *Movie Reader,* London: November Books, 1972, p. 12.

6. See Wollen, *Signs and Meanings in the Cinema.*

7. V. F. Perkins, 'Film Authorship: The Premature Burial', *CineAction!* 21/22 (1990), p. 59.

8. Robin Wood, 'Reflections on the Auteur Theory', *Personal Views,* revised edition, Detroit, MI, Wayne State University Press, 2006, p. 231.

9. Ibid., p. 57.

10. Steve Neale, *Genre and Hollywood,* Routledge, 2000, p. 51.

11. Ibid., p. 105.

12. Stanley Cavell, *Themes Out of School: Effects and Causes,* Chicago, IL: University of Chicago Press, 1988, p. 242.

13. 'The idea is that the members of a genre share the inheritance of certain conditions, procedures and subjects and goals of composition, and that in primary art each member of such a genre represents a study of these conditions, something I think of as bearing the responsibility of the inheritance. There is, on this picture, nothing one is tempted to call *the* features of a genre which all its members have in common.' Stanley Cavell, *Pursuits of Happiness: The Hollywood Comedy of Remarriage,* Cambridge, MA: Harvard University Press, 1981, p. 28.

14. Indeed, in a recent book on science fiction cinema, Christine Cornea suggests that the genre is *best* appreciated in relation to critical formulations of fantasy: 'Taking my cue from both Todorov and Jackson, I believe that science fiction is most usefully understood as a genre that relies upon the fantastic. I would also offer a further reformation of these two models, which I think is perhaps more useful in terms of the science fiction film: I would suggest that science fiction is a genre that is demonstrably located in between fantasy and reality. My usage of the term fantasy rather than the fantastic is meant to open up this model to further connotations beyond the stricter usages in literary theory.' Christine Cornea, *Science Fiction Cinema: Between Fantasy and Reality,* Edinburgh: Edinburgh University Press, 2007, p. 4.

15. Jane Feuer, *The Hollywood Musical,* second edition, London: Macmillan, 1993, p. 68.

16. Joseph Andrew Casper, *Vincente Minnelli and the Film Musical,* London: A. S. Barnes & Co., 1977, p. 165.

17. V. F. Perkins, 'Moments of Choice', *Rouge,* 9 (2006), http://www.rouge.com. au/9/moments_choice.html (accessed 12 November 2010).

18. For a detailed consideration of these two films in the context of the imagined worlds they construct, see James Walters, *Alternative Worlds in Hollywood Cinema: Resonance Between Realms,* Bristol: Intellect, 2008, pp. 55–79.

19. Susan Smith, *The Musical: Race, Gender and Performance,* London: Wallflower, 2005, p. 42.

20. Ibid., p. 41.

21. Ibid., p. 49.

22. Stanley Cavell, *Philosophy the Day After Tomorrow,* Cambridge, MA: Harvard University Press, 2005, p. 68.

23. Casper, *Vincente Minnelli and the Film Musical,* p. 135.

24. Cavell, *Philosophy the Day after Tomorrow,* p. 72.

25. Ibid., p. 73.

26. Such moments are not unique in cinema, in musicals or even in Astaire's career, however. See for example the famous sequence from *Royal Wedding* (Stanley Donen, 1951) in which he dances up the walls and across the ceiling of his room.

27. Walters, *Alternative Worlds in Hollywood Cinema,* pp. 169–90.

28. For a full account of the reception of and critical commentary upon *Brigadoon*'s representation of Highland practices and culture, see Colin McArthur, *Brigadoon, Braveheart and the Scots: Distortions of Scotland in Hollywood Cinema,* London: I. B. Tauris, 2003, pp. 94–122.

Chapter 4

1. And, of course, these titles highlight two other distinct traditions in fantasy cinema of this type: they are all adaptations of popular literary works and each features *female* children as its central protagonists.

2. Cary Bazalgette and David Buckingham (eds) *In Front of the Children: Screen Entertainment and Young Audiences,* London: British Film Institute, 1995, p. 1.

3. Peter Krämer, '"The Best Disney Film Disney Never Made": Children's Films and the Family Audience in American Cinema since the 1960s' in Steve Neale (ed.), *Genre and Contemporary Hollywood,* London: BFI Publishing, 2002, p. 185.

4. Ibid., p. 186.

5. Richard Dyer, *The Matter of Images: Essays on Representations,* London: Routledge, 2002a.

6. Richard Dyer, *Only Entertainment,* London: Routledge, 2002b, p. 3.

7. Andrew Britton, 'Blissing Out: The Politics of Reaganite Entertainment' in *Movie,* 31/32 (Winter), 1986, p. 4.

8. Robin Wood, *Hitchcock's Films Revisited,* New York: Columbia University Press, 1989, p. 33.

9. Robin Wood, *Hollywood from Vietnam to Reagan ... and Beyond,* New York: Columbia University Press, 2003, p. xiii.

10. Martin F. Norden, 'America and its Fantasy Films: 1945–1951' in *Film and History,* 12(1) (1982), p. 8.

11. Ibid., p. 2

12. Ibid.

13. Ibid.. pp. 6–7.

14. Ibid., p. 2.

15. Britton, 'Blissing Out', p. 2.

16. Ibid., p. 10.

17. Ibid., p. 37.

18. Krämer, p. 186.

19. Warren Buckland, *Directed by Steven Spielberg: Poetics of the Contemporary Hollywood Blockbuster,* London: Continuum, 2006, pp. 130–53; Krämer, p. 187.

20. Kristin Thompson, 'Fantasy, Franchises and Frodo Baggins: *The Lord of the Rings* and Modern Hollywood', *The Velvet Light Trap,* 52 (2003), p. 46.

21. Christine Cornea, *Science Fiction Cinema: Between Fantasy and Reality,* Edinburgh: Edinburgh University Press, 2007, pp. 112–15.

22. Wood, *Hollywood from Vietnam to Reagan ... And Beyond,* p. 158.

23. Ibid., p. 147.

24. Cornea, p. 116.

25. Wood, *Hollywood from Vietnam to Reagan ... And Beyond,* p. 154.

26. J. M. Barrie, *Peter Pan and other Plays,* Oxford: Oxford University Press, 1995, first published 1928.

27. J. M. Barrie, *Peter and Wendy,* http://www.gutenberg.org/etext/26654 (accessed 12 November 2010).

28. Ibid.

29. From 20–21 November 2007, the University of Lincoln, England, hosted a conference titled 'Spielberg at Sixty', which effectively provided a focus point for this trend. The conference has given rise to a special issue of *The New Review of Film and Television Studies* on the topic of Spielberg (volume 7, issue 1, 2009).

30. Buckland, *Directed by Steven Spielberg,* p. 1.

31. Nigel Morris, *The Cinema of Steven Spielberg: Empire of Light,* London: Wallflower Press, 2007, pp. 176–91.

32. Ibid., p. 191.

33. James Walters, *Alternative Worlds in Hollywood Cinema: Resonance Between Realms,* Bristol: Intellect, 2008, pp. 56–62.

34. Ibid., p. 74.

35. Josh has a birthday during his time as an adult.

Chapter 5

1. Stanley Cavell, *The World Viewed: Reflections on the Ontology of Film,* enlarged edition, London: Harvard University Press, 1979, p. 85.
2. Ibid., p. 86.
3. See V. F. Perkins' exemplary articles, '*Letter from an Unknown Woman* (on the Linz sequence)', *Movie* 29/30 (1982); 'Ophuls contra Wagner and Others', *Movie,* 36 (2000a); '"Same Tune Again!" – Repetition and Framing in Letter from an Unknown Woman', *CineAction* 52 (2000b); Robin Wood's key chapter ('Ewig hin der Liebe Glück: *Letter from an Unknown Woman*' in *Personal Views,* revised edition, Wayne State University Press, 2006); Stanley Cavell's extensive discussions of the film ('Psychoanalysis and Cinema: Moments of *Letter from an Unknown Woman*' and 'Postscript' in *Contesting Tears: The Hollywood Melodrama of the Unknown Woman,* Chicago University Press, 1996) or George M. Wilson's instructive narrative analysis (George M. Wilson, *Narration in Light: Studies in Cinematic Point of View,* London: Johns Hopkins University Press, 1986). This is by no means an exhaustive list but it does represent a variety of approaches to the film, each built on careful attention to its style and structure.
4. Wilson, *Narration in Light*, p. 104.
5. Deborah Thomas, *Beyond Genre: Melodrama, Comedy and Romance in Hollywood Films,* Moffat: Cameron & Hollis, 2000, pp. 32–42; George Wilson, 'On Film Narrative and Narrative Meaning' in Richard Allen and Murray Smith (eds), *Film Theory and Philosophy* (Oxford University Press, 1999), pp. 221–38.
6. Robin Wood, 'Robin Wood on *Bigger Than Life*', *Film Comment*, 8(3) (1972), p. 58.
7. Ibid., p. 56.
8. Thomas, pp. 37–8.
9. While Ophuls' and Ray's films convey aspects of character fantasy through a sophisticated and nuanced *mise en scène,* Koster displays no such filmmaking skill in his realization of *Harvey.* Indeed, the film runs very much like a straightforward screen version of the Pulitzer Prize-winning play from which it is adapted, with the camera functioning mainly as a passive device for framing scenes as if they were taking place within a proscenium arch. Whilst this may translate as a fairly negative comment about Koster's directorial skill on this film, his neutral strategy of representation provides a degree of space and freedom for the actors' performances to find their register and impact. This varies from James Stewart's inwardly projected style, which infuses his character with the hesitancies, repetitions and spontaneities of everyday action, to Josephine Hull's highly theatrical style, which makes clear the actress' translation of her performance from stage to screen.
10. Nicole Markotic, 'Punching up the Story: Disability and Film', *Canadian Journal of Film Studies*, 17(1) (2008), p. 3.

Chapter 6

1. George M. Wilson, *Narration in Light: Studies in Cinematic Point of View,* Baltimore, MD: Johns Hopkins University Press, 1986, p. 40.
2. Ibid., p. 43.
3. For a fuller consideration of the potentials and possibilities contained within particular fictional worlds see James Walters 'Making Light of the Dark: Understanding the World of *His Girl Friday*', *Journal of Film and Video*, 60(3-4) (2008b), pp. 90–102.
4. Robin Wood, *Personal Views: Explorations in Film,* Detroit, MI: Wayne State University Press, 2006, p. 27.
5. John Gibbs, *Mise-en-scène: Film Style and Interpretation,* London: Wallflower, 2001, p. 40.
6. V. F. Perkins *Film as Film: Understanding and Judging Movies,* New York: Da Capo, 1993, p. 120.
7. Ibid., p. 117.
8. Jeffrey Crouse 'Fueled by Enthusiasms: Jeffrey Crouse Interviews V.F. Perkins', *Film International*, 3 (2004), p. 23.
9. Gibbs, *Mise-en-scène*, p. 40.
10. Perkins, *Film as Film*, p. 119.
11. Ibid. pp. 121–2.
12. Ibid. p. 121.
13. See for example Camille Paglia, *The Birds,* London: British Film Institute, 1998, or Robin Wood's chapter on the film in his book *Hitchcock's Films Revisited,* New York: Columbia University Press, 2002, pp. 152–72.
14. Ibid., p. 122.
15. I would like to thank Andrew Klevan for introducing *Still Life* in his research group, 'The Magnifying Class' at Oxford University. I would also like to thank fellow members of the group for their stimulating discussion of the film.
16. A further scene, in which a tower block is seen to collapse in the background of a shot, possesses a related element of unreality but is contrastingly motivated by an event that could conceivably occur within the characters' fictional world.
17. Booklet accompanying the British Film Institute DVD release of *Still Life*, pp. 8–9.
18. Mark Sanderson discusses this sequence in detail in his short book on the film, *Don't Look Now,* London: British Film Institute, 1996, pp. 33–41.
19. David Butler, *Fantasy Cinema: Impossible Worlds on Screen,* London: Wallflower, 2009, pp. 82–3.
20. Kristin Thompson discusses this sequence extensively in her chapter 'Stepping out of blockbuster mode: the lighting of the beacons in *The Lord of the Rings: The Return of the King*' in Tom Brown and James Walters (eds), *Film Moments: Criticism, History, Theory,* London: British Film Institute/Palgrave Macmillan, 2010, pp. 144–8.

21. Kirsten Moana Thompson, 'Scale, Spectacle and Movement: Massive Software and Digital Special Effects in *The Lord of the Rings*', in Ernest Mathijs and Murray Pomerance (eds), *From Hobbits to Hollywood: Essays on Peter Jackson's* The Lord of the Rings, New York: Rodopi, 2006, p. 287.

22. Ibid., pp. 283–99.

23. Butler, *Fantasy Cinema*, p. 84.

24. Moana Thompson 'Scale, Spectacle and Movement: Massive Software and Digital Special Effects in *The Lord of the Rings*', p. 285.

Bibliography

Allen, R. and Smith, M. (eds), *Film Theory and Philosophy*, Oxford: Oxford University Press, 1999.

Altman, R., *Film/Genre*, London: British Film Institute, 1999.

Armitt, L., *Fantasy Fiction: An Introduction*, London: Continuum Books, 2005.

Arthur, P., 'The Living Dead', *Film Comment* September/October (2007).

Attebery, B., *Strategies of Fantasy*, Bloomington, IN: Indiana University Press, 1992.

Barrie, J. M., *Peter Pan and Other Plays*, Oxford: Oxford University Press, 1995.

Bazalgette, C. and Buckingham, D. (eds), *In Front of the Children: Screen Entertainment and Young Audiences*, London: British Film Institute, 1995.

Bazin, A., *What is Cinema?* translated by Hugh Gray, Berkeley, CA: University of California Press, 1967.

Bazin, A., 'The Life and Death of Superimposition', in B. Cardullo (ed.), *Bazin at Work: Major Essays and Reviews from the Forties and Fifties,* London: Routledge, 1997, p. 73.

Bellin, J. D., *Framing Monsters: Fantasy Film and Social Alienation*, Carbondale, IL: Southern Illinois University Press, 2005.

Bennett, J. and Brown, T. (eds), *Film and Television After DVD*, London: Routledge, 2008.

Bogdanovich, P., *Fritz Lang in America*, London: Studio Vista, 1967.

Bottomore, S. (1999), 'The Panicking Audience? Early Cinema and the "Train Effect"', *Historical Journal of Film, Radio and Television*, 19(2).

Britton, A., 'Blissing Out: The Politics of Reaganite Entertainment', *Movie* 31/32 (1986).

Brown, T. and Walters, J. (eds), *Film Moments: Criticism, History. Theory*, London: British Film Institute/Palgrave Macmillan, 2010.

Buckland, W., *Directed by Steven Spielberg: Poetics of the Contemporary Hollywood Blockbuster*, London: Continuum, 2006.

Butler, D., *Fantasy Cinema: Impossible Worlds On Screen*, London: Wallflower, 2009.

Cameron, I. (ed.), *Movie Reader*, London: November Books, 1972.

Casper, J. A., *Vincente Minnelli and the Film Musical*, South Brunswick, NJ: A. S. Barnes & Co., 1977.

Caughie, J., *Theories of Authorship*, London: Routledge & Kegan Paul/British Film Institute, 1981.

Cavell, S., *The World Viewed: Reflections on the Ontology of Film,* enlarged edition, London: Harvard University Press, 1979.

Cavell, S., *Pursuits of Happiness: The Hollywood Comedy of Remarriage*, London: Harvard University Press, 1981.

Cavell, S., *Themes Out of School: Effects and Causes*, Chicago, IL: University of Chicago Press, 1988.

Cavell, S., *Contesting Tears: The Hollywood Melodrama of the Unknown Woman*, Chicago, IL: University of Chicago Press, 1996.

Cavell, S., *Philosophy the Day after Tomorrow,* Cambridge, MA: Belknap Press of Harvard University Press, 2005.

Chanan, M., *The Dream that Kicks: The Prehistory and Early Years of Cinema in Britain*, London: Routledge, 1996.

Charney, L. and Schwartz, V. R. (eds), *Cinema and the Invention of Modern Life*, Berkeley, CA: University of California Press, 1995.

Christie, I., *The Last Machine: Early Cinema and the Birth of the Modern World*, London: British Film Institute, 1994.

Cornea, C., *Science Fiction Cinema: Between Fantasy and Reality*, Edinburgh: Edinburgh University Press, 2007.

Crouse, J., 'Fueled by Enthusiasms: Jeffrey Crouse interviews V. F. Perkins', *Film International* 3 (2004).

Dickens, C., *Christmas Books*, London: Wordsworth, 1995.

Donald, J. (ed.), *Fantasy and the Cinema*, London: British Film Institute, 1989.

Dyer, R., *The Matter of Images: Essays on Representations*, London: Routledge, 2002a.

Dyer R., *Only Entertainment*, London: Routledge, 2002b.

Eisner, L., *Fritz Lang*, New York: Da Capo Press, 1976.

Elsaesser, T. (ed.), *Early Cinema: Space Frame Narrative*, London: British Film Institute, 1990.

Feuer, J., *The Hollywood Musical,* second edition, London: Macmillan, 1993.

Geraghty, L. and Jancovich, M., *The Shifting Definitions of Genre: Essays on Labeling Films, Television Shows and Media*, Jefferson, NC: McFarland & Company, 2007.

Gibbs, J., *Mise-en-scène: Film Style and Interpretation*, London: Wallflower, 2001.

Gibbs, J. and Pye, D. (eds), *Style and Meaning: Studies in the Detailed Analysis of Film*, Manchester: Manchester University Press, 2005.

Gordon, I., Jancovich, M. and McAllister, M., *Film and Comic Books*, Jackson, MS: University of Mississippi Press, 2007.

Gunning, T., *The Films of Fritz Lang: Allegories of Vision and Modernity*, London: British Film Institute, 2000.

Harvie, C., Martin, G. and Scharf, A. (eds), *Industrialisation and Culture 1830–1914*, London: Macmillan for The Open University Press, 1970.

Jackson, R., *Fantasy: The Literature of Subversion,* London: Routledge, 2003.

Lakoff, G. and Johnson, M., *Metaphors We Live By,* Chicago: Chicago University Press, 1980.

Lebeau, V., *Childhood and Cinema*, London: Reaktion, 2008.

LeBel, S., '"Tone Down the Boobs, Please!": Reading the Special Effect Body in Superhero Movies', *CineAction*, 77 (2009).

Leitch, T., *Crime Films*, Cambridge: Cambridge University Press, 2002.

Markotic, N., 'Punching up the Story: Disability and Film', *Canadian Journal of Film Studies*, 17(1) (2008).

Mathews, R., *Fantasy: The Liberation of Imagination*, London: Routledge, 2002.

Mathijs, E. and Pomerance, M. (eds), *From Hobbits to Hollywood: Essays on Peter Jackson's* The Lord of the Rings, New York: Rodopi, 2006.

McArthur, C., *Brigadoon, Braveheart and the Scots: Distortions of Scotland in Hollywood Cinema*, London: I. B. Tauris, 2003.

Morris, N., *The Cinema of Steven Spielberg: Empire of Light*, London: Wallflower Press, 2007.

Neale, S., *Genre and Hollywood*, London: Routledge, 2000.

Neale, S. (ed.), *Genre and Contemporary Hollywood*, London: British Film Institute, 2002.

Norden, M. F., 'America and its Fantasy Films: 1945–1951', *Film and History*, 12(1) (1982).

Paglia, C., *The Birds*, London: British Film Institute, 1998.

Parkinson, D., *History of Film*, London: Thames & Hudson, 1997.

Perkins, V. F., '*Letter from an Unknown Woman* (on the Linz Sequence)', *Movie,* 29/30 (1982).

Perkins, V. F., 'Film Authorship: The Premature Burial', *CineAction,* 21/22 (1990).

Perkins, V. F., *Film as Film: Understanding and Judging Movies,* New York: Da Capo Press, 1993.

Perkins, V. F., 'Ophuls contra Wagner and Others', *Movie,* 36, 2000a.

Perkins, V. F., '"Same Tune Again!" – Repetition and Framing in *Letter from an Unknown Woman*', *CineAction,* 52, 2000b.

Perkins, V. F., 'Where is the World? The Horizon of Events in Movie Fiction', in J. Gibbs and D. Pye (eds) *Style and Meaning: Studies in the Detailed Analysis of Film,* Manchester: Manchester University Press, 2005, p. 19.

Perkins, V. F., 'Moments of Choice', *Rouge,* 9 (2006).

Popple, S. and Kember, J., *Early Cinema: From Factory Gate to Dream Factory*, London; New York: Wallflower, 2004.

Purse, L., 'Digital Heroes in Contemporary Hollywood: Exertion, Identification and the Virtual Action Body', *Film Criticism,* 32(1) (2007).

Rabkin, E., *The Fantastic in Literature,* Princeton, NJ: Princeton University Press, 1976.

Sanderson, M., *Don't Look Now*, London: British Film Institute, 1996.

Schatz, T., *The Genius of the System: Hollywood Filmmaking in the Studio Era*, New York: Pantheon, 1988.

Smith, S., *The Musical: Race, Gender and Performance*, London: Wallflower, 2005.

Stratyner, L. and Keller, J. R. (eds), *Fantasy Fiction into Film*, Jefferson, NC: McFarland, 2007.

Syal, M., *Anita and Me*, London: Flamingo, 1996.

Thomas, D., *Beyond Genre: Melodrama, Comedy and Romance in Hollywood Films*, Moffat: Cameron & Hollis, 2000.

Thomas, D., *Reading Hollywood: Spaces and Meanings in American Film*, London: Wallflower, 2001.

Thompson, K., 'Fantasy, Franchises and Frodo Baggins: *The Lord of the Rings* and Modern Hollywood', *The Velvet Light Trap*, 52(Fall) (2003).

Todorov, T., *The Fantastic: A Structural Approach to a Literary Genre*, New York: Cornell University Press, 1975.

Walters, J., *Alternative Worlds in Hollywood Cinema: Resonance Between Realms*, Bristol: Intellect, 2008a.

Walters, J., 'Making Light of the Dark: Understanding the World of *His Girl Friday*', *Journal of Film and Video*, 60(3–4) (2008b).

Wilson, G. M., *Narration in Light: Studies in Cinematic Point of View*, Baltimore, MD: Johns Hopkins University Press, 1986.

Wollen, P., *Signs and Meaning in the Cinema*, London: British Film Institute, 1967.

Wood, R., 'Robin Wood on *Bigger Than Life*', *Film Comment*, 8(3) (1972).

Wood, R., *Hitchcock's Films Revisited*, New York: Columbia University Press, 2002.

Wood, R., *Hollywood from Vietnam to Reagan ... And Beyond*, New York: Columbia University Press, 2003.

Wood, R., *Personal Views: Explorations in Film,* revised edition, Detroit, MI: Wayne State University Press, 2006.

Index